CEO Tools is for *every n*

At last, here is every manager's ....ng up the nuts and bolts of business.

Just a twist of a wrench can literally change your world. Think about securing the bolts on an aircraft engine. The right tools and techniques are paramount.

In business, it's the same. Every manager needs just the right business tools and know-how to be successful. This is a "go-do-it" book, not just some more "how to" lessons. You can use the tools today to be more successful.

This book is from Kraig Kramers, an eight-time veteran CEO, who puts easy-to-use management tools directly in your hands to make more money and improve your individual success immediately. Kraig is a nationally acclaimed speaker with over 10,000 managers and CEOs using the tools already. This book is about tools for tightening up the nuts and bolts in *your* group, department, or business for customers, people, productivity, profits, and results.

Whether or not you ever want to be chief executive or are now a CEO, this book is for you.

Pre-publication praise for *CEO Tools*

"Kraig Kramers is a sound winner. When you read *CEO Tools*, I think you will agree." **Ken Blanchard,** Coauthor of
The One Minute Manager® and
Whale Done!™

"Kraig delivers a wealth of practical 'take-home' material. He motivates CEOs and managers to take *meaningful* action now." **Richard Carr**, President and CEO
TEC Worldwide

"Being a CEO or manager in the 21st century without having these valuable tools in your tool kit – would be like playing in the NFL without your helmet. Must reading for *every* manager!"

Red Scott, CEO (retired)
Fuqua Industries, Inc. (NYSE)
and Norman Vincent Peale
Humanitarian, Horatio Alger Society

"This is the best step-by-step guide to doing more and better business I have ever read." **Susan Harte**, Sr. Business Writer
Atlanta Journal-Constitution

"CEO TOOLS is the playbook for every manager and CEO looking to build a winning strategy in business. Kraig diagrams the X's and O's for business success with the best of Super Bowl winning coaches."

Glenn Hemmerle, former CEO
Crown Books, Athlete's Foot, Pearle
Vision, and Miracle-Ear

"Kraig Kramers' book is simply pure genius. It offers both skills and strategy that can be implemented at all management levels. Whether you're a first line supervisor or CEO, this book will foster both *understanding and action*. Have several copies in your company library – your return on investment will be enormous!"

Ron Fleisher, CEO of Creative
Bottomline Solutions, Inc. and CEO
of four other companies earlier

"When CEOs run into business problems, they go back to the basics. This book provides a complete systemic model to keep your enterprise on track and avoid managerial pitfalls."

Clark A. Johnson, CEO (retired)
Pier 1 Imports

"Lee Iacocca told the U.S. Congress that 'Even a master craftsman would be hard pressed to produce top results using broken, rusted or non-existing tools.' Kraig Kramers delivers a veritable power tool kit for managers who seek proven, productive solutions to the fundamentals of producing extraordinary results with everyday people. A new business classic in the making."

Jim Cecil, CEO
The James Cecil Company

CEO Tools

The Nuts-n-Bolts of Business for Every Manager's Success

CEO Tools

by

Kraig Kramers

Gandy Dancer Press

CEO Tools: The Nuts-n-Bolts of Business
for Every Manager's Success

Published by: **Gandy**
              Dancer
              Press
P.O. Box 2190
Stockbridge, GA 30281
Phone (770) 389-5768
Email: *info@ceotools.com*

ISBN 0-9725720-0-7
Library of Congress Control Number: 2002114255

Cover Design by **GBA/SourceLink**
Internal Graphics and CD Designed by **I.B.I.S., Inc.**

Gandy Dancer Press books may be purchased at a discount for educational, business, or sales promotional use. For information and **quantity discounts**, please contact us at the address or email address above.

Printed in the United States of America
First Edition: December 2002

10 9 8 7 6 5 4 3 2 1

Dedication – The heroes behind *CEO Tools*

This book is dedicated to every employee at eight companies who made my job as chief executive so much easier by responding to the *CEO Tools* presented in the following pages. Often they created or improved the tools. Sometimes they challenged them, and me. Thank goodness. These employees caused their companies to outperform their industries in every respect, sometimes once, but more frequently on a recurring basis year after year. Here are the people, past and present, who made my life so much easier:

The Employees of Courtesy Coffee in San Diego and Nationwide
The Employees of National Airmotive Corp. (aircraft engines) in Oakland CA
The Employees of Munson Sporting Goods Company in Costa Mesa CA
The Employees of Metro One Telecommunications in Portland OR
The Employees of Corporate Partners in Lake Oswego OR and Atlanta GA
The Employees of Snapper (lawnmowers) in McDonough GA and Worldwide
The Employees of Guarantee Insurance Resources in Marietta GA
The Employees of Graphic Arts Center (printing) in Portland OR and
across America

If you were at these companies at the time of my involvement, or before or after, thank you for everything you did, day-in-day-out. Thank you, too, for your support as I went on to the next challenge.

This book is also dedicated to the parent companies and their officers and employees who helped us accomplish what we did. Please refer to the Acknowledgments near the end of this book for specific individuals and corporations who deserve recognition for allowing our teams at each of these companies to learn, create, and improve the *CEO Tools* for every manager's use everywhere.

Of course this book is possible only because of the customers and suppliers and community and shareholders of those companies. These people were among my greatest teachers. Thank you all, including Gladys Groocock, a long-time resident of Portland, OR, who always reminded us of our community responsibilities. You'll meet a few of these folks in the following pages.

CEO Tools – Table of Contents

Look for this symbol in the book's margin, indicating that the tool is included in a ready-to-use form on the enclosed CD. Some of the tools are automated for use by you and those around you with IBM-compatible PCs via a desktop-ready icon for "click-n-use."

Preface – What's in this book for you as manager or CEO?

The twist of a wrench can quickly change your world forever. Consider the probable consequences of over-tightening the bolts on an aircraft engine.

In business, it's the same. Thrust suddenly into a major, floundering printing company, my most immediate and daunting challenge as CEO was getting a new, non-functioning six-million-dollar printing press to work. Our experienced VP of manufacturing said this was the only press he had ever seen set up with such low bear pressures. We decided to over-tighten the bolts on the press, even though the manufacturer warned us it would seize up and void the warranty. Our reasoning was simple: the press didn't work anyway, and even though a $6-million investment was at stake, we would fail as an ongoing business if we didn't get this particular press going. It was a monstrous press and one that had already sealed my predecessor CEO's demise. The good news is, it worked.

Just a few twists of the wrench made all the difference in the world. The same is true in all aspects of business. Using a few business tools in the right way often means ongoing success in a short time. It's all about having the right business tools and actually using them. This book is about the right tools and how to turn both easy and tough decisions into action; it's about tightening-up *meaningful* nuts and bolts in your business.

So, specifically what's in this book for you?

Let's say you're a manager or executive in an organization somewhere. You wonder: why is it that some enterprises experience immense ongoing success while others drone on in mediocrity, day after day, year after year? The answer is to make your business situation *meaningful,* make it fun again, make it come to life for everyone. There are tools for doing this, and that's what's in this book for you: easy-to-use tools to instill meaning in your enterprise and insure success for you as manager.

These are "go-do-it" tools, not just more "how to" lessons. These are tools that fit comfortably in your hand. They're CEO tools for managers that match virtually everyone's management style. Maybe you're not sure what your management approach is. Perhaps you want to change it. Then what's in this book for you is a proven seven-step management process and style. Each process step corresponds with one of the seven core chapters in which a dozen or so tools are meticulously described to make that management step meaningful again, successful again.

Actually, you may have tried a few of the tools to tune up your organization's performance in the past. Perhaps these tools haven't made it into your regular tool kit because of marginal success in the past or maybe just not knowing how to really make them work. What's in this book for you, then, is a set of straightforward implementation instructions to insure successful application of the tools. Consider the following tools to pique your interest:

Key customer-impacting jobs. What if the key people in your business suddenly began giving your customers more than any competitor could? What if you could give customers "superb meaningful performance?"

What gets measured gets done. Sure you've heard this, but did anyone ever tell you there were three steps to making it work? What would happen if you were measuring just the one or two things that would enable growth at four times your industry's average growth rate?

One-page business plan with *unique business proposition.* What if everyone around you knew what the game plan was and executed their parts perfectly?

Trailing 12-months charts. Did you know that most charts and many numerical comparisons actually lie to you? What if you had a special kind of chart that always told you the truth, and what if it tracked what *causes sales growth* to happen? Then could you manage what *causes growth?*

Quarterly priorities sharing. What would happen if your management team members shared their five most-important priorities with each other and helped each other achieve them? Wouldn't a lot more get done? What performance might result if this happened all the time?

Each of these tools is easy to use and is certain to improve your impact as a manager as well as your business results. That's what's in this book for you.

Disclaimer – What's <u>not</u> in this Book?

This book and CD are intended as a learning experience with information about business and management. The book and CD offer insight but not definitive roadmaps and do not guarantee success. While use of the book/CD does not assure success, numerous organizations continue to garner great ongoing results with the tools.

NO SOFTWARE SUPPORT: The CD is provided without software support and without provision for human interaction to help with its use. Consulting, for a fee, is available – contact Corporate Partners through the publisher. Please refer to the Customer License Agreement provided on the CD, containing additional important provisions and limitations. Internet sources included in the book and on the CD are now available but may not be available in the future.

Neither the author, nor the publisher, nor anyone else associated with preparation, production, or delivery of the book or the CD shall bear any responsibility or liability to any person or entity with respect to any damage or loss of any kind whatsoever resulting from use of the tools and concepts presented in the book and/or the CD, whether directly or indirectly.

If you do NOT wish to accept total responsibility for your personal use and the use by your organization of the tools and concepts offered in the book and/or CD, and accept the additional provisions provided above and in the CD License, please return the book and CD to the publisher for a complete refund. Please sign your name below and return this actual page with original receipt to indicate you want a refund and that you have kept no copies of the book, CD or tools and that you will not use the tools.

Publisher: *Gandy Dancer Press*
P.O. Box 2190
Stockbridge, GA 30281 U.S.A.
Phone (770) 389-5768
Email: *info@ceotools.com*

Your name, address & phone:

_____

_____

_____

_____

CEO Tools

The Nuts-n-Bolts of Business for Every Manager's Success

CEO Tools

by

Kraig Kramers

Gandy Dancer Press

xviii

$$\$\$\$$$

<CLICK> icons on the
enclosed CD to try special
automated tools identified
by the following symbol:

(CEO Tool)

Introduction – Business Tools for More Profits Right Now

Having exactly the right tools for the job makes everything so much easier. Do you have, for example, a Black & Decker® Electric Screwdriver for tasks not suited to the much slower, manual variety? Is there a Cuisinart® as well as a chef's knife in your kitchen? Or have you ever seen an air-powered impact wrench used on your automobile wheel lug nuts instead of what automakers laughably supply as a wheel-wrench? Success in business isn't simple: it's a rapidly changing, complex game, in which you want exactly the right tools to propel your company's performance with customers, people, and – ultimately – profit.

So, start right now with just a handful of the right tools for improving your managerial performance, increasing productivity all around you and growing profits. Here are a few tools from the seven management process steps from chapters one through seven:

1. Make goals meaningful motivators. Try setting really *big audacious goals* (BAGs) together with your people. Big results happen by reaching higher, not by setting perfect, purely logical goals. Add fun to assure success. Make it okay to fail, okay to fall short of BAGs while still striving. You'll beat budget like a drum! Then celebrate success; else your next BAG won't work. As chief executive officer at Graphic Arts Center (GAC) printing in Oregon, my job was made easy by this tool for 17 consecutive quarters of record-setting profit growth. Here's a second tool: write a *1-page business plan* explaining your overall goal, your vision and

Big Audacious Goals

1-Page Business Plan

1

your action plans, and then give copies to all employees. Share your business targets to help everyone focus on

CEO Tool
1-Pg BP

what's important. Translate to key employees what they can do to achieve the jointly accepted goal shown in your 1-page business plan. For four years this tool guided our growth at GAC printing, taking us from $60 million in sales to $120 million. Our industry grew at only single-digit rates.

2. Communicate for meaningful results. Start by listening mightily to every employee at every level of your business. Don't assume people at the bottom don't have good ideas. The best tool here is *walk the four corners (W4C)* of your business for 20 minutes every day, asking your people how to improve the company, how to fix

Walk Your Four Corners

problems and how to seize opportunities. If you ask often and listen hard, they'll shower you with solutions. By the way, don't forget to ask them how they are, too. My first week at Snapper lawnmowers, the employees gave me exactly the right tools to turn this behemoth from a $50 million loss in one year to a $13 million profit the next. It was simply W4C and *asking them how – not* telling them how.

3. Track what's meaningful. Break your long-term goals into workable chunks with the *Quarterly Priorities*

QPM: Top Management Tool

Manager (QPM), the single most powerful management tool in *any* business. Spell out your own top five priorities for the next 90 days, the big meaningful ones, the stepping-stones to your vision. Show the list to your key people for feedback and buy-in; then get their top five priorities as well. Coach and

CEO Tool
QPM

support progress during the quarter. Jointly share final results and repeat the process for the ensuing quarter. Apply the QPM to get results. The QPM startled us at GAC printing by making a permanent change in our mindset about the industry norm of losing money in the first quarter every year. Another tool is the *Trailing 12-Month Chart (T12M)*,

2

the single most meaningful measurement tool in business. It's a rolling annual total chart that reads instantly and true for every key business indicator. You must try T12M, so jump to chapter three now for a quick test-drive.

CEO Tool
T12M Chart

4. Anticipate the future – then realize it. Determine your *right growth rate* by seeing how fast your company can grow while not running out of cash. Use your computer to model sales increases of 10, 20 and 30 percent per year, keeping an eye on the cash account shown on your projected balance sheet.

CEO Tool
Right

At the point the modeled sales increase causes cash to approach zero, you've reached maximum growth. Now ease back a few percent to leave a buffer zone of safety. Then put pedal to metal for greater growth to pump up profits. Don't run out of cash as most do: slowly, then suddenly! Try this tool soon.

5. Place and coach winners. The most meaningful tool here is *key customer-impacting jobs.* Look inside your company and find the three or four jobs that have the biggest impact on customers. Get those jobs exactly right by putting winners in them and agreeing on what constitutes superb

> Key
> Customer-
> Impacting
> Jobs

performance for your customer. Then give your key people the tools, training, compensation and recognition to produce that level of performance. Stand back: the fuse is lit for a profit explosion! This tool galvanized our growth at Guarantee Insurance Resources in Atlanta, propelling a profit gain of 31% in one year at this already super-profitable medical insurer.

6. Get organized to get results. Create a *one-page company calendar.* It's a list of all the important goals, projects and dates for the next 12 months. Give copies to all employees. Now

CEO Tool
CoCal

they can manage their own time instead of you managing it. This calendar also points employees at the work needed to make your business successful. Revise and republish the company calendar regularly so that employees can always plan ahead for the next 12 months. At Courtesy Coffee in San Diego, this tool facilitated 100% sales growth in just two years while competitors saw only nominal improvement.

7. Celebrate every success. Try *recognition buck$,* a nifty tool for praise and recognition. It provides fun ways for employees at all levels to recognize each other for outstanding job performance. Give this simple recognition buck$ form to all employees; encourage them to praise others. Maybe add a reward, like an expense-paid weekend away with spouse for those who get recognized most, and for those who recognize others the most. Recognition was the underlying tool for making GAC printing the leading fine color printer in America for over eight years.

Every one of these tools will work to better your business right now. In subsequent chapters you'll find useful details for applying the tools. Since each of us must do things our own way, please plan to fine-tune each tool so that you're comfortable using it the way you do things. And encourage people in your company to do the same, within appropriate guidelines that you set. Many more money-making tools lie ahead, with two enhancements: a *management process* which adds context to using the tools, and the *state of we* in which everyone works in sync and attains superstar dream-team success. When realized, *we* puts and keeps your company at the forefront of your industry.

It's been challenging and fun during my career to discover these CEO/manager tools. Yet even greater fun was the revelation that there was a management process in which the tools had a distinct, sequential place. This is much like the way you would build something from wood. As an example, to final-sand a piece of wood before it is properly cut to size with saws is usually fruitless. First we measure twice, then cut once, sand an awful lot, and then finish the wood. Quite a few tools are involved and there is a definite sequence, some patience, and a process. It's the same in business for consistent high-quality results: we need some kind of management process in which sequencing the tools will yield the greatest results. Each of the tools in this book will give you rewarding results on its own, but when taken together in a sequence, real magic occurs.

Many managers and CEOs give up on becoming excellent in certain business areas because they can't find tools that work, or the tools aren't easy enough or intuitive enough to use. Or maybe some business areas just aren't their forte. The goal in this book is to make it easy for you to implement the right tools that indeed exist for every business area and every business function, and to demonstrate that you yourself don't have to implement every one of them. That should be great news! Simply share this book with your key players and get them to implement tools that fit your organization, especially the ones that appeal to you but that are not your own personal forte. By doing this, you will almost certainly cover all the business areas needing attention, areas you might have been neglecting or even avoiding in the past.

There's also a quantum state in business that goes beyond the tools and beyond the process. It's an amazing level, where everything goes just right; everything becomes perfect harmony. Having experienced this harmony several times, it's really worth working to get there. When you're ready to conduct your business like a philharmonic symphony orchestra, there is a path. As CEO of eight companies in as many different industries and of as many different sizes, a flash hit me one day that there was more to business success than tools or process. It was getting to the *state of we.*

Remember the Johnny Cash song, *One Piece at a Time*? Most people don't recognize it by title, yet you'll smile when you recall the lyrics describing an auto assembly worker who builds his dream car "one piece at a time" by smuggling parts and bits out of the plant in his lunchbox. Whether you like Mr. Cash and country-western music or not, many such songs contain amazingly applicable management messages.

> **Implement the Tools "One Piece at a Time"**

One piece at a time is how big sustainable successes happen. At Snapper, the leading-brand lawnmower manufacturer, we found that re-starting the plant just wouldn't work following a major consolidation of three plants into one. Not only was everything in a different place in the newly configured plant, but new lawnmower designs, a new product-look, and a narrowed supplier group had virtually straitjacketed our workers' ability to assemble lawnmowers. Everyone was complaining about how Engineering's new designs weren't right, how Purchasing had bought bolts that were too short, how our Suppliers hadn't delivered what was ordered, much less on time, and how Marketing's new labels didn't fit or were too hard to put on straight.

Saturday 7:30 a.m.: Clad in blue jeans and ready to get dirty, the senior management team – including the CEO and seven senior Vice-Presidents representing as many different functional areas – arrived at the Snapper plant. We proceeded to hand-assemble a dozen different first-article lawnmowers, *one piece at a time*, discovering and correcting the problems as we worked, and rendering redesigns and emergency requests to suppliers on the spot. By Saturday night at

| "One Piece at a Time" is a GREAT Tool! |

10 p.m. enough had been done to free up the bottlenecks so that the plant could begin humming by midday on Monday. That one "piece" involving hands-on assembly by us Ivory Tower types set the example for everyone else at Snapper to quit grousing and get back to building lawnmowers. By no means was it the only piece in making up our version of the dream car, but it sure jump-started things and put us on the path to a *state of we*.

It also reminded us that most problems in business have their origins in lack of coordination and communication among people.

| Communicate to the Right Person |

Snapper's workers saw that their management was willing to get their hands dirty to discover that the reasons lawnmowers couldn't be assembled was because people who understood the individual problems were not talking to each other, or for certain weren't talking to the *right* each others. Above all, management means coordination and communication, done one piece at a time, but done until the dream car is built, and then built over and over again the right way.

6

That single management tool at Snapper worked and worked really well, all by itself. It energized employees to begin coordinating and communicating better. They began instigating problem correction on the spot on their own, made recommendations more readily, and went back to work making great Snapper lawnmowers.

The Magic of We

What you're about to experience is a complete tool-chest of tested and on-point management tools that make more money, that catalyze customer care, that enhance employee enjoyment, and that just make it fun to be in business. Each tool stands on its own. Taken together, the tools will soon carry your organization from *us and them* to that magical place we're calling *we*. That *we* is Johnny Cash's dream car.

Having the right business tools creates consistently successful business performance. Yet to realize ongoing superlative results requires a solid, well-practiced management process. To move even further up the scale, consistent, high quality, unassailable, superlative results requires the state of we. *We* is more than team and more than high profit for a year or two. It's where everyone around the business, meaning employees, customers, suppliers and community are totally in sync, totally aligned. Let's not get the metaphorical cart before the horse: first, the management process.

Tune Up *Your* Management Process Today

What's your management process? What right tools get you results as a manager? What's the sequence in using those tools? If someone had asked me these questions ten years back, no ready responses would have come forth, and even hypothetical answers would have been hard to formulate. While having been a successful CEO in more than half-a-dozen different businesses, I couldn't have told you exactly what created results for me. Yet, there was a singular, step-wise management process and there were definite results-producing tools in each process step. It was decidedly disconcerting to learn my successes came from these tools and process, and that it wasn't just me.

Certainly, this management process won't work perfectly for everyone – although it sure works for me. But even if mine doesn't fit you to a "T," hopefully you'll be motivated to take a closer look at what you do to get results in your business, and then take action to improve it. After all, we hear that golfing sensation Tiger Woods works on his backswing every day and look where that's gotten him. Here's our management process to improve the sequencing of your tools:

The Seven-Step Management Process

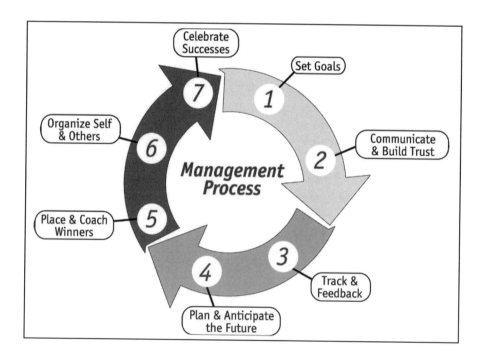

Seven-Step Management Process

1. **Make goals meaningful motivators.** What do goals mean in your business? Are they used to motivate? How are you having fun with goals? What are your people focused on, if not goals? As author Hannah Moore so aptly observed: "Obstacles are those frightful things you see when you take your eyes off the goal." Are your people seeing obstacles? Or, are they motivated deep down by the goals, hurdling over every obstacle that gets in the way?

2. **Communicate to get meaningful results.** Without a healthy level of trust in a company, communication stops cold or goes underground. And vice-versa. How are you building both trust and communication? What tools do you use regularly? Clark Johnson, the retired CEO of Pier 1 Imports, said it so well: "Communication can rise only to the level of trust in an organization."

3. **Track what's meaningful.** Tracking is about measuring and regularly feeding back meaningful indicators to those who can improve the outcomes you desire. What do you track? Is it focused, few, and fervent? How do you make it information and not just more data? What are your measurement and feedback tools? Will Rogers said it best: "Even if you're on the right track, you'll get run over if you just sit there." How do you track both results and runaway or surprise situations?

4. **Anticipate the future and then realize it.** Have you decided how fast to grow your business? How do you manage "what *causes* sales?" What are your target opportunities and when will you seize the moment? George Steiner, the granddaddy of modern planning, put it so well: "Planning is looking into the future, changing

your own current behavior, and then creating better results." Are you doing all three?

5. **Place and coach winners.** Every manager should be good at this, but most aren't, presumably because we're not taught it in college or in business until we learn it in the post-graduate school of hard knocks. What can you do to improve yourself and those around you at placing/coaching? Jerry Goldress, the preeminent turnaround guru, talks about "putting superstars in game-breaker positions." What are your game-breaker positions and who's making sure you have matching superstars? How frequent is the coaching for your key people? Who's attending to this in your company? Check out the great movie *Hoosiers* to get more insight. It's just the best management movie ever made and a box-office hit, too. Keep a pad handy to jot down management messages and leadership lessons.

6. **Get organized to get results.** Lou Lundborg, the super-successful chairman for decades at BankAmerica, sought only two characteristics in those he hired: a high energy level and an ability to *organize self and others*. How do you stay organized? How do you organize others? What are your organizing and process-improving tools? When did you last upgrade them?

7. **Celebrate every success.** Are you having fun? Are you making sure those around you are enjoying their work? How? How often? Do you measure employee satisfaction and pro-act to keep it high? Most large, successful public companies do. That might surprise you. Many of them even measure the number of fun events and the happiness of employees on an ongoing basis. Herb Kelleher at Southwest Airlines proved irrefutably that "employee happiness creates customer happiness," while certain others (for instance, Delta Air Lines and United Airlines) seem to have headed in quite the opposite direction in both constituencies in recent

years.   Which airline would you rather fly, if you actually had a choice?

As leaders, most of us appear to be unaware of our own management processes. It's like your backswing in golf: you can't see it, yet it has a direct and profound impact on your accuracy and distance. In business, these are called performance and longevity. Our management backswing evolves as we work through our careers, and then one day, usually quite by accident, we discover that we have something we use all the time. Even then, however, we rarely think about the steps involved, kind of like that old "sharpen the saw" adage. Everyone knows that a sharp saw cuts far better than a dull one. And most of the time we're so focused on cutting down trees that we don't take a few moments to step back and sharpen the saw. When we do stop and sharpen, the number of trees cut by the end of the day far exceeds what we would have cut without honing our tools.

Imagine that you are videotaping your management backswing: what does it look like, what are the stages or steps you go through, what do others say your weak spots are? How can you tweak your management process to yield greater returns?   Getting answers to these questions, and taking a more deliberate look, leads to new performance levels.

> Fine-Tune Your Backswing

Through such introspection we always see how to improve our own business game.

So let's ask again: *What's your management process? What tools get you results as a manager? What's the sequence in using your tools?* You can answer these questions to help improve your existing management process, or maybe it's easier to adopt or adapt parts of the management process we've offered here.

Getting to a Culture of *We*

Everyone wants to jump right to *we* and just skip over the management process and the organizational development that entails. You can't just jump to *we*. Consistent application of a few tools in

11

each critical area will get you there. So there is a short cut, after all, and it involves embedding your own management process using some communication and recognition tools. After some time working on it you'll get to *we* surprisingly quickly. The military calls this "time-in-grade."

Now it doesn't occur overnight, but it does indeed occur. You score some small successes here and a few more there, and one day, probably as you're walking the four corners of your business, you discover you have generated this "we" feeling inside your company.

| The "We" Culture |

Suddenly everyone's happy just making it happen. Customers win big at this point. No longer will you hear the "us versus them" or "that's not my job" mentalities so common in so many companies. Instead, you begin to hear, "wow, we sure took care of Jane Customer today!" and "tough day, but we got it done!" Or, "production is a little behind but don't worry, we'll get there." It may be hard to pinpoint the exact moment the transformation occurs. But you'll know when it does because it's like a locomotive under full steam; it's rolling, and you can't stop it. You won't ever want to, either.

| Happy People Make Happy Customers |

It takes hard work, dedication, consistent application of a management process plus a commitment to continual learning to achieve the *we* culture. When you do, your organization can accomplish anything it sets out to achieve and no competitor can touch you. Obviously, it's worth the extra effort.

Use the Tools = Take Action *Now!*

| First Use Measuring Tools... |

Owning the right tools isn't enough. Owning good, sharp tools isn't enough. They need to be used. We managers must take action with some sharp *implementation* tools because some other special *measuring* tools are telling us to take action. Action brings results. Nobody running a business ever made big bucks by just thinking, intellectualizing or talking about doing something. There's no question that communication will

12

improve performance and is the grease for speeding along ongoing results, but big sustainable things happen only by taking action – action that's augmented and coordinated by ongoing communication. In order to achieve goals, we have to get out there and act. This means doing things to set the example as well as making things happen through others.

...Then Use
Action
Tools

Turning that around, action without purpose and direction often creates adverse results. Being effective means doing the *right* things, taking the *right* action. How would you like to create a system – and tools that work within that system – to help you take the right action almost every time to get the results you want? Sounds simple and it is. It's about reading the signals, taking action and making more money. The rest of this book is dedicated to you – and to your endeavors to hone the right system for you with the right tools for you.

Track Key Indicators	Use Tools & Take Action	Make Money
👥📈	☺🛠️➡️	$🔼

Chapter 1 – Make Goals *Meaningful* Motivators

A goal is like a dartboard – you get points for just being on the board. You don't have to hit the bull's-eye every time to score. One of the CEO's "musts" is to make goals so meaningful that they move everyone to action, to try to score. True for all managers, not just CEOs. When goals become meaningful motivators, magic happens. The dartboard analogy helps most everyone see how to move toward action, how to score, and how to make meaningful, magical results.

At Graphic Arts Center, a major commercial printing company, everyone understood the goal of doubling sheet-fed printing sales from $12 to $24 million annually over the ensuing two years. Sheet-fed represented about 20 percent of our total volume. This meant accelerating growth in this product segment to about six times the industry growth rate over a two-year period for this Portland-based printing company. *Everyone* at GAC understood the goal: customers, employees, managers, suppliers, and even our community.

What made doubling sheet-fed volume so meaningful? Why did everyone buy into it so well? Simply put, the doubling of sheet-fed would generate enough profit to buy all new sheet-fed printing presses. Those new presses really had big meaning to each constituency. For customers they represented state-of-the-art machinery that would produce the very best printed products. For employees the presses were new and exciting to use, to show off, and to brag about. Suppliers loved them, too, since they gobbled paper and ink even faster. Our friends and neighbors knew this meant prosperity for the community, including more jobs and lower

> Set
> Meaningful
> Goals

emissions. We communicated hard so that everyone really grasped the *meaning* of doubling sheet-fed in two years. As a result, every constituency helped move us toward that goal.

In the first few months at the printing company, we set another meaningful goal: we wanted to explode away from our flat year-to-year $60 million in sales and become a $100 million per year industry leader. Why one hundred million? When first asked this question, my answer was an immediate, spontaneous, yet straight from the heart: "Why? Because $100 million's a noble number!" People laughed when I first said it, and so did I. Reflect on it for a moment and it becomes obvious: people think of you differently if you say you're a $100 million company as opposed to saying we did $99 million last year. You enter a new league. All of a sudden you're playing with the big kids.

It's the CEO's job, and yes, every manager's job, to lead in the setting of meaningful direction. And then make the message about that goal even more meaningful through the tool of

| Communicate Meaningful Goals |

communication. How did we communicate it at GAC? Well, the message was literally everywhere: signs on walls shouting out the goal, everyone talking about the goal at every meeting, managers reiterating it as we "walked the four corners" of our business, and customers and suppliers echoing the familiar strain. More sheet-fed meant getting the best printing presses. Rapid growth meant being a winning team.

Customers, employees and suppliers always want to be part of being a winner. In those early days at GAC – early for me since GAC was a 90-year-old company – we saw Esprit, Victoria's Secret, Nordstrom and many other brand names give us more print jobs in response to our new big goals, we saw Crown Zellerbach and James River give us better paper prices, we saw our own people giving it extra hours and extra effort.

Goals should be at a minimum envisionable and always challenging to be effective. The doubling of sheet-fed in two years at GAC was indeed a challenge, since it was way over 40 percent per year compound growth. Yet the seven regional sales managers said they could do it and wanted to try. They knew it was challenging and to them, it was fun. They also knew that they had grown at similar rates in the past and even though the numbers were smaller back then, they knew it would be exciting to take this new challenge. They could envision the challenge and see that maybe, just maybe, they could make it happen.

Go, Make It Happen

Can the challenge ever become a hallucination? You bet, and in fact it did in the second year of the turnaround at Snapper lawnmowers, where the lesson of setting goals just a tad too high was taught to me once again. The big audacious goal we had set for Snapper that year was so far out of reach three months into the year that it became de-motivating. This happened because we were forced to cut back on volume into our pipeline of distributors and dealers so that we wouldn't overload them with product relative to what consumers were buying at retail. We tracked this very carefully each week, and we just had to face curtailment. We suddenly were experiencing a *hallucination* instead of the big audacious fun goal we had all agreed to pursue. We needed to back down to more realistic goals. So we told employees and the parent company about the cutback. Nobody really liked the bad news, especially our parent company. But by replacing the old, overreaching goal with a new goal, we continued to stay challenged and kept on making money.

Goals become most meaningful and managers can repeat their successes by celebrating the goal's accomplishment, or even its near-achievement. In fact we failed to meet the goal of doubling sheet-fed at GAC printing from $12 million to $24 million in that second year. The actual number was $23.9 million. Yet we celebrated the success big-time, and in so doing cemented an ongoing commitment to have fun with new challenging goals. Celebration made those big goals a regular way of life.

Celebrate Meaningful Goals

Nothing leads to success like having clear, written, *repetitively communicated* goals. Nothing! Unfortunately, in most companies the goals are

Repetitive Communication Tool

ambiguous and relatively unknown to anyone outside the senior management team. And often, even that senior management team sees only a vague, unclear picture of the goals. To get where you want to go, everyone – yes, *everyone* from the person who sweeps the floor at night to the CEO – has to know what the company goals are, why they're important, and what needs to be done in their own individual jobs to achieve those company goals.

How goals are set also has a tremendous impact on both individual and overall organizational performance. By far the most important lesson to be learned here is to *encourage people to set their own goals.* Sounds a bit weird, huh? Well, how often have we gone into planning sessions with goals we thought were fairly aggressive, just to find in amazement that our management team tosses them out the window and insists upon much more difficult objectives?

> **Encourage Reaching Individual Goals**

Equally amazing, a good many CEOs and managers have never really seen this same phenomenon of the team wanting to reach higher, usually because they've been setting, selling and even hammering their own unrealistically low goals and even then getting resistance at that low level. The term "sandbagging" comes to mind. The curious thing is that, as long as a few essential factors are in place, most people will always set higher goals and achieve much more, given the chance. Don't tell people what they could or should or ought to accomplish. Work jointly at goals and encourage them to decide for themselves. Then support them and provide resources for achieving their goals: that's the job of management. Clark Johnson, while CEO at Pier 1 Imports during its explosive growth years, captured it so clearly: "My greatest nightmare is not setting the hurdle high enough with my team."

There are six fundamental principles that can improve your goal setting in this third millennium and assure having aggressive goals for every one of your people. You stand a much better chance of getting where you want to go with this straightforward process:

> **Goal Setting Process**

1. Use the budget as the base. Set it as the minimum acceptable performance for your company or group in the year ahead – make it the do-or-die basis for sales, costs and expenses. Set realistic, achievable, but somewhat challenging goals. It should be a reaching but reasonable budget, meaning you need to go some to get it, but it is fairly do-able. Otherwise it discourages your employees from the get-go, even before getting started.

2. Then, together and a few days later, set some bigger, more audacious goals that are higher and much more difficult, but position these so it will be fun to go for them and just fine if you fall short. Include a compensation scheme that accelerates above budget. Think of the big audacious goal as the bull's-eye of a dartboard, where everyone still gets points for missing the center but hitting the dartboard. Make it fun. The budget is a box that surrounds your dartboard as a zone where it's okay to throw your dart. You even get budget-accomplishment points if you miss the dartboard but are still in the box.

   It's Okay to Miss the Bull's-eye!

3. Never set goals in isolation from the organization. People work harder to achieve goals they participate in creating themselves, especially in a group.

4. Test your goals against company values and against your business strategy to assure that they are in sync. If not, toss those goals out and try again. Check out chapter four for some nifty strategy tools.

5. Once you have arrived at meaningful goals, communicate them again and again. Then communicate them some more. Repetitive communication is what's needed. There will be a number of tools in the next chapter to help with repetitive communication.

6. Praise and reward behavior that supports the goals, remembering that if you can't measure it, you can't reward it. Show your achievers that you care by providing positive feedback. This will automatically prime them for the next round of achievement.

To get meaningful goals to create results every time involves jointly setting the goals, communicating about them often, measuring results, and praising the performance of people. If you have a few folks who can't seem to write a goal, here's a little teaching tool for goal setting. Show them VERB+NOUN+DATE on a flipchart. Beneath that write a goal, such as: Take sales from $60M to $100M in 3 years. Then show how Take is the verb, sales from $60M to $100M is the noun, and in 3 years is the date. Then cement their understanding by writing underneath that the following ultimate Verb+Noun+Date goal, namely DO IT NOW! Everyone who's ever seen this remembers how to write a goal and how to teach goal setting.

> Goal Tool:
> V + N + D

How about taking a look now at a few tools for setting organizational goals to achieve results beyond your wildest dreams?

Set a Single *Overall Goal* with Your Team

What if we set an overall goal and everyone bought into it? Let's explore an *overall, big-picture goal* to communicate to everyone. The idea is to provide a "north star," an unshakable and immovable compass bearing to guide everyone's efforts. This overall team or company goal goes far beyond budget or projections and typically has a time frame longer than a year. Remember at the printing company when we stalled at $60 million in sales? We set a three-year net sales goal of $100 million. By focusing on that overall company goal, we grew at about 20 percent a year while our industry advanced at less than a third of that.

> Overall
> Goal

How do you get people to go for the gold, to embrace commitment? Do these four things:

1. Eliminate the fear of failure,
2. Make the goal a target (dartboard with bull's-eye), not a "must-do,"
3. Make that bull's-eye a stretch, and above all,
4. Have fun going for it; cheerlead along the way.

Here's how it might work for you. Sit down with your management team and create a reasonable, workable budget. Make it clear that missing budget is not an option; then align the compensation plan so that everyone will be happy making the budget. So now you've nailed down the budget. Let this sit for a few days. Let it sink in. Then call your team back together and say, "the budget is the budget and it's set in stone; we're not going to mess with it. But let's have some fun now! Let's set a bigger goal that goes way beyond the budget and let's just have a good time going for it. If we don't hit it, it's okay. But by reaching beyond budget, we'll stretch some and go at it only so long as it's fun. We'll leave the compensation scheme open-ended upwards, so that as we go above budget and approach the goal, everyone will make a lot more money." Then open it up for discussion. Make it okay to fall short of the goal. You will be absolutely amazed at how high your people will reach.

Ralph Waldo Emerson reasoned: "People who reach higher, achieve more." Even way back then it wasn't rocket science. Emerson's been gone for over 100 years. Miracles will happen by design when you put the four critical goal-setting elements for overall goals in place as described above. Of course, be sure you have the right people in the right positions. Our job as manager or CEO has now been transformed into that of leading rather than selling and/or shoving people toward goals or even worse, complaining that our people didn't even get close to the goals after the fact. Once the dust settles, it's always *us*, not them. Always. So turn it around.

Always Reach Higher!

But what if our people just won't go for more reaching goals? Either we need new people or a new leader. My suggestion is that it's more often the latter and that you be the first to recognize it. What to do about it? Grow yourself as a leader as provided in chapters five,

23

seven and eight.   Maybe terminate one or two of the lowest
performers to get everyone else's attention. But don't do nothin'.

Big Audacious Goals

If you really want your people to accomplish amazing things,
try setting *big, audacious goals* with them. The best BAGs are those
that are acceptable challenges, like making a buck in what has always
been a loss month. A BAG doesn't necessarily have to be stated in
terms of total revenue or dollars. Your BAG can also
target number of units sold, or number of happy
customers, or number of client cases successfully
resolved. It can be any measure of quality or customer satisfaction, or
just about anything that leads to outstanding performance for the
organization as a whole. Regardless of what you decide to target and
measure, the secret to success is making sure everyone in the
company understands the BAG, has fun going for it, and stays
focused on it with laser-beam precision. This means setting a very
clear goal and then communicating it over and over and over again.
Once you get it right, titanic things happen.

Set Big Audacious Goals

Just before joining GAC printing as its chief executive, the
company had hit the wall after several consecutive years of very
healthy growth. Sales had gone flat and stayed that way, despite slow
but steady overall growth within the industry. When a company stalls
out like that, many things happen. People get bored and frustrated
because they don't feel challenged or successful any more. Profits go
down because expenses keep climbing when sales don't. The sense
of fun and challenge evaporates into thin air. Pretty soon the winners
leave. (Why is it that losers never leave?) The company drops into
complacency and then decline.

My decision as group VP at the parent company and as
overseer of the printing group was to intervene before GAC reached
the point of disastrous descent. It dawned on me that this was a great
opportunity to leave the parent and actually go run GAC. My first
week there, GAC happened to be staging its regular quarterly sales

management meeting with its seven regional sales managers from around the country. My first question at this meeting was, "how do we get things going again?" Startled, one sales manager asked, "you mean growth?"

"You bet – growth is great fun," I responded.

Another observed: "Your predecessor never talked about growth. He was stuck in the drone zone." What he meant was the pace of the pack can't exceed the pace of the leader. Think about a dog-sled team for a moment as the extreme example. Too many CEOs and managers relax into complacency or coasting. Remember, the only direction you can coast very long is downhill, and even that ends pretty quickly.

> **No Drone Zones!**

GAC's managers looked at each other for a few moments, uncertain about what to say next. Finally one ventured, "we know how to grow – sheet-fed print jobs. Those orders produce twice the gross margin as web-press print jobs. And another thing, web-press orders have three-to-nine-months' lag time before printing and billing. Sheet-fed orders get printed, shipped and billed in just a few days."

"How fast could we grow sheet-fed?" was my next, natural question.

Another manager spoke up. "Our competitors average four to eight percent growth per year for sheet-fed, but we could double our production in two years if we get aggressive. We've grown that fast before."

Now *that* would get anyone's attention. My knee-jerk response was, "let's go for it!" The managers began talking excitedly in side conversations. You could feel the energy rising in the room.

But someone in the back of the room spoke up over the din, "hold on folks, hold on. We need new sheet-fed printing presses. No way could we double production without them."

Immediately my comeback was: "Well we can't just rush out and buy new presses – we're barely profitable as it is!" And after a moment of thought, quickly added, "I went to the John Housman School of Business." Of course there isn't such a place – my MBA was from Stanford University. Well, everyone remembered Mr. Housman when I then referred to his Smith Barney TV commercials, "we need to do it the old fashioned way, we need to *earn* it."

Their next question was, "do you mean we have to first achieve the $24 million in sheet-fed sales and then we'll get new sheet-fed presses?"

I responded, "well, what if we set out growing sheet-fed as fast as we can, and after three or four months if we're on track to double in two years, we'll go buy our first new sheet-fed press? And it'll be state-of-the-art, a Heidelberg Speedmaster 6-color, 40-inch press." They really liked the idea of earn it as you go. It was logical and a challenge. People love challenges, as long as they're framed in a sensible, believable way.

| Earn It As You Go! |

"And we'll keep on getting a new press every few months," I continued, "as long as we can keep growing at that pace of doubling every two years." After all, you just don't want to go out and fill up a room with eight $1.5 million printing presses before proving that you can earn, or justify, them. Everyone at GAC bought into the concept. We all excitedly went to work on it.

Several weeks later, the parent company came to see us to inquire about how we might be doing at getting GAC going again. They brought the senior management team of the parent company plus the three other printing company presidents, who had been in printing their entire working lives. My role at the front of the room was to dazzle them with how we would get GAC immensely profitable immediately, including the sheet-fed doubling strategy. The other three printing company presidents insisted we couldn't grow much faster than 12 percent or 14 percent per year, that the doubling of sheet-fed in two years, which amounts to over 40 percent per year, was truly impossible.

Here's a quick flashback: our parent company president had brought in Dick Vermeil about a year before to talk with us, and Mr. Vermeil allowed as how "I Will" (commitment) was at least as important as "IQ" (smarts or intelligence) every time. Now some may not recognize Dick Vermeil's name, but he had been the very successful coach of the Philadelphia Eagles™ football team for a bunch of years, retired for a while, then came back to coach St. Louis. For several years not much good seemed to happen, at least not visibly with the St. Louis football team, and some people were saying, maybe Vermeil's lost it. Maybe that "I Will" stuff doesn't work anymore. Well until the 1999 Superbowl which was won by Mr. Vermeil and the St. Louis Rams™. It seemed that Dick Vermeil was back with a vengeance! He was right and still is: you need both "IQ" and "I Will" with a tad more of the latter. Without the commitment to make it work and the smarts to make it work, you might as well pack up and go home. Luckily, we had both at GAC printing.

Get Commitment

Yet despite our best efforts, we learned that those other experienced printing company presidents also knew what they were talking about…well, up to a point. Indeed, you can't double sheet-fed in two years. As mentioned previously, by the end of the second year we had only hit $23.9 million in sales, missing our target by a horrifying one percent! The moral of the story, of course, is that if we had set the goal at $18 million, a still quite daunting target, we would never have come even close to $23.9 million. Without the big audacious goal of doubling sales in two years, we never would have gotten as far as we did. Thanks to setting a BAG, we almost hit $24 million, and the last two or three million dollars of sales volume were almost pure profit.

The very best part was how much fun we had chasing after that goal. Every time we captured an order for sheet-fed, someone would run down the hall shouting, "sheet-fed, sheet-fed!" followed by a chorus of hoops and hollers from everyone there. Not so much because anyone encouraged it but because we didn't *dis*courage it. As president, my job was to create an environment for fun and let everyone else decide

Create Fun Opportunities

how to have fun. They did, and they will every time. Why not try it yourself?

Here's another example of how a BAG can turn a company around. A few years ago the Snapper lawnmower company was hemorrhaging red ink. It had lost money 18 months in a row, and in one year had managed to produce a preposterous pre-tax loss of $54 million on only $165 million in sales. In the month prior to my becoming Snapper's CEO, it lost $9 million at the pre-tax profit line.

In those circumstances many would consider hitting the break-even point within the next 12 months an absolute miracle. Having previously experienced extraordinary results at GAC with audacity, we set our sights on a much larger target at Snapper.

For the coming year our BAG was $250 million in sales with pretax earnings of $20 million. That's an audacious goal all right: 50 percent sales growth and increase the bottom line by $74 million in one year. It might seem like a hallucination even for a healthy company, but especially for one poised so precariously on the precipice. And it was particularly audacious at a time when the entire industry had declined for five years in a row and was showing every sign of continuing its descending spiral for several more.

Once again we missed our big audacious target, and once again we laughed all the way to the bank. That year we managed $248 million in sales with a pretax profit of $13.7 million versus the $250 million and $20 million goals. And once again this re-emphasizes the value of reaching for the stars. If we had settled for a more reasonable goal, we wouldn't have even come close to our actual results. So, aim high and don't kick yourself if you fail to reach the target; in fact, celebrate. You don't want to fail on the budget and most short-term operational goals, but it's okay to miss the mark on your BAG. So many companies are focused on one level, when instead an acceptable minimum called budget, and great performance called BAG, can provide a zone of attractive results that accommodates both an uncertain outlook and unforeseen or uncontrollable outside influences. You always do better when you aim for a far-reaching goal and you can have a lot more fun in the process. Always remember to celebrate your BAGs so you set the stage for the next one.

The 1-Page Business Plan

There isn't a simpler, more effective tool than the 1-Page Business Plan for getting employees focused on a big audacious fun goal or any other major company or departmental goal, and then for communicating how each of them can contribute to reaching it.

| 1-Page |
| Business |
| Plan |

As managers, our job is to get our employees to "take the hill," to accomplish the primary goal of our company, division or functional area. But in many businesses, the employees don't even know what the hill looks like, much less how to get to the top of it. Few things are more demoralizing than devoting huge amounts of time and energy to capture a hill only to discover once you get to the top that you have taken the wrong hill, in other words, tackled the wrong objective. The 1-page business plan ensures you capture the right hill. It points people in the right direction by providing a clear, compelling prescription: "Here's what we want to do and here's how we want to do it." Put your 1-page business plan in all employees' hands so they can power the organization to the top of the right hill. Talk to them frequently about its contents to reiterate its direction. You might also distribute it to your customers and suppliers so they'll help you make it happen. Customers gave us additional print jobs and suppliers gave us volume discounts once they understood the commitment and challenge represented by our 1-page business plan. We showed them how it was good for them: remember at the beginning of this chapter how new printing presses were good for all our constituents?

Ideally, the 1-page plan should have four sections, but you certainly could add an extra section or two to yours to include mission or vision or your own special thing. You can also change the following four key elements of a 1-page business plan to suit your own needs at the time:

29

1. The **unique business proposition** defines who you are as an organization and what you do in no less than superlative terms. It should describe your company in a way that can make you a market leader and help your people understand the business. Example: Snapper is the #1 brand of lawn-mowers sold through servicing dealers in America.

2. **Purpose** identifies your customers and how you serve them. You must be the best in the world at this, or else be lowest price and commodity status.

3. The **goals** section states your *overall goal* and can also include one or two other key company-wide performance objectives. As an example, our goal is to take GAC from $60 to $100 million in sales over the next three years.

4. **Strategy** explains in general, yet fairly focused terms, where the company needs to go and how everyone will get it there.

What might your 1-page business plan say? How can you put it together? How can you get everyone in your company or group plugged into it?

A sample 1-page business plan is presented on the following page and it's one that really worked at GAC printing. Keep it simple, put it in the hands of all employees, and use it to get them to focus on achieving the goal.

Also, regularly talk with your people about the plan as you walk your four corners. Explain their roles and their specific actions that will lead to success in achieving the 1-page business plan.

GAC GRAPHIC ARTS CENTER

UNIQUE BUSINESS PROPOSITION

Graphic Arts Center is the leading fine color commercial printer in the United States. We serve America's most dynamic businesses with top quality printing of advertising literature, specialty catalogs and annual reports.

PURPOSE

Graphic Arts Center's purpose for being in business is to care for its customers' needs before, during and after delivery of the printed job, and to do that better than any other printer.

GOALS

Graphic Arts Center's immediate goal is to grow to $100 million in annual net sales. We also aim to achieve a return of 25% pretax return-on-equity and 6% pretax return-on-sales.

STRATEGY

Graphic Arts Center's strategy is to extend its leading position in the web and sheetfed commercial printing market in the western United States while expanding its position of market leadership in commercial sheetfed printing in the Northwest. At the same time, Graphic Arts Center will continue to enhance its reputation and position nationally as the top quality catalog and annual report producer.

Our plan is to grow by at least 20% annually through greater penetration of the market segments we know best. We will continue to add to our professional salesforce, which is the largest and best commercial printing sales organization in America. We'll continue to use state-of-the-art technology to serve the quality and delivery needs of our customers. And we will continue to penetrate large metropolitan markets where we are not yet fully represented.

To accomplish this strategy, Graphic Arts Center will continue to attract, train and retain the most talented and customer-conscious employees in the industry.

Finally, our strategy will be undertaken while always putting our customers' needs first.

A different approach is offered in the book entitled *The One Page Business Plan* published in 1998 by Jim Horan. Whichever format you choose for your plan, please do give concise written guidance to your people to help them achieve your joint goals. Getting it all on one page is always a good thing to do when communicating a concept or direction to a group of people. It's crisp and to the point.

31

The Top Five Goals

As an adjunct to the 1-page business plan, the *top five goals* tool gets your senior management team focused. Again, this goes on

Top
Five Goals

one page and lists the company's key financial and performance objectives. Break it into two categories, short-term and long-term objectives, and include five goals in each. For example, during my first year at GAC printing our top five goals identified the following:

Short-Term Objectives
- Achieve pre-tax return on sales (ROS) in upcoming Q3 = 5.5 percent.
- Achieve net sales in the new Fiscal Year of $72 million (+15 percent).
- Upgrade sheet-fed productivity by 20 percent in the new Fiscal Year.
- Reduce receivables days to 55 days from 63 average in the new Fiscal Year.
- Get the Toshiba non-functioning "monster" press running within 3 months.

Long-Term Objectives
- Increase pre-tax ROS to 8 percent average over the next three years.
- Have a long-range product/market direction defined by year-end.
- Develop at least one unique feature or proprietary format for each new press.
- Replace and standardize all sheet-fed presses within two years.
- Achieve $100 million in sales from our current $60 million within 3 years.

Notice we chose five goals each for short-term and long-term, not two nor 20 each. With only two everyone will become bored, and 20 will lead to chaos and confusion where everyone works on all of them and none is completed. Five is just right.

Depending on your management style and corporate culture, you may or may not want to distribute your top five goals to everyone in the company. It's been very valuable to make these goals available to all senior managers, but rarely does it help much to give these out to the rank and file. It's often just too much for them. The principal purpose of top five goals is to be sure you focus on all the short-term and long-term initiatives for the company, and most importantly that some senior manager, some champion, has taken ownership of each one.

> Champions
> for the Big
> Goals

A good reason not to share these goals below the top is that they may contain a goal or two that deals with highly proprietary, confidential or even scary topics. An example might be a goal that talks about reorganizing the company. When people know something like that will be happening to them, but don't know when or what, they worry and stop focusing on work. Productivity declines, and that's the opposite result you want from your top five goals. We'll touch on this in depth in chapter two.

Nowadays many companies, especially those practicing the various forms of open book management, have very open cultures. In those situations it may make sense to share this kind of information at all levels. But this is one instance where you, as president or manager, have to decide what's right for your folks. Please pick one way or the other, not both. In other words, don't choose to be inconsistent. Either way, you'll find the top five goals to be an effective tool in supporting your 1-page business plan and in keeping everyone working together in concert.

Now the most incomparable tool for getting people to focus and work together comes next. It's simply 13 words that place your company ahead of all the rest.

Unique Business Proposition

What does your business really sell, from the customer's viewpoint? What do you really do better than anyone else? That uniqueness is usually whatever it is that's a big source of pride to your people. More important, do your employees, customers and suppliers know and clearly understand what it is that you do so well?

One reason goals work so well is that they keep people focused. But even the best goals won't do any good if your lead people focus on the wrong things. Often we don't set goals well enough and don't communicate them well enough, causing those

around us to go off in their own individual, uncoordinated directions. Either havoc or no progress at all is the usual outcome. By focusing goals toward the company's unique business proposition (UBP), we assure a coordinated outcome. This UBP is your niche, the thing you do differently, and most importantly, the thing you do best of anyone in the entire world! It's the fundamental place pride flows from for our people.

To assure you set goals that go in the right direction, try defining your niche dead-on. Work toward getting crystal clear on the difference between what you think you sell and what your customers are really buying.

For example at GAC printing, after much discussion, we realized that we didn't just sell high-end commercial printing; we sold the positive image-piece that promotes our clients' sales and profits.

The UBP *Defines* the Company's Focus

They called what we did "GAC quality" and it had become the industry standard. It connoted more than quality, reflecting the value-added nuances we were able to suggest in the final design of the printed piece. That distinction made a tremendous difference in how we promoted our products and services and how we interacted with our customers. It also provided needed direction when setting our company goals.

GAC's entire unique business proposition, as accepted by management and all constituencies, was: *GAC is the leading fine color commercial printer in the United States. We serve America's most dynamic businesses with top quality printing of advertising literature, specialty catalogs and annual reports.* The words "fine color" were the generic replacement for "GAC quality" and we got the whole industry, meaning customers and competitors, to use them.

Here are a few more thought-starters to get you going on your own unique business proposition – many thanks to Jeffrey Gitomer, the well-known speaker and author for his influence in making this list possible:

- **Don't sell drill bits – provide perfect hole-makers to your customers.**
- **Don't sell insurance – offer financial security to businesses, protecting them against misfortune.**
- **At Snapper, don't sell lawnmowers – sell beautiful lawns.**
- **Don't sell Courtesy Coffee – sell the 6:00 a.m. waker-upper.**
- **Don't sell Munson's sporting goods – sell the fun of the sport.**
- **Don't sell cars, don't sell transportation – sell prestige (luxury cars).**
- **Don't sell repairs or service – sell worry-free performance.**

As part of this exercise, it helps to ask questions like: What is unique, different, unusual, or compelling about our company that differentiates us from all of our competition? What does our company really do? How do our customers describe us? Why do they say they keep coming back or come to us in the first place?

The unique business proposition is the backdrop for everything your company does, for every goal it sets. Without a unique statement, you as leader hem and haw over what it is your business does, your people feel directionless, and goals are not well directed. The UBP is

CEO Tool
1-Pg BP

the underpinning of the 1-page business plan and very foundation for the company or team vision. Think of it this way: if the president or CEO or manager can't say in 13 words that *Snapper is the #1 brand of lawnmowers*

CEO/Manager
Sets the
Pace

sold through servicing dealers in America, then who can or will in your entire organization? And where is your company headed without this clear articulation? To really make a big point of it, the UBP defines the company's prime focus. Check the CD/Desktop tools to structure your unique business proposition.

Use What Really Motivates (*The Harley*® *Hot Button*)

Setting ambitious goals is one thing; achieving them is another. To get an individual superstar to reach for new frontiers, find out what really motivates that person. It's something special that the person really wants or needs but either can't or won't buy for him/herself. Offer that something as a reward for hitting a big audacious target. The reward should never be money. Bucks are vastly over-rated as a behavior modification tool. You have to pay a competitive salary and offer incentives just to keep top talent, but in most cases, money isn't much more than a base motivator. Think about Maslow's hierarchical pyramid of needs for a moment; money is near the most basic, bottom level of that triangle.

Instead, we're talking about *dreams* here. Everybody has something they long for but either can't afford or can't bring

| Harley® Hot Button |

themselves to spend the money to get. It could be a trip around the world, a Harley-Davidson® motorcycle, or a hot tub on the back patio – anything that fulfills a long-held desire. If you really want to motivate people, identify their dreams and find ways to help fulfill them. When you do, there is nothing they can't accomplish.

At the printing company, our top regional sales manager, Ken Clark, had recently added a big, beautiful music room to his home.

| Offer *Tiered* Rewards |

After about two years, however, it still sat empty. Ken and his wife both loved classical music and had in mind a fine grand piano for their music room. But something other than money had kept the music room empty for quite some time after it was completed. Could it be that the extravagance of writing a $30,000 check for a piano just seemed too much? Maybe buying a Steinway felt just a bit too showy? Whatever it was, we decided to offer Ken a two-tiered incentive plan. If he could get his region to $5.5 million in sales and a profit of $795,000 in the upcoming quarter that year, GAC would present Mr. and Mrs. Clark with a world-class Kawai grand piano valued at $11,000. But if Ken could produce $915,000 of profit, his music room would be filled with the sonorous strains of a Steinway Music Room Grand Piano, the very same version that Vladimir Horowitz had in his New York apartment for so many years. It was worth over $32,000 at the time.

Now this really lit a fire under Ken! But setting a challenging goal is only half the equation. In order to make sure your people achieve it, follow through with plenty of encouragement and enthusiastic support. People often start out with a bang, but as obstacles get in the way, their excitement and belief in their ability to attain the goal can wane quickly. Remember the admonition of author Hannah Moore: "Obstacles are those frightful things you see when you take your eye off the goal." Again, our job as president or manager is to help everyone stay focused on the goal.

> Reinforce Successes Along the Way

During the quarter, we kept encouraging Ken in his endeavor by sending him the latest Steinway catalog, awarding him a state-of-the-art metronome after his first month of success, and offering support and "atta-boys" at every opportunity along the way.

> Eliminate Obstacles in People's Minds

Ken achieved the piano, and within two weeks of the end of the quarter we flew in the best piano setup person and best piano tuner from Los Angeles to install the Steinway properly in the Clarks' music room. After all, why scrimp at the end? You don't just deliver a Steinway, you *install* it. That Steinway piano was absolutely stunning in the Clarks' music room.

At the end of the period, Ken had exceeded the target by generating $938K of profit against the $915K goal. The look of pride and pleasure on Ken's face when that piano arrived made it all worthwhile. Talk about win-win situations! GAC made a tremendous profit that year and we helped one of our most valued people realize a longtime dream. It doesn't get much better than that.

There are several questions to consider when using *The Harley Hot Button*. First, have ready an answer to what happens if your Ken falls a little short, say reaches 99 percent of goal. Our response was a letter in the file that said if Ken hit 90 percent or more of the target, we'd still offer him the Steinway but he had to write a check for the difference (one percent of $32,000 or $320); the file copy was witnessed at the start of the program even though Ken never knew about it. Second, who pays taxes on the piano? The right answer is to gross it up and write a check to Ken for the taxes, including the tax on the check you write to him. Third, be sure to deliver the reward, the Steinway in this case, in a timely manner. When people work that hard to help achieve your goals, they expect you to hold up your end of the bargain. That means following through and delivering the reward without delay. Besides, the closer you link the reward to the behavior, the more you influence the behavior the next time around.

We could easily have called this tool the Steinway Caper, but *The Harley Hot Button* seems to fit. Earlier, Gerry Kivland, our regional sales VP in Seattle, had risen to a similar occasion and as far as I know is still tooling around on his beautiful motorbike.

This chapter proposes a few new approaches in your company, like an overall goal, big audacious goals, a one-page business plans, getting commitment through *I will*, the unique business proposition, no drone zones, Steinways, Harleys and substantially improved profitability by taking a different approach to goals. But what it's really all about is having fun! Put fun with direction back into your company using these tools for making goals more meaningful to everyone. The next chapter offers some ideas for communicating the meaningful goals better, getting more take on them. To wrap up, a list of *Top 10 Tools for Meaningful Goals* follows to recap the tools from this chapter. The list also offers a few new ones to spark your imagination further.

REACH FOR MEANINGFUL GOALS!

Top Ten Tools for *Meaningful* Goals

1. Business unit's *overall goal*. Jointly pick an overall, big picture, meaningful goal to communicate to everyone in your company. By focusing on our $100 million sales goal when we were at $60 million, we accelerated GAC printing at 20 percent a year in an industry that grew at single-digit percentages.

2. Big audacious goals (BAG). Have some fun by setting some really reaching BAGs within your overall goal. We grew a product line from $12 million to $23.9 million by challenging ourselves with an impossible BAG of doubling it in two years. Make it okay to fall short of the BAG as long as you beat budget.

3. Reinforce the *meaning* of goals along the way. Use *repetitive communication* about goals and give everyone "you go girls" and "atta-boys" along the way. Goals will happen as if by magic and everyone will enjoy what they're doing.

4. Get commitment on goals. Work with everyone (employees, customers, suppliers and community) to get commitment on goals. Dick Vermeil very appropriately said it best: "The 'I Will' factor is as important as 'IQ'."

5. Top five goals. Identify and agree with your team on five very specific short-term and five very specific long-term goals. These will focus them on what really needs to be done. Two goals are too few and will result in boredom. Twenty are too many and will result in chaos. Five is just right!

6. The Harley hot button. To achieve really remarkable results, identify a thing a person really wants or needs but won't or can't buy, like a Harley. Offer it as a reward for achieving a BAG and really support that person's effort.

7. Goal writer 101a. Teach "noun + verb + date" to write a goal. For example, _Achieve $500K Pretax Profit in the First Quarter 2001_. The most obvious verb + noun + date is _do it now!_

8. One-page business plan. Create a one-page plan to plug all employees into a common direction. Let it shout out your

CEO Tool
1-Pg BP

unique business proposition and your goals, purpose and strategy. Give it to everyone and reinforce its message regularly through repetitive communication.

9. Unique business proposition (UBP). "Can you tell me what your company does?" When asked this question, most

CEO Tool
UBP

employees, managers and even CEOs give a very generic answer. Instead, pursue a niched, differentiating answer to this question – you'll then have your definitive vision and mission. Example: "Graphic Arts Center is the leading fine-color commercial printer in America."

10. What gets measured gets done. Identify a three-year overall goal, break it down month by month, track it and communicate it to everyone monthly for big, consistent results. We call this _tracking_, with more detail to come in chapter three.

Chapter 2 – *Communicate* to Get Meaningful Results

Not getting any communication is far worse than getting bad news. The country-western group Lonestar does a tune entitled *No News* that is right on point. The lyrics dolefully lament: "My level of anxiety is just a product of no news" as the protagonist waits and waits and waits to hear from his beloved. Employees of too many businesses in America identify too well with no news. In fact, most employees wonder what the company is all about most of the time because we managers aren't communicating.

Lack of consistent communication creates lack of trust. Intermittent, partial, and flaky communication also creates distrust. Trust and communication can become a vicious cycle when ignored by managers. Or, trust and communication can become your most valuable tools.

> Communication and Trust Are Siamese Twins

Lack of communication leads to what my late mentor Kurt Einstein, business leader and psychiatrist, referred to as the universal uncertainty condition: "When the human mind doesn't know, it assumes negative." And when we humans assume negative, we quickly become distrustful. In turn, that distrust leads to further feelings of being not in the know. It's a bad cycle with an easy answer: communicate frequently and work to build trust. Such a simple solution, yet so rarely practiced by most management teams. Business writer Brian McDermott captured it: "Trust ties to profits in the workplace. Eighty-six percent of employees say that *lack of trust* stops them from doing their best." What a staggering statistic. Eighty-six percent! This chapter provides a number of tools for communicating better and improving trust dramatically, yet we all seem to stall a bit, thinking that trust is the hard part. Actually, every one of us has a terrific tool for building trust, namely our *relationship-building* skills. We all have these skills but they're almost always directed outside our organizations. Spend a few moments each day putting that laser-beam smile and relationship-building skill to work inside with your fellow employees. You'll be amazed at the improved trust and communication levels you achieve.

Relationship Skills Build Trust

Values: The Tools That Align *Everyone* for Success

Trust levels are directly proportional to how company values are practiced. It's not just how well we identify and communicate those values, but how well they're acted out every day. At one point, my career landed me in the corporate planner job of a Fortune 500 firm. Unfortunately, the firm was faced with making serious cutbacks at the time. My immediate responsibility was to plan and implement the selling off and closing down of a third of the operations while merging the remainder of the company into a larger, also public, forest products firm. It's never fun eliminating jobs and laying people off, but in this case we had no choice. The company had made several serious mistakes in the distant past and had no chance of surviving on its own without this downsizing/re-engineering strategy. We accepted the unpleasant but inevitable task of shrinking the company down to a size and position where it would be attractive to an acquirer.

Values Form the Foundation for Communication

Over our objections, the president began a series of incremental cutbacks. It's much better to make one big cut and get it over with, but the CEO decided to handle it differently. He was being *mis*guided by the Personnel Department. As the process of making the cuts went along, that personnel department – today it's called HR and tends to be much more humane – would publish updated company phone directories every so often. Whenever a new directory came out, every one of us dropped whatever we were doing and rushed to get a copy to see if our names were still in it. *Unbelievable but true* – the company published the internal phone directory ahead of making the actual cuts.

How much trust could this possibly engender in employees? You could put all the trust in that organization into a thimble and still get your finger into it.

To make matters worse, none of us managers dared approach the CEO on this subject because the VP of personnel had become that CEO's executioner. To lock horns with that VP would have immediately sealed our own fates. Nor were we much inclined to communicate at all amidst the resulting strong feelings of distrust. In a closed environment, where you don't have open, honest communication paralleled by trust, you can't stop such nonsense. We couldn't do anything about those phone directories that devastated trust in that organization.

Contrast that strange situation with a company that places a premium on openness. When you walk into the lobby at Automated Logic Corporation (ALC), just north of Atlanta, one of the first things you see is a large framed copy of their values statement hanging on the wall. Underneath sits a nice stand filled with smaller copies, and anyone who walks in is encouraged to take one. Not surprisingly, ALC has a high regard for openness. Rather than having offices or cubicles, every employee – including the president – sits in an open bullpen. The company has set up a few glass-walled offices as conference rooms when groups of people need to have meetings and not disturb those in the main areas. Other than that, everything takes place out in the open.

Distribute, Live, and Communicate Your Values

Not that every company needs to go this far, but this represents a good example of how one company lives and breathes its values, rather than just displaying them on the wall. The company is quite successful and their culture of openness genuinely works for them. At the end of this chapter, you'll find the *Top 10 Tools for Aligning Values* to sharpen up the definition and daily application of

Top Ten Values Tools (end of chapter)

values in your company. Also shown at chapter-end are examples of several superb values statements from my friends and clients. One of these, W.H. Bass, succeeds through their values. This highly successful construction company tests every major decision against their values – this has been one of their great secrets to success for a decade-and-a-half in business.

Here's a model for thinking about how values fit with everything else in your company:

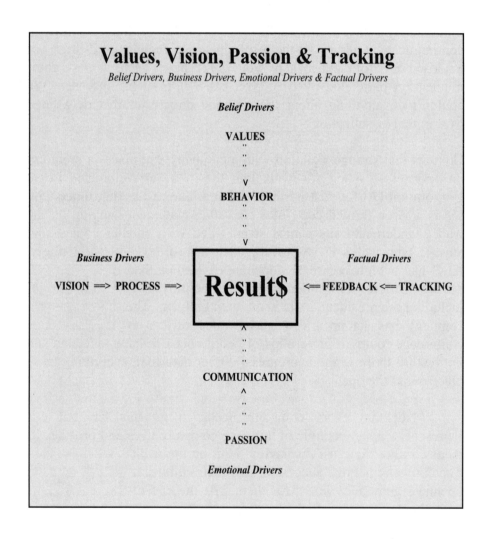

There are at least four sets of drivers that create results in business: we've labeled them business drivers, emotional drivers, factual drivers and belief drivers. Most companies start with the founder's vision as the business driver. It leads to processes like creating a product and selling it, which in turn lead to results like sales growth and profit dollars. The emotional driver consists of our passion for the business and product or customer, which in turn generates communication about those things, again getting results. Factual drivers are the numbers, but more importantly tracking mechanisms, that allow feedback to people in an organization, causing them to get results.

Then there are belief drivers, which are the different values we all bring to the business that drive our behaviors which in turn once again get or don't get results. It's this last area that is usually ignored by management, especially since we think we can just post the values and then things will be rosy. Not so! We need to teach them, use them, tell stories about them, and make them a part of what causes results to happen in our companies. We need to coax them into a cohesive culture: it's here that you can make a difference by getting all your people on board. Check out the *Top Ten Tools for Aligning Values* plus examples of different value sets at the end of this chapter. Getting improved results using these tools may astonish you.

Walk the Four Corners (W4C)

It is amazing how much employees know. Not just our direct reports, but front-line people and people at the very bottom. Because they're in the trenches doing the work day-in and day-out, they have the answers to just about any problem that arises in or about your business. Plus they know of opportunities you never pictured in your wildest dreams. However, they generally won't tell you how much they know unless you ask. My favorite tool for getting employees' best ideas is called W4C: walk the four corners. It's not quite Sam Walton's "management by walking around," which was mainly a message-sending tool, yet W4C is somewhat akin.

47

Every day, get out of your office and spend 20 minutes walking the four corners of your enterprise. Stop with one person, two at most, and ask open-ended questions like, "what do you see that we don't see? How can we make this better for our customers? How can we improve productivity in this area? How can we grow faster?" Then stand back and listen. Your people will give you all the answers. The people in a company always know how to make it better, but we CEOs and managers have isolated ourselves and are listening too selectively. We have our special filter eliminating certain input and we're typically listening only to those advisors at the top. Very often, we just don't even ask. Or worse, we assume those at the bottom don't use their brains. It's an awful thing to say, but we assume many don't have brains just because they're low-wage earners, or that they don't care enough to think. It just isn't so.

Snapper lawnmower manufacturing had been losing money eighteen months in a row when the parent company asked me to come in as CEO. The "snappin' turtle" was upside-down with its legs up in the air, flailing away, expending all kinds of energy in an effort to right itself. But it was getting absolutely nowhere. My entire first week on the job was spent walking the four corners and asking people one question, "how do we get this snapping turtle flipped over, wound up and going again?" In no uncertain terms, they told me exactly how to grab that turtle, flip it over, crank it up and start making money again. Forty-five days later we turned profitable and never saw that turtle on his back again.

Walk Your Four Corners Every Day (W4C)

Here's an example of what they told me on one of my four-corners walks. The director of advertising at Snapper didn't hesitate for a moment when asked: "What worked in the past to get consumers to really go for our products?" He expounded on how we used to advertise in *Reader's Digest* to get spectacular results, that our current spending of $15 million per year on TV media wasn't working, and that it would take $30 - 40 million to be effective on TV. What an easy decision! We immediately cut TV to zero, even though we had nearly a million bucks tied up in new television ads using TV actor Kelsey Grammer – whom we "excused" from being our spokesperson. Instead, we spent just under a million in *Reader's*

Digest with spectacular sell-through results at the consumer level. It turns out that the magazine had a readership of around 100 million people, so the reach was incredible. Picture a big foldout, multi-color ad flying out every time someone picked up *Reader's Digest* in the dentist's office. It's a no-brainer, some might say, but not without the input from walking the four corners.

Using nearly identical ideas that our employees came up with, we returned to profitability right away and just kept on "makin' bacon," a red-neck colloquial metaphor for money. Please understand this remarkable turnaround had little to do with me and everything to do with the employees knowing what needed to be done and wanting to do it. Someone just needed to ask them, listen, and then coordinate the effort. Don't ever overlook the power of W4C. And when you do walk your four corners, don't forget to include your customers and suppliers. They'll tell you more about your business and each other than you ever dreamed of knowing. Moreover, one great way to find out about your competition is to ask your suppliers. They know more about your competitors than your competitors know about themselves. After all, suppliers are studying your competition hard to figure out how to sell to them. And on a similar track, what would your customers say if you asked them why they do business with you? Walking four corners can be an executive's best tool for gathering business intelligence of all kinds and for staying in touch with that part of the real world often overlooked or unseen.

Mayor Rudy Giuliani is a modern American hero. He kept walking his four corners in the days, weeks and months following the shocking 911.01 tragedy in New York City. We can all take a long and valuable lesson from him. Many people in his same situation near the end of their formal tenure might have just gone along with the flow. Instead he got out there, walked the four corners, learned about what was happening first hand at ground zero, listened and then acted. Again and again

Un-Isolate Yourself!

his actions were perfect responses to the situations because he stayed in touch.

We CEOs, and some senior managers, have a tendency toward deafness. By that I mean we isolate ourselves from the information we need to hear, and we listen selectively when we do hear it. We also have a tendency to glaze over, meaning that when someone is telling us something we think we've already heard, our eyes glaze over and our mind goes elsewhere to work on other things. Whether conscious or unconscious, these behaviors send subtle but substantial messages to our employees. Unfortunately, they send really wrong messages most of the time. Here's a perfect example of how a seemingly small, unintentional incident can send the wrong message throughout the entire organization.

Suppose I'm sitting in my office working on a financial report on the PC. Someone appears in the doorway and says, "hey Kraig, I need to talk to you for a minute." Engrossed in my computer, I barely look up and reply, "I'm right in the middle of this big Excel file. Come back later." What have I just done? I've unintentionally sent a permanent message to everyone in the company, way beyond just that one person, not to interrupt Kraig when he's on his computer. The fact that the message was unintentional is totally irrelevant. It went out anyway, loud and much too clear. What was the real message sent that day? "Kraig's not willing to listen when we've got something important to tell him."

As CEOs and managers, we send these kinds of messages every day without even thinking about them. With some effort and dedication, we can change our behavior so that we do these things less often. It starts with being more aware of our effect on employees and making a conscious effort to send messages that build trust and enhance communication. We won't ever achieve perfection, but we can move the needle dramatically in the right direction. Remember that employees pay very close attention to *everything we do*. For example, they not only watch where we park our cars but also how we park our cars, and then relate rumors about it to others. To communicate effectively, we need to plug into that and be more aware of and sensitive to the effects our behavior and our communications have on employees.

We who are CEOs have been convinced that it's lonely at the top. Well, Kathy Mattea's country-western hit song is right on: *It's Lonely at the Bottom Too!* It turns out, it's lonely everywhere if we're not interacting with each other. Walk your four corners and go talk to the folks at the bottom. They'll shower you with solutions.

Always Be Prepared

Thanks to the Boy Scouts of America® for teaching us the great *Be Prepared* slogan at a tender young age when we'd remember it and live by it. When we communicate and build trust, we create a wonderful atmosphere of openness. That openness, however, has pluses and minuses to it. The increased productivity far outweighs the negatives, but always be prepared for the unexpected.

One Monday morning in the dead of winter I arrived at Snapper lawnmower at my usual time (about 7:00 a.m.) and began climbing the stairs to my office in total darkness. As I reached for the light switch at the top of the stairs, the hair on the back of my neck suddenly stood up. I couldn't see or hear anything, but somehow I knew someone was there with me. I flipped on the switch and just about jumped out of my skin. There sat one of our younger employees, looking like something the cat had dragged in. Many thoughts raced through my mind, mostly fear of the unknown, a quick flashback to no news. Most of all, I wondered why was he was there, what he wanted, and whether I should assume the full Ninja position, whatever that might be.

It turned out the young man had blown his entire Friday paycheck on cocaine and applied it liberally to do the same to his mind. Monday morning rolled around and he was flat broke and still wired on coke. He needed to talk to someone and, because we had chatted several times

> **Be Ready for Anything!**

on my walk-the-four-corners, he chose me. We went into my office and I talked him down a bit. My administrative assistant showed up shortly and hurried the head of human resources over to handle the situation appropriately. The young man wasn't even a regular employee, but a temp assembly-line worker. Yet he felt safe talking to me. Once past the initial scare, I considered the situation a positive rather than a negative. You never expect to encounter that kind of thing, and you certainly don't like to see anyone on drugs. But the fact that he felt comfortable coming to me spoke enormously about our open, communicating culture.

You're probably curious about that employee's outcome. We cajoled some employee assistance out of our insurance carrier for him, but he still didn't make it. Eventually he was terminated.

Repeat the Message and Tell a Story

In order to work, communication must be *repetitive*, especially on the things that seem obvious to you. For example, suppose you

> Repetitive Communication Tool

identify a goal of going from $60 million to $100 million in sales over three years and hold a big meeting to propose the goal and discuss it. Everyone understands, and even buys into the goal and comes away from the meeting fired up to make it happen. But let's say you don't mention the goal again for six months. What will happen the next time you walk your four corners and ask people, "what's our main corporate goal? What are we trying to do, big picture?" The main response will be a shrugging, "I dunno." A few will vaguely remember the $100 million goal, but they will think you didn't mean it

> Repetitive Communication Makes It Happen!

because you haven't said anything about it since then. Most will have forgotten about it altogether. This should be a real "aha!" for everyone. Face it, communication must be repetitive to be effective. More importantly, when you talk about the goal again and again and again, it will happen as if by magic.

Here's a good example of how repetitive communication can get the job done. At the printing company, we had always lost money during our fiscal first quarter – April though June. No matter what we tried or how hard we worked, the seasonality of the business never failed to get the best of us. In fact, GAC printing lost money every first quarter in 94 out of the entire 95 years it had been in business. Talk about consistent but unhappy track records! Intrigued by the one *profitable* first quarter, I had lunch with my predecessor despite my direct involvement in his termination. He said he had accomplished the seemingly impossible feat of making money in the first quarter by establishing very specific sales targets with each salesperson, which was very uncommon in the printing industry. Based on that one piece of evidence, we resolved to take that same step and several more to forever make the first quarter profitable.

Ask What Used To Work!

That year, the management team agreed to set a goal of making a profit of $1.00 during the first quarter. That's right, just a single greenback. That may seem like an overly modest goal until you consider that we lost nearly $750,000 in the first quarter of the previous year. Three months later we had thrown off the shackles of the past and earned a very healthy profit of $209K for the quarter. That's nearly a million dollars more profit added on a year-to-year basis, but historically it was just accepted that we must lose money in the first quarter. After all, the whole industry went into the tank at that time each year, so why shouldn't we? Please don't ever be led by this sort of sheep like following-the-herd mentality. Remember, industry average is really only mediocre.

So, how did we do it? Through ongoing, repetitive communications, telling a consistent story and keeping people focused on the goal. First, we made the goal as clear, as simple and as direct as possible. Our motto, mantra and mode of operation became Q1 = $1.00. We used a one-dollar bill as the main prop in our story. The U.S. dollar makes a fabulous communication tool because it's loaded with neuro-linguistic programming. People recognize it instantly by sight in that appealing visual of "green." They also respond to the sound of money. Can't you just hear the sound it makes when you snap a crisp new bill between your hands. And, money also feels unique to the touch. Neuro-linguistic programming involves all three modes: sight, sound and touch in a powerful communication tool described in the end-of-chapter tool kit. Even with their eyes

Communicate using Neuro-Linguistic Programming

closed, folks know when you put money in their hands. Above all,
money talks. It gets people's attention. So when

Q1 = $1.00

talking to employees about goals, hold up a dollar bill
and verbalize Q1 = $1.00 (phonetically it's Q-one equals a buck).

That was just for openers. Before the quarter began, we also communicated via letters to all our customers, suppliers and employees, identifying our goal and asking for their help in achieving it. Mary Hughes at Victoria's Secret gave us a $500,000 print job just because we shared Q1 = $1.00 with her. Suppliers gave us modest but still meaningful price concessions once they understood why. During the quarter, we sent regular "cheerleading" memos and letters to these same constituencies reporting on our progress toward the goal. They responded by helping more! We made up large lapel buttons for everyone. What did they say? You guessed it: Q1 = $1.00. We hung signs in the plant, and on home office and sales office walls to remind us all about the goal, and we sent out "buck$" memos to heighten the hype. Through this strategy, we earned $104K in April, lost $19K in May, and rebounded to earn $124K in June, for a record first quarter total of $209K of profit.

We celebrated for a solid month when we achieved that buck! A catered lunch for the entire company kicked it off on all three shifts. We placed a huge sign on the front of the building and smaller signs all around the plant proclaiming:

Our banker called that morning to say GAC was his only client where he could read their quarterly financial results from the freeway driving to work!

We presented Q1 plaques to key players. The management team walked their four corners as a group to thank and congratulate every employee on all three shifts in all 387,000 square feet of buildings. It was a very long and very rewarding day for the officers as GAC's employees responded with equal enthusiasm. We sent thank-you letters to all employees, customers and suppliers and put stuffers in paycheck envelopes together with real one-dollar bills. In every way possible, we let employees, customers, and suppliers know how much we appreciated their hard work and support in helping us achieve the goal. This virtually guaranteed subsequent successes.

> *$1.00 = We Made It!*

> **Use Symbolism As a Dynamic Tool**

Even before we finished celebrating, we set a new goal for the second quarter, Q2 = $2.00. This was truly symbolic since we were aiming at $1 million, and the second quarter had always been profitable. Actually, my idea was Q2 = $1 million, but everyone told me not to flaunt our profitability in the second quarter. Well, everybody at GAC was really getting into it now. We made $1.5 million in the second quarter. We kept this up for all sixteen quarters of my tenure at GAC and always beat these big audacious fun goals. As Admiral Foche, famous French naval hero exclaimed: "Toujour audache!" (Be always audacious!) Maybe we were setting those goals too low, but something suggests it wasn't only the audacity of the goals but also the consistent communication, trust building and *we* spirit that made it all happen.

> Q2 = $2.00

Here's another example. A recent client of mine in North Georgia wanted to reduce his manufacturing costs in the coming year by a penny per pound of product produced, a seemingly modest goal. Considering that such a goal represented 12 percent of his total costs, however, it would be a real stretch for this division. To communicate the goal to employees and solicit their ideas for improvement, the division Vice President came up with the slogan *LBS = -1¢*. He then put the slogan at the top of a suggestion sheet and distributed it to all employees. Once a month, he wrote a letter to update everyone on progress toward the goal. He also held a monthly meeting to report progress to all employees to communicate better with those that preferred auditory over visual feedback. And before the year began, this VP pre-announced they would also set aside 25¢ on every dollar saved and promised to divvy up the pool of money at the end of the year among all employees.

Using this strategy, the company achieved savings of 1.02¢ per pound. This added half a million dollars in pre-tax profit to the bottom line! Not bad for a corny tool like *LBS = -1¢*. So what's the moral of this story? Identify an area in your company where you can try this kind of simple, repetitive communication and big audacious goal. You will have fun, make money and open your people's eyes to the kinds of things they can accomplish by having fun.

CEO's or Manager's Monthly Letter

One of the best tools for getting your message out to the troops on a regular basis is the CEO's or Manager's Monthly Letter, with the purpose of repeating the goal month in and month out so that people never lose sight of it. Despite the trend toward online and Email communications, print the letter on paper and give a copy to every employee. If you send it via Email, your employees will print it out anyway, which wastes their time and costs more. Or worse, some will forget to print it, which means they won't read it, defeating the purpose of the communication tool.

> CEO's/Manager's
> Monthly Letter
> for Repetitive
> Communication

Obviously you need to vary the message a bit each month to keep it fresh and interesting. In addition to repetitive communication, the CEO's or manager's monthly letter also presents an opportunity for praising performance-producing people while thanking everyone else. The idea is *thank people for effort* and *praise them for performance.* This monthly letter is your tool for keeping everyone informed from your perspective and gives you the chance to talk about customer successes. Following is a sample CEO/manager monthly letter from my tenure at the insurance company:

CEO Tool
CEOMoLtr

56

GUARANTEE INSURANCE RESOURCES

TO: All Employees
FROM: Kraig Kramers
SUBJ: "Getting to Know You"
DATE: January 9, 1995

It's a pleasure to join GIR and I look forward to getting to know each of you and learning a lot about GIR's business from you. Sheri will contact you to set up individual meetings so that we can get to know each other. Because there's only one of me and many of you, these initial meetings will need to be short. To make the meetings more effective, let me ask that you think in advance about what GIR and its people can do to improve what our customers receive in terms of product, response, communication, service and anything else of value or importance to them. I'm also interested in any other thoughts or input you may have on any subject.

It's the beginning of a New Year and a time for setting goals. During January, GIR's management will be looking very hard at where we're headed, how the market is changing, and how to improve the outcome for the company in 1995 and beyond. We'll also be setting goals in addition to the obvious ones for the year. *Your* input and thoughts about GIR's future are very important and are encouraged both now and anytime. GIR's Advisory Committee, comprised mainly of client TPAs, meets this week to provide specific input to us on what *they* would like to see from GIR in the future.

Our immediate goal is to ***increase written premiums by 20%***, month-by-month, over last year. Since we haven't focused on this target quite this way, it may take a few months for us to get on track. We'll keep you informed as we move along, and we'll also let you know as our review of the market and strategies come into better focus.

As of right now, we're running ahead of last January and we're approaching the desired 20% gain for the month. For those of you who are making this happen, THANK YOU and keep up the great work! For everyone else, let's dive in and support the effort to beat the $14.4 million underwriting goal for January. Since it's the first month of a new year, *now's* the time to get ahead rather than struggling to catch up later in the year. Every little bit of extra effort somehow counts bigger in January, so give it your very best shot!

It will be my practice and pleasure to write an All Employees letter similar to this one every month. This will not in any way replace or second-guess "The RE-source" but rather should be an additional way of keeping everyone more informed about GIR. Hopefully the editor of *The RE-source* will allow me to write an article for that publication now and then in addition to this monthly letter!

Again, it's great to be with you and I look forward to spending some quality time with each of you very soon.

With best regards,

Kraig

Kraig W. Kramers
President and CEO

One-to-One with Direct-Reports

To build trust, which in turn enhances communication within your management team, try a regular, short one-to-one session with each direct report. Each meeting should take no longer than 20 to 30 minutes and interaction should be on only non-business things. Start out on a weekly basis for five or six weeks and then make it a monthly luncheon where you talk about what else is going on in your lives. Try always to talk non-business, making this a relationship-building meeting. If you drift into business discussions, the meeting degenerates into an accountability session. This half-hour should be a trust-building time. Schedule these meetings in ink on your calendar and permit no interruptions during the meetings. More than anything, your people value your interest in them and your uninterrupted time and attention.

One-to-One Meetings to Build Trust

Why have such meetings? Because they build trust and relationship. Start out by asking in a friendly, yet neutral conversational tone, "how's it going?" Don't ask, "how are you doing?" because that has all kinds of accountability overtones to it. Remember these meetings are targeted to build trust and relationship, not to pursue accountability issues. Simply "how's it going?" will work just fine. Then let your direct-report lead the conversation from there. The goal is to get your direct reports talking about anything but business. If they start in on a particular project or trouble they're having with a particular employee, quickly switch the subject to their golf game or family or some outside interest. The idea isn't to pry into their personal lives but simply to form deeper personal relationships. People who share things other than business become much more involved, caring and accepting – those words sure sound like trust to me.

Weekly Employee Update

How about a few more easy-to-implement tools for repetitive communication? Try the many interesting, consciousness-raising reminders available to you, like the monthly letter discussed above, or perhaps a *Weekly Employee Update* assembled by your administrative assistant with news about customers, employee successes and how you're doing against goals. Mail it to everyone each week. This is a great tool for companies with remote locations as it keeps everyone current on what's happening everywhere weekly.

> Weekly Employee Update

There's more at chapter-end in the *Top 10 Communication Tools*. Get everyone around you, all the functional and department managers throughout the organization, to work on communicating this way. Talk about what's going on and mention the goals repetitively. Your people will become more productive and you'll reduce the most monstrous of goals to mere child's play.

> See Top 10 Communication Tools (end of chapter)

Personal Notes Home

One of the most powerful of all communication tools is the *Personal Note Home,* a little note of recognition that the manager simply mails to the person's home. It's a fun surprise to receive such notes, and they're never forgotten by recipients. These notes are both communication and recognition, and that has a lot to do with their remarkable impact. The easiest such note to write is:

Dear Bill,

Great job!

With best regards,

Kraig

9-21-01

You both know what the note says without spelling specifics, yet it takes only a moment to pen and it has huge impact.

Here's the challenge with Personal Notes Home: we can't randomly write such praises since they've not yet become a habit. *Random habit* has a certain oxymoronic ring to it, don't you think? To remind yourself to do these incredibly motivating communications, use Post-It® notes and entries in your calendar to earmark certain note-writing days. At GAC printing it became a regular habit to do these every month – that was about sixty 30-word notes each month for the 48 months of my tenure there. At this point, you're saying to yourself, how can any CEO or manager devote such huge time chunks to such a thing? Guess the best answer would be: as much as it takes because the payoff is huge. And why is the payoff so big? Simple really: people love to know how they're doing. It's the number one question on everyone's mind: "How we doin', boss?" and "How am I doing, boss?" Of course, people will never ask the "I" question that directly, but they sure do want to know.

> **Personal Notes Home Both Recognize *and* Communicate**

An even better answer to why write such notes and letters is that it only takes about three hours a month to write the 60 personal notes, the CEO's/manager's monthly letter, and the one-page monthly operations report, which you'll see in chapter six. You get good at it very quickly, and you learn to get organized because of it. This in turn leads to knowing your people better, which in turn results in improved productivity and much better communications.

We've heard that Mary Kay Ash of Mary Kay Cosmetics would write 30 to 40 notes like these every day. Legend says it fueled her success. Similarly, Pier 1 Imports CEO and chairman Clark Johnson wrote a weekly letter to all associates for over seven years. He stuck to one subject: customers! Go take a look at Clark's phenomenal track record during those years; for nearly two years he was opening a new store every single week. Repetitive communication pays off. Regular personal notes of recognition pay off. Really successful managers and companies use these tools almost religiously.

The Power of "We"

When you work hard at building trust and communication, and then manage in a way that establishes an open atmosphere, amazing things happen. My first year at GAC printing, we had a third-quarter goal of 5.5 percent pretax return on sales. One day while walking my four corners, Ed Marsden, our lead first-shift press operator on GAC's number one Heidelberg sheet-fed press, stopped me to ask, "hey Kraig, how are we doing on that 5.5 percent thing?"

My response was: "We're doing fine, Ed, but we're not quite there. About 5.3 percent right now."

He responded enthusiastically, "don't worry, we'll pass the word and we'll all push a little harder. We'll *make* that 5.5 percent!"

I thanked him, and encouraged him with, "that would be really neat. Keep up the great work!" and went on my way. While walking away I mentally pumped my fist into the air and I exclaimed "yes!" almost out loud. Because at that exact moment, *us and them* had just become *we*. The people of GAC had not only bought into the goal but had now made it their own. Rather than a random collection

> Get to "We" By Building Communication and Trust

61

of individual efforts, we had become a unified team, working as one toward the same distinct goal. And this was in a union environment that later experience taught me was tougher than the Steelworkers Union at Snapper. To get a quick view of how to accomplish this in your company, watch the movie *Hoosiers* made in 1986 about a 1950's Indiana high school basketball team. You can buy it on videocassette almost anywhere for under $10 and it's worth 1,000 times that amount. Watch it, then show it and teach it to all managers around you.

> **Best Management Movie: *Hoosiers***

It goes to show that with the right communication on a repetitive basis, anything is possible. The key is to use as many communication tools as possible and keep chipping away at the goal. Each communication tool generates its own momentum. When you get enough of them put together so that the message comes through loud and clear, the feeling in your company becomes we rather than us and them. And once you get the power of we working in your company, no competitor can touch you.

Practice Openness via Frequent Communication – It Builds Trust

For many managers, CEOs, and especially owners, openness and honest communication may feel difficult. We just don't think the folks around us will understand, or worse that they'll use the information we share in a negative way against us. But the truly great companies have always done it this way. My first job out of graduate school in 1966 was with Corning Glass Works. Even way back then Corning was voted one of the 50 best-managed companies in America every year. Its version of openness took the form of quarterly meetings with all managers to explain not only the financial results but also what had caused them, with full discussion among employees. This made for a very open culture.

While attending Stanford Business School, I had the good fortune to work for Hewlett-Packard® as an assistant overseas sales manager. Even back then there was a very open culture, and my visual recollection of vice presidents sitting in the bullpen with their people is still vivid in my mind. Bill Hewlett and Dave Packard walked their four corners, which is where that undoubtedly became my tool, now that it occurs to me. Bill and Dave are gone and things have changed some with the huge growth of HP, with the coming and going of various CEOs. Yet HP seems to still be a very open company due to its culture of communication and trust. Without question, that openness was a significant contributor to HP becoming the great company it is. The concepts of openness, trust and communication form the foundation for all great companies. Why not make your company even greater by applying these concepts with the tools we've described here?

We began this chapter offering the precept that people presume the worst when they don't get news of any kind. Jim Wisner, the great leader of Financial Securities Corporation offered it up rather whimsically: "Very seldom is there an announcement that nothing has happened."

This chapter has been about communication and trust, perhaps the most overlooked and underutilized of management tools. How can you apply and improve the use of these tools everywhere in your company?

COMMUNICATE MORE FOR MORE RESULTS.

Top Ten Communication Tools

1. CEO's or manager's monthly letter. Get your message *to everyone*, building trust, teamwork and results. People like to know whether they're making it, so tell them what's going on. Remember, what gets measured *and communicated* is what gets done.

CEOMoLtr

2. One-to-one with direct-reports. Try prescheduled, uninterruptible, individual weekly meetings with each direct-report for 20-30 minutes to assure trust through relationship development. Talk only non-business. This should never be an accountability meeting!

3. Personal notes home. Send individual cheerleading and congratulatory notes home to reinforce results. It's an amazingly powerful tool.

4. Share business plans with *everyone*. This dramatically enhances trust, multiplies your communication tenfold and really gets everyone going in the same direction. Use the 1-Page Business Plan for this purpose.

5. {Q1 = $1.00} or symbolism. Set a goal of making just $1.00 in your worst or loss quarter or month, communicate it broadly, and participate in helping those around you achieve it. Hold up a one-dollar bill, referring to it as you speak. Hand out $1 bills. Make your symbolism visible and frequent.

6. Weekly employee update. This one-pager cites key happenings with customers and talks about employee performance. Each week try to tell a little story about how someone lived up to a key company value with that customer. What else could be as important? Email or fax this weekly to all your people, especially at remote locations, just to stay in touch.

7. Use NLP as a tool. Use sight, sound and feel (Neuro-Linguistic Programming) to supercharge your communications. Example: ***Heard*** *you might be* ***looking*** *for new ways to* ***touch*** *your customers.* We humans switch among these sight-sound-feel modalities and only receive messages on the wavelength we're on at the moment. The best communicators use NLP. Try this – you'll be amazed at your accelerated attention and buy-in from those around you.

8. Monthly superstars letter. Write winner-praising letters to the group of people who make the rubber meet the road in your company. Recognize the winners, don't even mention the laggards and send the letter to all.

9. Repetitive communication. Yes, take it to the street frequently. Find every excuse to reiterate goals and direction. Try to be doubly redundant. Consistency and repetitiveness will dramatically enhance effectiveness. Don't know who said it, but "repetition results in retention."

10. Feed everyone's effort. Volunteer your personal support to each person's effort to beat the goal. CEOs and managers should have a serving attitude when it comes to others efforts and successes.

Top Ten Values-Aligning Tools

1. Get values input from all stakeholders. Start by getting input from every employee and all your other stakeholders on values. Then sort for a consensus of a few core values.

2. Study others' value systems. Incorporate as many other published values as possible, but still end up with only one page and as few values as possible.

3. Try Ron Fleisher's (speaker and consultant) great three-value system. A wonderful, yet simple value set comes to us from this author, speaker and five-time CEO: *1) The customer is our first focus always; 2) Revenues less expenses equals profit; and 3) Promise what the customer wants and needs, then over-deliver.* Work each word and phrase – there's a wealth of vision and mission in these three values.

4. Include bits of everyone in the published values. Buy-in won't occur unless you get a bit of everyone in the final values statement. But don't let this water down your values. Nor should values be pure consensus; rather, get input democratically and decide the values autocratically.

5. Publicize only values you're sure of. In the beginning, publish only the values you're absolutely sure of. Any that you can't live up to 100 percent should be left aside. Don't include a value you can't live up to totally and completely.

6. Repeat the values – preach your values everyday. Wall plaques that emblazon the values aren't enough. Find different ways to reiterate the message over the years. Have copies in your lobby for all stakeholders; put them on your website, your fax cover page, every Email. Make the extra effort to communicate values repetitively.

7. Test all decisions against your values. Each and every day, test your decisions against your values. Teach others to do the same.

8. Be willing to upgrade your values. We can't all be perfect. You may need to upgrade your values over time. Remember that you can never downgrade them without criticism and severe loss of credibility. So think hard before upgrading.

9. Publish your own cardinals. These are rules of the road for running the business based on values. Publish them so everyone can see how *you* live by them. Kraig's are shown on the page following the three value statement examples shown below.

10. Values, vision and passion. Values are the starting point after you have vision and passion. Many businesses lack one of these three vital ingredients. To maximize your success, work on all three. CEOs: promote or hire a COO with passion if you've lost yours.

Here's a footnote or two about setting business values in a company. Get values input in a democratic way from everyone involved: employees, customers, suppliers, and community. Then set the values autocratically. The story of the thoroughbred racehorse designed by committee comes to mind; don't you get this clear mental image of a three-hump camel? Take a look at the values statements on the ensuing pages. They sure are appealing and the values are alive and successfully guiding all three companies.

Values of W.H. Bass, Inc.

These values serve as the basis for how we as a company make our decisions, plan for the future and are the standard we use for measuring success.

▼ **STRIVING FOR EXCELLENCE IN SERVICE:**
We will provide a level of service for our external and internal customers which exceeds their expectations and is always increasing.

▼ **PROVIDING QUALITY OF LIFE IN THE TRUEST SENSE OF THE WORD:**
As a company, we are a structure which affords the opportunity for people to be all that they can be; being responsible to the only resource God has entrusted us with - our people - and striving to be a team that everyone is proud to be a member of.

▼ **WE WILL SEEK TO WORK WITH ONLY THE HIGHEST QUALITY CLIENTS**:
Defined as a client who is the best in our niche, a client who treats us with respect, a client who shares our level of ethics and gives us the respect we earn, and a client who allows us to achieve a reasonable level of profit.

▼ **FINANCIAL STABILITY:**
Achieving a level of profits by maximizing our percent mark-up and weekly job profits, by maximizing each profit center, by minimizing our General and Administrative costs, and achieving a level of financial stability by minimizing debt and obtaining sound financial ratios.

▼ **MAINTAINING INTEGRITY**:
Never should we allow ourselves to fall into a position where there is a sacrifice of integrity or place our clients or suppliers into a position to do the same.

▼ **CHOOSING THE MOST SIMPLISTIC APPROACH:**
We will always "challenge" our decisions to insure they are result-oriented and not process-oriented. We will always seek the most simplistic approach to the situation which will best serve our client.

▼ **OUR COMPANY SPIRIT**
We are a group of entrepreneurs who have teamed together with a common focus. We are people who are driven by a passion for a high level of success, individuals who are decision makers in control of our own destinies. It is our desire to attract people with this common spirit.

GROEN BROTHERS AVIATION
- CORPORATE VALUES -

As a corporation and as individuals, **we will always do what is "right."** Doing the right thing isn't always easy. It is easy, however, to know whether or not a course of action is right. If we have to ask ourselves, "is this right?" we already know the answer.

We will be each others staunchest allies. In a world filled with change, our relationship with each other will be a constant we can count on. As members of this team, we will always support each other. We will never undermine a fellow team member, and we will not tolerate it of others.

We will listen. We will listen to each other, our customers, our suppliers, and any other source of information and knowledge. We know that we must continue to learn. We believe that knowledge is power. We will learn all we can about our industry and its needs. We will find out what our customers want, and we will give it to them.

We will be accountable. Each one of us is accountable for our own actions. When we commit to a course of action there will be consequences. We accept the consequences of our actions and our inactions. We realize that we are not perfect. When we err, we will admit our error and learn from it.

We will treat everyone with respect. We will respect the dignity of each other, our customers, our suppliers, and everyone with whom we come in contact.

We will continue to strive for perfection. Each task we attempt will be measured against perfection. Even though it may seem impossible to achieve this goal, we will never willingly give up trying. We will demand excellence from ourselves and from each other.

AUTOMATED LOGIC CORPORATION

Our Mission

Leadership in the Building Automation Industry by 2002. Our customers, our competitors, and our ALC family are our three judges. Unanimous consent is required.

Our Values

Localness There is a 16th century principle which says:

> *It is a violation of 'The Right Order'*
> *for a higher level to intervene at the lower level*
> *when the lower level*
> *can solve the problem itself.*

Those functions that can be performed at a local level should be.

Managers All managers shall imprint themselves daily with the following:

- I will listen.
- I will not shoot the messenger.
- Management is always the problem.

Differences Our individual differences can enhance or negate each other. If we constructively share our differences, in pursuit of a worthy goal, they become our source of strength for superior achievement.

Customers They sustain us. As fair exchange our customers will enjoy in return:

- Quality product
- Value for their dollar
- Timely response
- Good counsel and support
- Fairness and respect

To provide our customers with less is to sabotage our own survival.

Quality If our customer is still pleased with us on the day our product is worn out, obsolete, or replaced, we will have met our quality goal.

Rules An organization must have structure to operate efficiently, so a few simple rules are necessary. But when a rule is in conflict with fairness, fairness will always prevail. We will not stand on rules, we will stand on fairness.

Failure It is a *stepping stone* to achievement when it is:

- unique,
- small, manageable,
- and intelligently considered.

It is a *stonewall* to achievement when it is:

- repetitious,
- large, unmanageable,
- or poorly thought-through.

Improvement Like the products we produce, our individual jobs are comprised of many components, and for every component there is a time for improvement. There are always at least three or four components of our job whose time for improvement is now.

Openness We have open book management, an open office plan, and a 360 degree review process. If we err, it will be on the side of awareness versus unawareness.

Communication

- Clarity
- Candor
- Constructive purpose

Without all three, it is a waste of time.
With a heavy dose of each, miracles can happen.

Kraig's Business Cardinals

Most CEOs have a strong interest in assuring a clear understanding of the culture and ethical conduct expected in their businesses. One good way of doing this is for CEOs to set down on paper what they believe in, how they measure others and what they generally hold of value. These might be called the CEO's business "cardinals" and these are mine:

1. **Always** treat people **right** yet tell them **performance** is **expected**.
2. Focus on **big, audacious goals** and on **tracking** success.
3. Help people **set and take action** to achieve goals.
4. **Communicate** company performance **regularly** and truthfully.
5. **Celebrate successes** and then set new goals.
6. You'll only **manage** what you choose to **measure**.
7. **Customers first**, then plant and machinery.
8. Know **what** it is the company **really sells**.
9. Create a **climate of trust** and **communication**.
10. Build **genuine value**, not paper profits or sales hype.
11. Bet on the **person**, not the idea or the product.
12. **Never** compromise quality for price or profit.
13. You only get **one chance** to make a first impression.
14. Do **first things first**, second things never.
15. Make **time for people** who want to see you right now.
16. Repeated **recognition** will enhance repeated **performance**.
17. Lead people, manage things.
18. Take responsibility for **momentum**.
19. **"About right"** now is far better than "exactly wrong" later.
20. One improper compromise can collapse a career or a company.
21. **Honesty** is **still** the best policy -- cover-ups create catastrophe.
22. Do the **"right thing"** rather than "just doing things right".
23. Always play "what if".
24. Tell the **bad news first**, never last.
25. It's too easy to cut price and **much too hard** to bring it back.
26. Keep all your eggs in a **bunch** of baskets.
27. Invest your time with **winners** -- not with losers.
28. Go to your strengths when the going gets tough.
29. A little success can create a lot of overhead.
30. Anything you can **dream**, you can **do**!

> **"I think I can – I think I can –I think I can.
> Up, up, up. Faster and faster and faster the
> little engine climbed, until at last they
> reached the top of the mountain."**
> Watty Piper *The Little Engine That Could*^{TM}

Chapter 3 – Now *Track* What's Meaningful

"Are we gaining momentum or losing steam in our business right now? What actions are we taking in response to that first question?"

If you can't instantly respond to these two questions, you're not on track. The greatest killer of businesses is the lack of *responsive tracking* and, in turn, lack of *anticipatory action* resulting from the lack of tracking or just non-action.

> **Build a Truly
> Responsive
> Tracking System**

How many companies have been in the midst of going public when they had a profit hiccup, an unexpected loss or severe drop in profitability? How many have been in the middle of a re-financing when some unforeseen event embarrassed the company, causing deep concerns with lenders and owners?

Two years prior to my becoming CEO at Graphic Arts Center, this printer was in the midst of an Initial Public Offering. Just weeks before the go-public date, the company had its first surprise loss month in years, and not a small loss at that. It was a total debacle. At GAC's parent company we cancelled the IPO, removed and replaced the president, and wrote off the rather sizable accrued expenses associated with the failed public offering.

What caused the unanticipated profit hiccup at GAC? It was simply the lack of responsive tracking to appropriately anticipate the future. Measuring results in my world includes taking a fresh look at the near-term future each

> **Prospective
> Results
> Tracking**

month. Let's call it *prospective results tracking* and it's the tool that keeps the GAC debacles from happening. We'll talk in depth about anticipation as a tool in chapter four, but first let's ask how tracking can obviate catastrophes like the GAC public non-offering and, even more importantly, actually produce profits beyond your wildest dreams.

Can you imagine watching a football game without a scoreboard? Or playing a round of golf without tracking your shots on a scorecard? Or not thinking ahead in basketball as to what the other team might do in the last minute of play? Or not looking up the fairway to see if there is a sand trap on the right?

Then why run a business that way?

Our top tracking tool for getting results to happen in any company and avoid the potholes is – what gets measured gets done.

WGMGD = What Gets Measured Gets Done

No, it doesn't stand for "<u>W</u>hat's <u>G</u>ood, <u>M</u>iller <u>G</u>enuine <u>D</u>raft®?" MGD® beer is good, but even better is: What Gets Measured Gets Done. You've heard the expression many times. Yet

Best Results
Tool: WGMGD

few things have a bigger impact on achieving your goals than measuring performance and letting people know how they're doing in relation to those goals. Employees aren't dumb. They watch what you pay attention to, or don't pay attention to, and they adjust their behavior accordingly. If you want to achieve your goals, measure the outcomes, track the performance along the way relative to the goals, and give feedback of your interpretations to your people. It's really that simple. But we need a tracking system to make sure we indeed both measure and give feedback. Surprisingly, if we don't also measure how often we give feedback, the feedback usually isn't given and WGMGD doesn't work.

No one ever told us that "what gets measured gets done" means more than simply just measure it. However, somewhere along the line it became crystal clear that there are three steps to WGMGD. A serendipitous surprise was that these parallel closely steps one, two and three of my seven-step management process from the first chapter. Maybe that's not such a coincidence after all. Here's how WGMGD works:

Three Steps To Success With WGMGD

1. Set an overall goal with your key people,
2. Communicate that goal repetitively and build trust, and
3. Track the actual against the goal and give feedback frequently.

You may recall at GAC printing we had set an overall goal of growing from $60 million in sales to $100 million in just three years. That's about 20 percent compound growth per year in an industry that's usually about four percent to six percent a year. The WGMGD formula taught us first to set that *overall goal* for the company. The goal of going for $100 million was then *communicated repetitively* to everyone, including customers and suppliers. *Trust* grew at GAC through honest qualitative feedback at frequent intervals to everyone about how the company was doing, indeed, how the employees were doing. And finally we *tracked* against the goal as we went along, with *feedback* to everyone in and around the company.

Here's how it played out. Remember the adage: "How do you eat an elephant? One bite at a time." The same holds true for big audacious fun goals and other major organizational goals like our jump from $60 million to $100 million over three years. That $40 million growth or $40 million elephant can cause major organizational heartburn taken all at once. But break the three-year goal down by year, and it's about $13 million per year. That's much more easily digested by your people. Spread that over 12 months, it's a bit more than $1 million per month. Try tracking monthly against the overall goal of getting to $100 million and tell employees how they're doing each month. Now people have a handle on this goal, a benchmark, a way of understanding how it's going or more appropriately, how we're tracking against the goal as we go along.

It now becomes very easy to track performance, determine whether you are growing at the proper rate and feed back the results

| Reduce Goals To Chewable Chunks |

to your people. When taken in small bites rather than trying to eat the whole elephant at once, people get a chance to chew and swallow so profit dollars increase steadily yet noticeably. This WGMGD thing never fails to work when approached using the three steps.

Here are some additional thoughts that will help keep WGMGD itself on track:

- *Measure the right things.* If we measure the wrong things, the wrong things will get done. Try some key profitable growth measures, like gross profit return-on-sales or gross profit return-on-investment (inventory plus receivables related to a product line). Whenever possible, focus on positive, growth-oriented measures. An example: turn a waste reduction goal ☹ into a percent good product produced ☺ measure. Or track percent retention (✚) instead of employee turnover (➖), or accounts receivable turnover (⬆) instead of A/R days sales outstanding (⬇). Another hint is to measure profitable sales growth and not just increased sales dollars.

- *Don't measure too many things.* Asking people to measure 20 or 30 different things only causes confusion. Instead, settle on two or three key things. As CEO or manager, you might want to have a sheet with 30 key indicators on it for your own tracking, but don't share the list with the entire company as it will confuse and de-focus them. Again, select one or two major measurements for the entire organization's focus.

- *Provide plenty of feedback face-to-face.* Measurement without feedback is like the proverbial tree falling in the forest – if no one hears it, did it make a sound?

People don't care so much about what we measure or how we measure it so long as you regularly tell them how we're tracking, how we're doing.

QPM = Quarterly Priorities Management

QPM is one of the most useful tracking tools in the entire business world, but even better, it's the single most powerful management tool. It has an amazing ability to keep you and your management team focused on your premier priorities plus it assures you're on track to accomplish them on time within, or often beating, budget. Best of all, the QPM is so easy to use! Start by identifying your top five goals/priorities for the next 90 days. The time period is critical here, so try not to shorten it to less than the three months. As CEO or manager, your focus on the long-term vision needs to be translated into how we will get from here to there for everyone in the company. The problem is that the day-to-day stuff keeps getting in the way.

> All-time Best Management Tool: QPM

The QPM page and the 90-day focus provide the perfect middle ground while answering the question, "what big things am I going to do over the next three months that will get us closer to our vision?" You're looking for the big, quarterly stepping stones that will take you and your team to the vision.

Many CEOs and most managers have a short horizon when it comes to running the business, typically a few months or one to two years. The problem is, those same CEOs and managers will have that same short horizon several months and two years from now, not having moved one inch toward their visions. Change that now! Focus on just those five big things you should do this quarter to get to that vision you keep saying you want to be at two to five years from now.

CEO Tool
QPM

Here's the basic QPM form to get started on a new way of getting to your vision:

USA Any Corporation
"TOP FIVE PRIORITIES"

Name:_____

Title:_____

PRIORITY RANK	CURRENT PRIORITY For Quarter Ending 03-31-xx	PROGRESS AND CURRENT STATUS	NEW PRIORITY For Quarter Ending 06-30-xx
1.			
2.			
3.			
4.			
5.			

At first, you may end up with 29 items rather than five – if so you're probably looking at activities rather than goals or priorities. Focus on just the five biggest things that lead to the vision. Here are mine at Graphic Arts Center for the first quarter:

Graphic Arts Center
"TOP FIVE PRIORITIES"

1st Quarter

Name: Kraig W. Kramers

Title: President & CEO

PRIORITY RANK	CURRENT PRIORITY For Quarter Ending 03-31-xx	PROGRESS AND CURRENT STATUS	NEW PRIORITY For Quarter Ending 06-30-xx
1.	Implement a plan to make Q 1= $1.00 that achieves $1.00 or more of pretax profit in the first quarter.		
2.	Get a $70 million sales plan written and bought into by quarter-end.		
3.	Meet 10 of top 30 customers by the end of February. Visit all 6 sales offices & meet 5 suppliers in March.		
4.	Identify a plan for resolving the "slack month syndrome" by March 30.		
5.	Get our "key indicators" identified and tracking defined by end-Feb.		

Next, after writing down your top five priorities in order of importance, give them to your direct reports in a meeting and ask for their honest feedback. Tell them, "here's what I intend to concentrate on for the next 90 days to help get us to our long-range vision. Are these five priorities the right ones for your CEO to be focused on?" Listen to their answers and take notes. Even if you disagree, write it down. That way you will at least consider their input rather than rejecting it out of hand. This also makes you appear to be a great listener, and perceptions are almost always realities.

> QPM Gets
> Buy-in and
> Communicates

At this stage, you really do want your people's objective feedback regarding your proposed priorities. After listening to what they have to say, hand out a blank form to each direct report – see the sample above titled QPM Tool. Say to them, "let's adjourn this meeting and meet again next week. In the interim, would you please write down your top five priorities for the next 90 days? Let's reconvene next Friday morning at 10:30 and share them with each other. By the way, it's not my intention to hold you accountable for your five priorities…we're all adults here and let me ask that you hold yourself accountable since Kraig tells me this is a great self-accountability tool."

Before that Friday meeting coach your direct reports, individually and privately, on getting their priorities just right and in sync. Coaching means helping them see the right priorities, both for them as individual managers and for the company. It's a bit of give and take, a bit of selling but never telling. The job of the CEO/manager is really only two things: helping to set the direction of the enterprise (e.g., goals and priorities) and then supporting and coaching those around you to achieve that direction.

When the team gets together on Friday, an amazing thing will happen. For the first time, everyone on the management team will know what is most important to each other. As a result, they will stop throwing obstacles in front of each other – hopefully only by mistake in the past. Up till now they didn't understand the impact on other members of the team from what they did. They didn't know what was important to each other. You may think your top people know these things, but they don't. Even if they talk to each other on a regular basis, they don't always talk about the right things. The problem with many teams is they lack "common cause." They're all running toward different goal lines or no goal lines. This QPM process establishes common cause, a common goal line. Now that your direct reports understand each other's priorities, they can truly come together as a team and help each other rather than being scattered or occasionally working at odds.

During the quarter, help your team make their priorities happen. Clip an article on sales planning for the Sales VP who's working on a sales plan that quarter. Offer to help that VP with the spreadsheet analysis for the sales plan if you're good at that.

At the end of the quarter, fill out the middle column on your own QPM form. This represents your report card to yourself about the things you said you would do in the first quarter. Here's what it might look like, continuing our example:

Graphic Arts Center
"TOP FIVE PRIORITIES"

Report

Name: Kraig W. Kramers
Title: President & CEO

PRIORITY RANK	CURRENT PRIORITY For Quarter Ending 03-31-xx	RESULTS AT END OF QUARTER	NEW PRIORITY For Quarter Ending 06-30-xx
1.	Implement a plan to make Q1 = $1.00 that achieves $1.00 or more of pretax profit in the first quarter.	Plan and implementation completed: Q1 = $1.00 and in fact pretax profit was $209K!	
2.	Get a $70 million sales plan written and bought into by quarter-end.	Sales targets set at Feb 21st. Draft of plan completed March 5th. Plan finalized and accepted March 23rd.	
3.	Meet 10 of top 30 customers by the end of February. Visit all 6 sales offices & meet 5 suppliers in March.	Customers met by March 30. Suppliers met by April 2. Offices complete on the 25th of March.	
4.	Identify a plan for resolving the "slack month syndrome" by March 30.	Solution is sales management and sales staffing. Will target a sales management plan for next quarter.	
5.	Get our "key indicators" identified and tracking defined by end-Feb.	Incomplete. Will be completed by the end of April.	

This report card, or results section, ties a ribbon around the past quarter and finishes it off. It furnishes a sense of finality.

Next, we're ready to go to the right-hand column and list our new priorities for the next 90 days. They will almost always be different than the past 90 days, yet one or two might carry over but not necessarily remain in the same priority position. Now let's take a look at the QPM for the next quarter:

Graphic Arts Center
"TOP FIVE PRIORITIES"
Name: Kraig W. Kramers
Title: President & CEO

| End 1st Qtr. | |

PRIORITY RANK	CURRENT PRIORITY For Quarter Ending 03-31-xx	RESULTS FOR LAST QUARTER	NEW PRIORITY For Quarter Ending 06-30-xx
1.	Implement a plan to make Q1 = $1.00 that achieves $1.00 or more of pretax profit in the first quarter.	Plan and implementation completed: Q1 = $1.00 and in fact pretax profit was $209K!	Orchestrate April PTE = $50K and achieve Q2 = $1,000,000 PTE.
2.	Get a $70 million sales plan written and bought into by quarter-end.	Sales targets set at Feb 21st. Draft of plan completed March 5th. Plan finalized and accepted March 23rd.	Revamp sales management organization by April 30th.
3.	Meet 10 of top 30 customers by the end of February. Visit all 6 sales offices & meet 5 suppliers in March.	Customers met by March 30. Suppliers met by April 2. Offices complete on the 25th of March.	Get "Project Swap" completed by the 30th of June, including one new sheetfed press up and running.
4.	Identify a plan for resolving the "slack month syndrome" by March 30.	Solution is sales management and sales staffing. Will target a sales management plan for next quarter.	Get AIC cost standards reset by the 30th of June.
5.	Get our "key indicators" identified and tracking defined by end-Feb.	Incomplete. Will be completed by the end of April.	Get the sheetfed strategy refined and formalized in a written marketing plan n.l.t. May 15th.

Notice the comment at the bottom of the "Results for Last Quarter" column about the incomplete fifth priority regarding key indicators; it was well underway and will be finished in April; it was not significant enough to carry over into the new priorities for the next quarter, and the sheetfed strategy outweighed it anyway as the new 5th priority for the second quarter.

Now take a copy of your fully filled-in form to each of your direct reports and ask them to complete their forms. Then schedule another meeting to share the completed quarterly priority management forms with each other.

Here's a critical point: please don't ever use these report cards to beat up on those who fail to achieve their priorities, since that will counteract the QPM's positive spirit. In addition, do not let your direct reports beat each other up over their lack of performance, but do indeed praise what did get done. Focus on the future while keeping the report cards on view for everyone in the room to see. That's all it takes – a controlled public display of people's performance. You will be astounded at how the performance levels in your company suddenly take off. You have probably heard it said best in nautical terms, "a rising tide carries all ships to new levels." Peer motivation is powerful in an organization. It is far stronger than superior-subordinate motivation.

| Peer Motivation is a Powerful Management Tool |

Obviously, if some of your people repeatedly fall short in their performances, you and your senior managers need to have coaching and accountability conversations with them, preferably in private. But if you have done a good job of placing winners in the right jobs, peer motivation will work wondrous results for you.

A couple of additional thoughts about the top five priorities: first, you probably shouldn't force this any further down than your direct reports. If they want to take it, in turn, to their direct-reports, that's fine. Encourage them to try it, but my experience is that some managers aren't great coaches and instead find other ways to accomplish their results. Second, top priorities aren't quite like big audacious goals or overall corporate goals, so think twice before making them public knowledge throughout the organization.

Suppose, for example, that one of your priorities involves reorganizing the whole company. It could cause serious morale and performance problems if people learned of an impending reorganization well before you have a chance to communicate it and explain the need for it and how it will work. Remember our earlier observations about no news and partial news? Despite this, your direct reports do need to know you're working on an upcoming reorganization so they can help you with the reorganization plan. It belongs on your quarterly priorities manager page but almost certainly not in the public domain yet.

Roll the QPM forward from quarter-to-quarter by refreshing the form – that is, move the last column to be first in the new quarter and clear the two right-hand columns so it looks like this:

Graphic Arts Center
"TOP FIVE PRIORITIES"
Name: Kraig W. Kramers
Title: President & CEO

2nd Quarter

PRIORITY RANK	CURRENT PRIORITY For Quarter Ending 06-30-xx	RESULTS FOR LAST QUARTER	NEW PRIORITY For Quarter Ending 09-30-xx
1.	Orchestrate April PTE = $50K and achieve Q2 = $1,000,000 PTE.		
2.	Revamp sales management organization by April 30th.		
3.	Get "Project Swap" completed by the 30th of June, including one new sheetfed press up and running.		
4.	Get AIC cost standards reset by the 30th of June.		
5.	Get the sheetfed strategy refined and formalized in a written marketing plan n.l.t. May 15th.		

The CD/Desktop helper associated with this book makes this really easy. Now you're ready for this management tool to become the best ongoing management system you've ever seen. It works from quarter-to-quarter keeping you and your team on track.

Here's an anecdote to help put the power of the quarterly priorities manager into perspective: a president friend of mine in Chicago used this with his charitable organization a few years back with spectacular success. The year before he used the QPM, his non-profit had raised about $25,000. The very next year, by using the QPM, they raised a whopping $700K plus. The QPM is just the best management tool around – so why not put it to profit-increasing use right now, today, in your business?

85

Trailing Twelve-Month Charts (T12M)

If I could only use only one tracking tool, it would be the trailing 12-months (T12M) chart. For openers, you can apply it to just about any meaningful indicator or measurement in your company. More importantly, however, *nothing* gives you a truer picture of what is going on in your company, historically, currently and prospectively. The T12M chart also allows you to identify potentially major problems and take remedial action long before they reach crisis stage. Let's return for a moment to the concept of anticipating the future here. Wayne Gretzky, arguably the world's greatest hockey player, responded this way to the question of why he is so good: "I don't skate to where the puck is. I skate to where the puck's going to be." That is what future anticipation is all about, prospectively seeing and being where the puck is going to be. The T12M chart will do this for you.

> **T12M Charts: The *Best* Tracking Tool**

T12M Charts

Most entrepreneurial CEOs and managers don't have financial backgrounds. They hate numbers and spreadsheets and financial analysis. But if you fit this description, please take heart: this is your tool. You just have to embrace the trailing 12-months chart because it will change your business life forever. Now, if you absolutely can't stand working with numbers, get your CFO or controller to create this chart for you. Whatever you do, you can't afford not to look at this chart on at least a monthly basis. Nothing will give you a better snapshot of where the company has been and, more important, where it is going. The immense importance of anticipating the future and getting a prospective picture can't be overemphasized. The trailing 12-month chart identifies future problems and opportunities, giving you the time to take action to fix things before they go awry or take advantage of a unique situation.

So here's how it works. Each dot on the following T12M chart represents the sales for the previous 12 months ending in that month. It's a rolling annual total of actual sales, entered monthly, that eliminates the seasonality effect in looking at your results.

Trailing Twelve Months (T12M) Chart

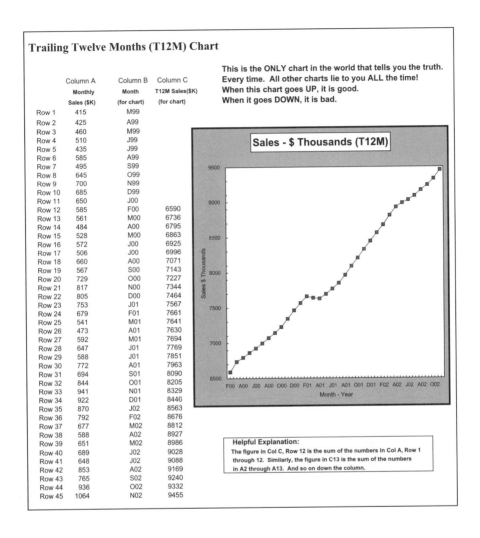

This is the ONLY chart in the world that tells you the truth. Every time. All other charts lie to you ALL the time! When this chart goes UP, it is good. When it goes DOWN, it is bad.

	Column A Monthly Sales ($K)	Column B Month (for chart)	Column C T12M Sales($K) (for chart)
Row 1	415	M99	
Row 2	425	A99	
Row 3	460	M99	
Row 4	510	J99	
Row 5	435	J99	
Row 6	585	A99	
Row 7	495	S99	
Row 8	645	O99	
Row 9	700	N99	
Row 10	685	D99	
Row 11	650	J00	
Row 12	585	F00	6590
Row 13	561	M00	6736
Row 14	484	A00	6795
Row 15	528	M00	6863
Row 16	572	J00	6925
Row 17	506	J00	6996
Row 18	660	A00	7071
Row 19	567	S00	7143
Row 20	729	O00	7227
Row 21	817	N00	7344
Row 22	805	D00	7464
Row 23	753	J01	7567
Row 24	679	F01	7661
Row 25	541	M01	7641
Row 26	473	A01	7630
Row 27	592	M01	7694
Row 28	647	J01	7769
Row 29	588	J01	7851
Row 30	772	A01	7963
Row 31	694	S01	8090
Row 32	844	O01	8205
Row 33	941	N01	8329
Row 34	922	D01	8446
Row 35	870	J02	8563
Row 36	792	F02	8676
Row 37	677	M02	8812
Row 38	588	A02	8927
Row 39	651	M02	8986
Row 40	689	J02	9028
Row 41	648	J02	9088
Row 42	853	A02	9169
Row 43	765	S02	9240
Row 44	936	O02	9332
Row 45	1064	N02	9455

Sales - $ Thousands (T12M)

Helpful Explanation:
The figure in Col C, Row 12 is the sum of the numbers in Col A, Row 1 through 12. Similarly, the figure in C13 is the sum of the numbers in A2 through A13. And so on down the column.

The first dot, lower-left on the chart, represents the total sales from March 1999 through February 2000, the next point represents total sales from April 1999 to March 2000 and so on. As you move across the page from left to right, you get a *rolling annual total*, shown on a monthly basis. Why is this so important? It's the only chart in the world that tells the truth, eliminates seasonality and points you to correct action.

> T12M Charts Eliminate Seasonality

Ordinary monthly charts only track one month at a time and go up and down from month to month with no relationship to prior performance – so they lie to you every month. There can be many reasons for going up or down, some good, some bad. Example: your

| All Other Charts *LIE* to You! |

ordinary monthly chart goes down this month; that might *not* be bad if it went down *less* than in the same month last year. If it went up this month, that might *not* be good, since it might have gone up *less* than in the same month last year! Yet an "up" on an ordinary monthly chart is universally viewed as "good." Ordinary charts give you a very limited perspective of the company's performance, usually incorrectly. Simply put, they lie to you. Even worse, you seldom get information about the direction of your company's performance from ordinary charts. It's funny: they taught us to do ordinary charts early, in about the fourth grade, but then never taught us to read them.

With the T12M chart, the only good direction is up. If it goes sideways or down, you know you have a problem. The T12M chart eliminates seasonality since each point has all twelve seasons or months, allowing every month to be compared with every other month. For the first time in your company's history, you'll see your sales and other business measures as they truly are. This may take a while to get used to since the charts you have looked at in the past contain seasonality you are used to seeing.

T12M charts provide a very easy read on any and all key indicators you may choose to track. No other chart does so much in one easily interpreted picture. An added advantage is that the T12M

| T12M Charts Are *Exception* Reports! |

chart also serves as an exception report. It's so easy to use that you can have 30 different charts arrive on your desk and you can review all of them in just three minutes. All you need to do is see if the chart is going up. If so, put that one aside. Any that are going sideways or down need your immediate attention because those tell you where the problems are. Take action on these. One glance tells you good or bad. Work immediately on the bad ones; nudge the good ones to be better.

T12M charts also make it easy to determine much sooner that a steady downward trend has begun. A couple of years back a CEO friend of mine who owns a PR firm in Atlanta called to say she wanted help getting her company to grow. She detailed how her company had slowed down right after the 1996 Olympics and how profitability had substantially waned as well. We took the data for 36 months of sales and did a T12M chart. Wonder of wonders, you could clearly see that this company's sales had stumbled five months before the Olympics, that in fact the Olympics had nearly nothing to do with it. More often than not, this is what we see with T12Ms. The real cause was internal: we changed the internal tracking tools, changed the compensation scheme, and put in some recognition-for-results tools. Today it's a healthy, growing, leading public relations firm making headlines of its own.

When starting out, put three years total on every trailing 12-month chart – two years of history and the current year. This gives you historical perspective and displays any true trend lines. Most companies compare the current year to last year, which is good because at least you're getting a comparison. Put two or three years of history on your T12M charts and that will be great, since it allows for much more accurate problem identification and analysis. Oscar Wilde observed that, "comparisons are odious" and he might have gone a little too far. They're okay, but let's go for great.

The first time you chart three years of sales for your company or operation, the graph will bounce all over the place. That's okay, because when you eventually straighten out that sales curve, it means you're running the company more efficiently and will make a lot more money.

The pictorial on the next page tells you everything you need to know to do your own T12M chart. If you click on the icon on the CD/Desktop Browser associated with this book, you will see this page displayed with complete instructions. You can actually use the format that follows to enter your data and generate your T12M charts in just a few minutes:

Example of Trailing 12 Months (T12M) Charting

HOW TO GET STARTED:
Example of charting 3 years of monthly SALES data on a T12M (Trailing Twelve Months) basis. You'll get a chart where each point is comparable to every other point. Look at this chart monthly to see things you never saw before about your business!

It's a ROLLING ANNUAL TOTAL tracked monthly. T12M charts will clearly tell you whether you're doing good or bad! Ordinary monthly charts often mislead and show little other than your seasonality (see example of it in the chart below). T12M charts eliminate seasonality and also show historical perspective, a true trendline.

Please see T12M on the CD/Desktop Browser for a detailed explanation of how to prepare your own T12M in just minutes.

	Column A Monthly Sales ($K)	Col B Mo-Yr	Col C T12M Sales $K (T12M chart)
Row 1	415	J-98	
Row 2	425	F-98	
Row 3	460	M-98	
Row 4	510	A-98	
Row 5	435	M-98	
Row 6	585	J-98	
Row 7	495	J-98	
Row 8	645	A-98	
Row 9	700	S-98	
Row 10	685	O-98	
Row 11	650	N-98	
Row 12	585	D-98	6590
Row 13	561	J-99	6736
Row 14	484	F-99	6795
Row 15	528	M-99	6863
Row 16	572	A-99	6925
Row 17	506	M-99	6996
Row 18	660	J-99	7071
Row 19	567	J-99	7143
Row 20	729	A-99	7227
Row 21	817	S-99	7344
Row 22	805	O-99	7464
Row 23	753	N-99	7567
Row 24	668	D-99	7650
Row 25	550	J-00	7639
Row 26	528	F-00	7683
Row 27	592	M-00	7747
Row 28	647	A-00	7822
Row 29	588	M-00	7904
Row 30	772	J-00	8016
Row 31	684	J-00	8133
Row 32	844	A-00	8248
Row 33	828	S-00	8259
Row 34	765	O-00	8219
Row 35	722	N-00	8188
Row 36	630	D-00	8150
Row 37	525	J-00	8125
Row 38	520	F-01	8117
Row 39	610	M-01	8135
Row 40	689	A-01	8177
Row 41	648	M-01	8237
Row 42	853	J-01	8318
Row 43	765	J-01	8399
Row 44	968	A-01	8523
Row 45	945	S-01	8640

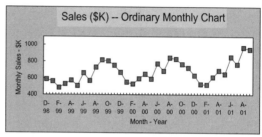

Sales ($K) -- Ordinary Monthly Chart

Sales ($K) -- Trailing 12 Months (T12M) Chart

Utilize this chart to track your business as you accelerate into high gear and high sustainable growth. A straight, long-term sales growth curve is more profitable because you'll find you are hiring and keeping people to do the work, rather than hiring and firing people as sales cycle up and down. Isn't it obvious that it's much more efficient to hire and keep? Work on turning your sales improvement into a straight line so it becomes much easier to predict and much more profitable. You'll also find that cash flow is more manageable once your sales growth exhibits a more orderly straight line on the trailing 12-months chart.

These charts are really not rocket science. You should just be able to hand the "how to" page shown above to your CFO or controller or numbers person and get back some T12Ms in a week. And, if by some chance that person can't get you the charts in a week? You probably should be in the market for a new CFO or controller or numbers person. Even easier, there's a CD in the back of this book with T12Ms in Excel format for your use. Simply open the T12M.xls file in Microsoft® Excel. It explains exactly how you can have your own T12M charts in minutes.

Take a look at that "how to" page again, the one with the ordinary monthly chart sitting above and perfectly aligned with the T12M. You're looking at a company with a seasonal downturn in September through February of each year. Let's say we are competitors, you and I. And you don't have the T12M but I do. Every year during the seasonal downturns, you muse, "oh, here we go again into the usual slowdown; guess it's time to cruise a bit, drop oars and catch our breath."

At my company, on the other hand, we spot the first down month on the T12M and say "whoops, time to tighten our grip and row faster." And, if we do it right, we'll take market share away from our competition. We call the salespeople and ask them to get two more orders each this week, we SPIF them (that is, provide them with a Special Performance Incentive Fee), and we ask them to go one extra for the Gipper. Guess what? Our sales now go up instead of down because we took action after seeing that first down-tilt on the T12M. Or rather, because we *pro-acted* after our *prospective tracker* told us to do so. You've got to have this T12M thing before your competitors do, or they'll kill you. Let's say it more positively: go clobber your competition by out-anticipating them.

> **Take Action Triggered by T12M Charts**

> **Clobber Your Competition With T12Ms**

91

Tracking What Causes Sales

Believe it or not, there is an even more important indicator than tracking sales or profits on the T12M, and that is tracking *what causes sales* to happen. In just about every business, the activities that cause sales to happen take place at least 30 days before you add last month's sales dot to the chart. This includes activities like

| Track *What Causes Sales* to Manage Way Ahead! |

new accounts called on, number of telemarketing calls, responses on a website, dollar value of requests-for-proposal in and/or out the door – anything that must take place in advance of the sale or that drives the sale to happen. Let's call this the key leading indicator (KLI) and by managing this you will get substantially enhanced growth.

At both the printing company and at the insurance underwriter, my primary leading sales indicator was dollar value of quotes per week. This happened about 80 days before the month's sales figure ever went on the chart at the printing company. At Guarantee Insurance Resources, the insurance company, it was three to four weeks in advance, which gave us a lot of pro-action time to get more sales whenever our key leading indicator showed signs of weakness. It's like the Early Warning System during the Cold War. We could

| Track *What Causes Sales* to Get Gargantuan Growth |

see a slowing happening in real-time using T12Ms, pro-act by encouraging more sales activity from our salespeople for a temporary period, and get back on track before we ever got off track. This really epitomizes prospective tracking.

At GAC printing, as long as we kept growing our dollar value of quotes per week, we knew that sales would continue to grow 80 to 90 days later. By using the trailing 12 months chart to track such key

| *The* Key Leading Indicator |

leading indicators, we could strive for a straight-line growth in sales. We got lucky, of course, and the straight line happened month-after-month, year-after-year at a growth rate more than four times that of our industry. Here's our T12M chart for sales, showing virtually straight-line performance:

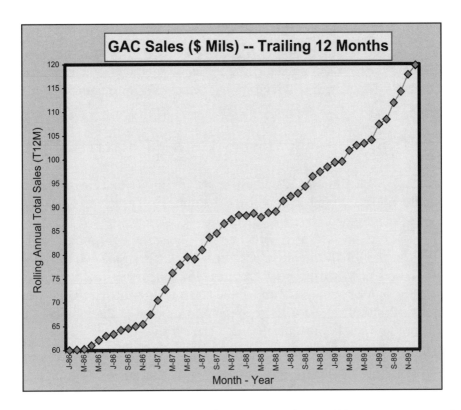

GAC Sales ($ Mils) -- Trailing 12 Months

Rolling Annual Total Sales (T12M)

Month - Year

So, what causes the rubber to meet the road in your company? What might your KLIs be: dollars of advertising? number of bids submitted? number of telemarketing calls? number of sales feet on the street? number of requests for proposal out the door? For my construction clients, what causes sales is total dollar volume of RFQs, or requests for proposal, in the door. For my retail clients, it's total dollars spent on advertising and direct mail pieces. For my distribution clients and office copier/computer-toner re-manufacturing client, it's total number of targeted telemarketing calls.

Identify your key leading indicators for sales and manage them using the T12M chart. Amazingly, your sales growth will take care of itself. It's simple cause and effect. Sales are the effect, caused by what happens 15 to 360 days earlier. The only difference with tracking what causes sales is that you should try eventually to track it on a trailing 52-week (T52W) basis rather than a T12M. That way you get a read-out every week instead of only once a month, allowing you to identify trends and take action even more quickly. This allows

> **Track KLIs Using T52W Charts**

you to out-think competition on a weekly basis. If you're not using this tool, start collecting data now. Learn to manage what causes sales and sales growth will happily happen almost automatically.

Next Step: 12-Month Moving Average Charts (12MMA)

Try the trailing 12-month chart for gross margin percent – actually it's a moving average of 12 months of gross profit dollars divided by 12 months of sales dollars (12MMA), expressed as a percent. It is the same concept as T12M, with all the attendant attributes. It's an exception report, very sensitive to change, eliminates seasonality, always tells the truth, and tells you much sooner. After what causes sales and sales itself, gross margin percent is the topmost key indicator to track in most businesses. Here's an example:

12MMA Chart

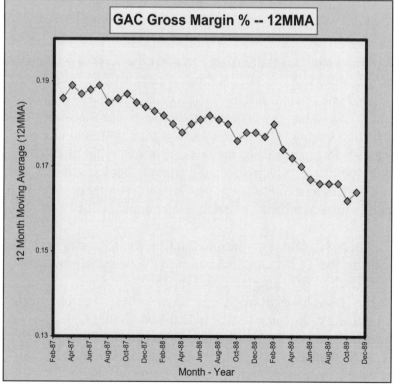

Notice that the gross margin is going down and you're saying: "Kraig, if you keep doing that much longer, you'll go out of business!" And you are right. But first please understand our strategy before judging our chart. Simply, our strategy is that we'll give away a little price to get the print jobs we want – very carefully, job-by-job, customer-by-customer, and only when we need to yield on price.

You can actually see a point where we stopped doing that and leveled the gross margin out and up a bit. At that precise point we had maxed out the plant's capacity, and it was time to stop the purposeful price erosion. Now, you saw the sales chart going straight up at a 20 percent rate a few pages back, so what do you think our pretax profit dollars chart looked like? Yup, straight up and growing even steeper than our sales.

T12M Charts Revisited

So here are the million-dollar questions: *What is your strategy? How are you tracking it?* And if you see yourself in the mirror with that deer-in-the-headlights look, well, then: it's time to grow your business. For help on your growth strategy, go talk to your people, walk your four corners. Maybe use a strategy meeting facilitator or a consultant. Once you've got the strategy pretty well nailed down, let me assure you that T12M charts – measuring the meaningful things – will be your best tracking tools.

What's Your Strategy? How Will You Track It?

Here is another real-life story of a company's actual sales experience that should convince you to start using T12M charts immediately. Following is an example of measuring meaningful things from a public company:

95

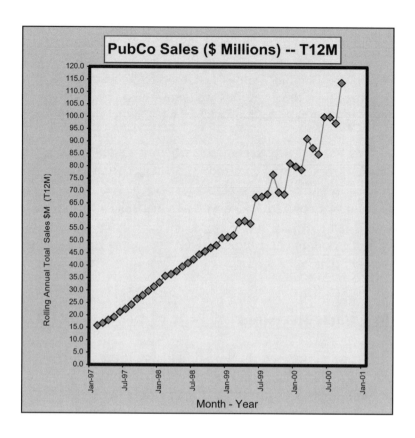

Notice that after consistent month-to-month growth for several years at very high rates, this company suddenly started suffering from the "3rd month" syndrome. That is, it fell behind on shipments in the first two months of a quarter and had to play catch-up in the third month to make quarterly numbers and keep Wall Street happy. Needless to say, this pattern then expands, as you can clearly see in the chart, and can quickly get to the breaking point. The senior management team saw this using T12M charts and fixed it before ever missing their numbers, thus avoiding a potential drop in stock price and being downgraded by the stock market analysts.

What else can we track with T12Ms and 12MMAs? My favorites for each financial category look like this, and if you can compare them to industry norms, and then beat them by a bit or a bunch, all the better:

Income Statement: Sales $, Gross Margin %, SG&A % of Sales, Profit $.

Balance Sheet: Stockholders Equity, Debt:Equity Ratio, Receivables Turnover, Accounts Receivable to Accounts Payable Ratio, Inventory Turnover.

Cash Flow Statement: Net Cash Generated (Used), Net New Borrowings.

Key Indicators: What Causes Sales, Customer Satisfaction Index, Employee Satisfaction Index, Product or Market Mix Change, Market Share, Profit Mix Change.

Base the early warning system for your business on these key indicators and you'll dramatically improve your profit and growth performance. Add key indicators that match your industry or niche and you'll easily leave your competitors in the dust.

Here's a final note about T12M Charts. If your sales flatten out, take action to reduce operating expenses right away or get sales up right away. Most managers just wait: this is "hope" and it's a four-letter word for pathological optimism. Act now – don't wait!

Monthly Superstars Letters

Contrary to popular belief, tracking tools don't consist only of boring charts and statistics. In fact, the more you can inject fun into the process, the more people will want to get involved. | Monthly Superstars Letter | The more people get involved, the more measurement and tracking will become an ingrained part of your culture. A favorite tool for tracking and reinforcing sales performance is called the Monthly Superstars Letter. Take a look at this example:

GAC

Memo to: **ALL SALES PERSONNEL**

From: **Kraig W. Kramers**

Subject: **June Superstars!**

Date: **June 28, 19xx**

You great Sales Superstars created the very best June GAC has ever had! Sales for the month were way over $7.2 million, including a tremendous $3.1 million of SHEETFED! You're up 18.5% over June last year.

Better yet, your job pricing and profitability came out over 100% of AIC. We want to thank you for those great results, and you in turn should thank your magnificent manufacturing team for the follow-through. Working together with them, you improved the "come-out" margin over the "go-in" margin by three percentage points!

There are 14 SuperStars this month and 11 for the quarter so far. Here are GAC's June SuperStars:

		June 19xx	Q2 So Far
Jack D.	Portland	+	+
Tanya I.	Portland	+	+
John M.	Portland	+	
George N.	Portland	+	+
William P.	Portland	+	+
Roland B.	San Francisco	+	+
Dave O.	San Francisco	+	
Michael S.	San Francisco	+	+
Jim T.	San Francisco	+	+
Paul W.	San Francisco	+	
Bob B.	Seattle	+	+
Richard V.	Seattle	+	
Chuck B.	Chicago	+	
Pete S.	Chicago	+	
Bill W.	New York	+	

Again, thank you for the big effort in June! It really paid off for GAC and our team. You're the best!

(continued on next page)

June Superstars
Page Two

RICHARD V. takes the near miss award this month with his super $292K actual for the quarter just missing his $310K target by 6%. And you know how close that really is when you realize that SEATTLE just missed their quarter target by only 1.3%! Congratulations to the individuals and the team in Seattle for being that close.

July and Q2 are looking a lot better thanks to everyone's effort in every region. But now is not the time to get complacent: remember we've got to get SHEETFED back up to 30% to get our profit performance on track for the year.

By the way, speaking of not becoming complacent, we have five winners so far in the YCDBSOYA contest! And we know no one at GAC ever succumbs to the implication of that acronym, but it's always good to remind ourselves to get up, get out and get on with doing our jobs with new vigor each day!

Earlier this week, the following SuperStars brought in great new sheetfed orders and solved the YCDBSOYA riddle:

1. Don G.	Los Angeles	10:42 a.m.	Monday	6-26-xx
2. Don S.	Portland	1:45 p.m.	Monday	6-26-xx
3. Dave O.	San Francisco	4:13 p.m.	Monday	6-26-xx
4. Greg W.	New York	1:13 p.m.	Tuesday	6-27-xx
5. Bob B.	Seattle	9:34 a.m.	Wednesday	6-28-xx

We're listening for the phone to ring from Chicago and Dallas...and we expect winners any moment! Each of the five SuperStars listed above won a brand new $100 bill, and we'll tell you more about the fun we had with them at the upcoming National Sales Meeting in two weeks. We're proud of you five and everyone else who's putting sheetfed over the top in July!

Keep at it, you're really making it happen at GAC!

With best regards,

Kraig

Kraig W. Kramers
President and CEO

If your vice president of sales doesn't do this on a regular basis, you're missing a real opportunity to recognize your winners and tap into the power of peer motivation with your salespeople.

Send this monthly superstars letter to everyone in the sales organization each month. Make it a snappy, energetic letter that truly conveys your excitement and your thanks for everyone's effort and especially praise for your superstars' performance. If your sales VP can't write great letters, designate a ghostwriter to help, but do get them written. Celebrate the winners in the letter, that is, those who hit

| Peer Motivation Tool |

their goals this month or quarter-to-date. Don't say a word about the laggards. In fact, don't even mention them at all. People can read between the lines; they know who is missing from the letter and why. Let the awesome power of peer motivation work for you, not against you. It works against you when you don't recognize results, since the performers start grousing about not being praised, which in turn slows down the whole sales group.

The monthly superstars letter also allows you to inject fun into the tracking process, which increases the "take" by everyone

| Inject Fun Whenever Possible: YCDBSOYA |

involved. People just get into it more if you make it fun – so how about a contest that's fun? On page two of the example letter above, we reported on the results of a contest in which we awarded $100 each to the first five salespeople who identified the meaning of the acronym YCDBSOYA. One hundred dollars doesn't buy what it used to, but it's the idea of winning that motivates; it stokes the competitive fires of good

| Winners Win at Everything: Great Hiring Tool |

salespeople. You can't have too many winners on your team and tools like these turn good performers into winners. A useful tool for identifying winners when you're hiring is to realize that winners win at everything, almost literally. Trust this tool in your hiring efforts.

To illustrate, the winner of the acronym contest at GAC printing was Don Gordon, who just happened to be the top salesperson five years in a row. Now you don't believe for an instant

| Focus on Winners |

that his winning the contest and being five-years best salesperson just coincidentally happened. And being top in sales isn't because Don had the biggest territory or the most experience, but because he is a *winner*. For instance, Don would take time out of his schedule to coach younger, less experienced salespeople when he could have instead made more money for himself by being out selling.

When you have superstars like that on your team, pay serious attention to them. Give them the opportunity to win, provide them the support they need and provide plenty of recognition for a job well done. At the same time of course, don't completely ignore everyone else. In many cases, average and even mediocre performers can improve with the right coaching and encouragement. But in general, you will get a lot more mileage out of your sales team by focusing your time and attention on the winners.

> Support
> Winners

Incidentally, YCDBSOYA stands for "you can't do business sitting on your ass," a somewhat crude saying that's been around a while but says it well. Yes it's possible to have fun and get a point across at the same time. Don't limit these kinds of contests to your sales team. People in other departments like to have fun, too. Why not come up with an acronym contest for your accounting department or support group? Put fun back into everything you do. Business is too serious and life too short not to go for the gusto.

Backlog Tracker Tool

Some companies measure sales performance on a monthly or quarterly basis. Why not do it also on a daily and weekly basis to get more advance reaction time? There's that concept of prospective tracking showing up again. For one, the nature of the work of selling makes it easy to track the performance more frequently. Number of sales closed, unit volume of sales, dollar amount of sales, number of sales calls made – these are all easy to quantify and measure on a daily or weekly basis. And, the more often you provide positive feedback, the more frequently you can guide and direct your sales force to the performance the company deserves.

A pair of really nifty tools for tracking salespeople's performance includes a "daily sales report of orders booked today" by salesperson and the "weekly sales report" which shows both the sales dollars by person and by region as well as the profit. It lists each

> Meaningful
> Daily & Weekly
> Sales Reports

101

salesperson's performance for the current month-to-date against targets, with a breakdown by product mix. At Snapper lawnmowers the weekly sales report showed walk-behind mowers, rear-engine riders, and lawn tractors sold; at GAC printing it reported sheet-fed vs. web printing orders captured. Even more important, it also measures how they did this time period versus the same time period

| Do Better Than Last Time |

last year. If your team does better this month than they did for the same month last year – and keeps that up in the long run – you can all giggle all the way to the bank. Of course, the other areas of the company have to do their part, but continual sales growth can take care of a lot of problems. In other words, strong growth of sales will overcome a bunch of shortfalls in other parts of the business. And, solid sales growth also tends to minimize the effects of seasonality in any business.

Best of the bunch for sales management is the *Backlog Tracker*, a monthly tally that shows you how you're doing

| Backlog Tracker |

prospectively months in advance. Following is an example of a backlog tracker that we used at the GAC printing. It allows you to see your backlog for upcoming months on an apples-to-apples basis versus exactly where you were at this time last year. All you have to do is take action to keep your backlog of sales for each upcoming month bigger than last year as you look at this report each week.

Now, maybe that's easier said than done, but if you have the backlog tool you will then start to figure out how to get more business

CEO Tool
Backlog

way in advance. Without a backlog tool, or some sales anticipation methodology that signals you about a slowdown of incoming business, you're really flying blind about the future. You're missing the opportunity to take action early for continual good results.

This tool can be found on the CD/Browser and is easy to adapt for use in your business. Let's take a detailed look at how this future anticipation tool worked in the printing company:

SALES BACKLOG TRACKER
Today's Date: 19-Dec-01
($ 000)   Updated each week.

Compares backlog for upcoming months
as of this week to the same point in time
last year. Permits apples-to-apples look
at the future, so you can change the future!

	Month	$ Sales Booked By Mo. This Year Thru 12/19/01	$ Sales Booked By Mo. Last Year Thru 12/19/00	Growth Sales $	%
↑ Historical Past ↓	Jan '01	$7,030	$5,055	$1,975	39.1%
	Feb '01	8,365	7,065	1,300	18.4%
	Mar '01	8,537	10,991	(2,454)	-22.3%
	1st Qtr	$23,932	$23,111	$821	3.6%
	Apr '01	$8,186	$6,733	$1,453	21.6%
	May '01	6,532	5,438	1,094	20.1%
	Jun '01	6,137	5,776	361	6.3%
	2nd Qtr	$20,855	$17,947	$2,908	16.2%
	Jul '01	$8,230	$7,027	$1,203	17.1%
	Aug '01	8,952	8,408	544	6.5%
	Sep '01	8,583	8,288	295	3.6%
	3rd Qtr	$25,765	$23,723	$2,042	8.6%
	Oct '01	$11,070	$7,706	$3,364	43.7%
	Nov '01	8,470	7,322	1,148	15.7%
NOW -->	Dec '01	8,219	5,256	2,963	56.4%
	4th Qtr	$27,759	$20,284	$7,475	36.9%
↑ Upcoming Future ↓	Jan '02	$8,794	$6,316	$2,478	39.2%
	Feb '02	5,954	5,805	149	2.6%
	Mar '02	6,168	3,527	2,641	74.9%
	1st Qtr	$20,916	$15,648	$5,268	33.7%
	Apr '02	$3,941	$3,734	$207	5.5%
	May '02	1,374	1,747	(373)	-21.4%
	Jun '02	502	1,274	(772)	-60.6%
	2nd Qtr	$5,817	$6,755	($938)	-13.9%

The third week Backlog Tracker report for December arrives on your desk and looks like the above example – it shows at least the next six months with the bookings for each month. The month of May might historically be your weakest month, showing on the report at $1.3 million this coming May vs. $1.7 million in May of last year as seen from the same vantage point of the third week in December. By now, dear reader, you've gotten this far, so you know it's time for action. Admittedly we have five months to do something, but it's no fun being behind and having sleepless nights over it, so let's do something about it now, way in advance. Yes, it's pro-action time.

Call the sales force, ask them to go out now in December, five months ahead of everyone else in the industry, and get May and June orders. Give customers the best price and best printing days in May-June. Let's lower price because we'll be faced with that anyway, given it's our worst month – our worst season. However, let's give our customers the best prices now because we have to anyway in May-June. This will beat out our competitors by doing it in December for May and June orders. Let's also set aside for those customers the best printing days because professional print buyers spend their entire lives in printing plants on weekends and nights, and they're more likely to award the job to us now in December because we're taking care of them as individuals and taking care of their companies as well. This approach resulted in filling up the plant for May-June when hardly any one of the 50,000 other commercial printers had ever done that. It's a lesson in how to clobber competition with the backlog tracker. It's almost as good as finding the cure for the common cold. So now, how can you adapt this tool to work for you?

Many companies can also track profit backlog by month on a weekly basis, just as sales were tracked above. Try it, as this allows you to actively change mix of business on the fly to maximize profitability. Again, this profit-mix tracker was successful during my stewardship at eight companies and with scores of clients.

Here's an afterthought about that worst season thing. Identify your worst season and try something different to fix it, like the actions

| Attack and Track Solutions to Your Worst Season! |

that beat down our worst month using the backlog tracker tool. At Snapper our worst season was the summer months, when almost no one manufactures lawnmowers. We changed this dramatically by turning our plant into what's called a "commercial manufacturer" of metal parts for others, including Blue Bird® buses and the two golf-car makers EZGO® and ClubCar®.

If you and your team brainstorm it, there's almost always a good answer or two to your worst season. Don't forget to walk your four corners and ask employees for ideas like this. They have them.

Daily Cash Report & Weekly Cash Re-Forecasting

My definition of an entrepreneur is someone who works seven days a week, 17 hours a day, and is always running out of cash. Unfortunately, many professional managers also run out of cash because they don't have the most basic tools of all, namely a daily cash report and a weekly cash re-forecaster.

The daily cash report will occupy precisely three seconds of your day, each day. Take a quick glance to see where you are on total borrowings and your maximum available line-of-credit, assuming you keep your cash account at some constant positive number, say $5,000. The point is that most of us borrow in business, so what we're really trying to do is not run out of credit line, rather than cash. What we really need to look at is "cash headroom" which includes both our available cash and the amount of availability in our line-of-credit.

By looking at it daily, CEOs and managers can stay in touch with when they're starting to get too close. They then can look at a few other things, like days sales outstanding on receivables or inventory turns, and take corrective action in plenty of time. There's that pro-active thing showing up again, namely taking action.

The format for cash tracking as well as cash re-forecasting follows and can also be found on the CD at Cash Tool. The form is pretty self-explanatory and there are brief instructions on use at the top of the page. Here's one format that works pretty well for keeping track of our cash headroom:

Your Company Name Here, Inc.
Daily Cash Tracking & Forecasting Report ($ 000)

Instructions: Issue report daily. Update the projection part of this report every Friday afternoon for as much of the near-term future as you can reasonably judge.

DATE	Actual					Projection				
	Receipts	IN Cleared	OUT Checks	Loan Advances	Loan Balance	Receipts	IN Cleared	OUT Checks	Loan Advances	Loan Balance
01-May-01										
02-May-01										
03-May-01										
04-May-01										
05-May-01										
06-May-01										
07-May-01										
08-May-01										
09-May-01										
10-May-01										
11-May-01										
12-May-01										
13-May-01										
14-May-01										
15-May-01										
16-May-01										
17-May-01										
18-May-01										
19-May-01										
20-May-01										
21-May-01										
22-May-01										
23-May-01										
24-May-01										
25-May-01										
26-May-01										
27-May-01										
28-May-01	Holiday					Holiday				
29-May-01										
30-May-01										
31-May-01										
01-Jun-01										
02-Jun-01										
03-Jun-01										
04-Jun-01										
05-Jun-01										
06-Jun-01										
07-Jun-01										
08-Jun-01										
M-T-D										
Budget										
B (W)										
Y-T-D										
Budget										
B (W)										
Week of 15 Jun										
Week of 22 Jun										
Week of 29 Jun										
Week of 6 Jul										

_____   Prepared By: _____   Copies To: _____   _____

Date

The weekly re-forecast included on the form above isn't much more complicated. Simply ask your financial person on Friday to re-forecast anticipated receipts and disbursements for each day of next week plus the same for the next four weeks by week, a total of the next five weeks

Weekly Cash Re-Forecast

altogether. Track actuals by day next week and repeat the exercise next Friday. Keep this up forever. Why? So you learn about your cash flows, improve your forecasting and your anticipation abilities, manage your cash inflows and outflows better, and most important of all, never ever run out of cash. Many thanks to Red Scott, the great leader of several public and private companies, for teaching us this essential tool.

CEO Tool
Cash

A few related tools you might consider: EDI, Ltd. in Atlanta is a unique engineering firm that uses a return-postage-paid postcard, sent to clients together with the invoice asking if there is any question about the invoice. This resulted in reducing past-90-days receivables from the high

> **Postcard with Invoice**

hundreds of thousands of dollars to the low tens of thousands. Another tool from Abe "Walking Bear" Sanchez (nationally-known speaker) is a way of tracking collections during the month so we're not waiting until month-end to find out we're not collecting fast enough. He calls it Collection Days Index (CDI). It simply tells you the percentage of what you

> **Try Abe's CDI Tool**

wanted to collect that you've actually achieved day-by-day as you go through the month. Try the postcard and the CDI in your company. Wasn't it in one of Ernest Hemingway's novels that one character says to another something like, how was it you went bankrupt? And the reply went something like: a little bit at a time, and then all of a sudden. Please don't let slow cash-creep trick you into suddenly facing bankruptcy!

Best Monthly Financial Formats

The very best, easiest to use, and most widely utilized monthly financial report is shown below in its income-statement format. Similar one-pagers are created each month for the balance sheet and cash flow summary. When we say most widely used, this includes most big

CEO Tool
BestFin

public companies and lots of really smart privately-held businesses of all kinds and sizes. This is one of those very special tools for zooming up to 30,000 feet and looking down to see how your business is really performing. The following is an example of the Best Financial income statement:

XYZ Manufacturing Company

INCOME STATEMENT SUMMARY as of 6/30/01

	Month Ended JUNE 2001	($000)			Year-to-Date (6 months)			Full Calendar Year (12 Months)		
Actual	Prior Forecast	Original Budget	Prior Year	OPERATING RESULTS	Actual	Original Budget	Prior Year	Current Forecast	Original Budget	Prior Year
9,597	9,927	7,753	10,151	**NET SALES**	142,071	116,209	104,157	**239,827**	247,336	165,614
6,275	5,807	4,424	8,612	**Cost of Goods Sold**	106,443	85,646	76,411	**170,073**	177,339	130,056
3,835	3,623	2,931	4,530	**Selling & Administrative**	30,042	26,105	38,433	**52,925**	51,883	82,507
10,110	9,430	7,355	13,142	**Total Costs**	136,485	111,751	114,844	**222,998**	229,222	212,563
(513)	497	398	(2,991)	**OPERATING INCOME**	5,586	4,458	(10,687)	**16,829**	18,114	(46,949)
2	183	33	94	**External Int Expense**	170	194	347	**473**	316	547
591	(169)	(79)	(124)	**Other Income (Expense)**	(2,579)	(2,603)	(3,816)	**(4,515)**	(4,704)	(7,482)
76	145	286	(3,209)	**PRETAX EARNINGS**	2,837	1,661	(14,850)	**11,841**	13,094	(54,978)
25	82	126	(1,034)	**Income Tax Provision**	928	542	(4,788)	**3,908**	4,200	(18,507)
51	63	160	(2,175)	**NET INCOME after TAX**	1,909	1,119	(10,062)	**7,933**	8,894	(36,471)
				PERCENT OF SALES						
34.6%	41.5%	42.9%	15.2%	Gross Profit	25.1%	26.3%	26.6%	**29.1%**	28.3%	21.5%
40.0%	36.5%	37.8%	44.6%	Selling & Administrative	21.1%	22.5%	36.9%	**22.1%**	21.0%	49.8%
-5.3%	5.0%	5.1%	-29.5%	Operating Income	3.9%	3.8%	-10.3%	**7.0%**	7.3%	-28.3%
0.8%	1.5%	3.7%	-31.6%	Pretax Earnings	2.0%	1.4%	-14.3%	**4.9%**	5.3%	-33.2%
0.5%	0.6%	2.1%	-21.4%	Net Income After Tax	1.3%	1.0%	-9.7%	**3.3%**	3.6%	-22.0%
				KEY STATISTICS						
4.40	4.20	3.90	2.60	Inventory Turnover (x)	3.90	3.50	2.80	**4.60**	4.10	2.80
1.63	1.52	1.51	1.48	Receivables Turnover (x)	1.51	1.40	1.64	**1.48**	1.59	1.47
1,253	1,250	1,250	1,015	Number of Employees	1,238	1,250	1,199	**1,275**	1,275	1,147
32.9%	31.9%	32.6%	32.2%	Effective Tax Rate	32.7%	32.6%	32.2%	**33.0%**	32.1%	33.7%
0.5%	4.9%	2.8%	-19.0%	ROTA (%)	2.7%	1.8%	-12.5%	**5.2%**	7.1%	-26.4%

As you can see on this best income-statement format, all the monthly data is in one easy-to-read place on the left, with almost

Best Monthly Financial Format

every comparison you'd want to make. The words are in the center so you don't have to use a straightedge like you probably do now with your normal detailed monthly printouts. Those accounting-oriented reports are very hard to read, and they provide data but not much information. We need management-oriented reports that give us information, and that's what this best financial format does. To further explain the format, you'll find on the right of the words are the year-to-date comparisons. Then on the far right is the most important summary you can look at: it's a comparison of this full year as *re-forecasted* this month, and it's compared to the budget and last year. This re-forecast includes actual figures so far this year plus the remaining months as re-forecasted or as budgeted, depending upon which you believe will most probably occur.

Every month when you look at these three columns on the right, you can re-assess new strategies and actions to either get back on budget or surpass budget by even more than you already might have done. Design a second page just like this format for your balance sheet and for your cash flow statement. Then you'll really be on top of things. Once again, here's a tracking tool that lets you pro-act to optimize your business performance. The CD Desktop software associated with this book offers all three financial-statement formats: income statement, balance sheet, and cash flow. Please modify and customize each of these to suit your needs and your key indicators or statistical preferences.

Top 5 Measures: Daily, Weekly and Monthly

Here's yet another tracking tool that keeps managers and CEOs at the top of their game. Just five measures will tell you what's happening daily, weekly, and then monthly, but each set of five is slightly different for each time period. Every night when finishing up at Snapper, our team would funnel five numbers to allow me to sleep better

| Top Five Daily, Weekly and Monthly Measures |

that night. Even when it was bad news, my sleep was better because at least what faced me the next day was known. It's the unknown that causes the mind to worry. Remember that wise mentor's words: "When the human mind doesn't know, it assumes negative."

The five *daily* measures at Snapper that allowed me to sleep each night were first, the daily cash amount – or more accurately the borrowings against the line of credit, second was the total number of lawnmowers sold that day at retail, and then three numbers representing how many lawnmowers we had manufactured that day: walk-behind lawnmowers, rear-engine riders, and lawn tractors.

Five different *weekly* numbers paralleled this input: 1-what our cash forecast looked like for the next week; 2-how well our customer service was working; 3-what our sales bookings were in dollars broken down by sales region, lawnmower type and profit mix; 4-where the grass was growing, so we could direct our advertising accordingly; and finally, 5-overall factory cost performance. Then *monthly* we looked at 1-the financials in summary form as described above; 2-overall customer satisfaction; 3-market share; 4-how well we were achieving our overall strategic initiatives; and 5-employee satisfaction.

By focusing on these key areas, any business can perform better. What are your top five daily, weekly and monthly measures? What do you think your competitors' might be?

Let's try to sum up tracking: it's the most under-utilized set of tools in management today. Measurement just to be measuring and misdirected measurement are probably the most abused sets of tools. If you track something that's going well, won't you want to try to repeat the experience? And once you know something's wrong using tracking tools, can't you then go do something to fix it? Well that's my strongly held belief. Yet many CEOs and managers don't understand or accept this, believing things just have to be the way they are. "Que sera sera," I suppose. But several events in my life disavow all acceptance of "what will be will be." Watty Piper's marvelous little book for kids *The Little Engine that Could*™ was one of those. Guess I'm still just a kid. Another was the Q1 = $1.00 experience described in chapter two: you don't have to lose money in those down months, even though the whole industry does. Managers and especially CEOs have to believe that we can always do better by trying, that we can make a difference. Track it, try something to fix it, try something different to fix it, but for sure do keep on tracking and trying.

A final point. One of my heroes has always been Albert Einstein. He made an astute observation: *Not everything that can be counted counts, and not everything that counts can be counted.* It's easy to agree with his first point, but his second leaves some room for

110

interpretation. It's my belief that everything we experience can be counted or measured, either objectively or subjectively. The latter may not always be accurate, but that's where my adaptation of Dr. Einstein's quote falls. Nevertheless, in business and in life, a subjective measurement or counting is better than no information at all. Recall that thing about no news from chapter two? Well here it is once again in the form of tracking…food for thought.

Count What
Counts in Your
Business

> ## What Gets Measured Gets Done
> ### when you
> ## TRACK ALONG THE WAY.

The Top Ten Business *Tracking* Tools

1. Quarterly priorities management (QPM). Set five quarterly goals or priorities tied into your vision; get your direct reports to do the same. Quarterly helps link the day-to-day to the longer-term, big picture. Review weekly and communicate these among yourselves to broaden teamwork and success toward your vision.

QPM

2. Trailing 12-month charts. These involve the sum of the prior 12 months, charted for three years. Use them 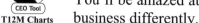 to track key indicators, especially gross margins. You'll be amazed at how this allows you to see your business differently.

T12M Charts

3. The *right* growth rate. There's a right growth rate for every business. Determine yours and grow at that rate. Any faster and you'll run out of cash; any slower and you'll get steam-rolled by those around you.

Right

4. Re-forecast sales, profit & cash-flow monthly. Not knowing you're about to grow too fast or suffer an ongoing string of monthly losses are excuses your banker will never understand. Try the ReFcast tool on the CD.

ReFcast

5. Track cash daily and re-forecast cash weekly. Cash crunches sneak up on most of us because we're not watching. Track your cash, don't grow too fast and stay well capitalized.

6. Communicate results to maximize results. People like to know whether they're making it, so tell them what's going on. But remember, what gets measured and gets *communicated repetitively* is usually what gets done.

Cash

7. Look at the future and **change the present.** Even if you can only look three days into the future, you can beat out your competition. Try it, you'll like it.

8. Identify your top five measures: daily+weekly+monthly. Know the most meaningful measures in your business and watch them like a hawk.

9. Per-unit measures. Sales dollars-per-unit will measure the price of your various products or markets or services. Finally you'll be able to see how your mix affects profits.

10. Monthly operations report. This is your personal report card that builds on a track record of results. You'll be surprised how you suddenly focus on the right things. See chapter six for full details.

What Gets Measured Gets Done, but *Details* Matter!

1. What gets measured gets done, but...if you don't tell anyone what you've measured as you go along, very little will get done.

2. What gets measured gets done, but...having the right measuring device or system or key indicator sure does help.

3. What gets measured gets done, so...if you measure the wrong thing, sure enough, the wrong thing will get done.

4. What gets measured gets done, but...if you're measuring too many things, everyone will get confused and nothing will get done.

5. What gets measured gets done, and...it matters *much less* how you measure it, and *much more* who and how you tell about it.

6. What gets measured gets done, yet...people don't care what measure you use. What they want to know is *how are we doing?*

7. What gets measured gets done, but...if your ongoing strategy is to trade margin for volume, you'd better have a tool that will warn you when to stop.

8. What gets measured gets done, but...practice only makes permanent, not perfect. If you don't recognize and reward results, they won't get repeated. Regular recognition will make perfect.

9. What gets measured gets done, and...it helps greatly if people believe their compensation is aligned closely with what's being measured and done.

10. What gets measured gets done, and...despite all of the above, you will grow your profits by measuring and telling about it now.

Chapter 4 – *Anticipate* the Future → Then *Realize* It

One of America's favorite country-western musicians, Vince Gill, knew what he was singing about when he recorded his platinum song, *There Ain't No Future in the Past.* Vince surely didn't have our chief executives or managers in mind when he first sang the tune. Nevertheless, his message has real meaning for the world of commerce. In planning and running our businesses, we should take lessons from the past, not live in it or with it. Nor should we live entirely in the present, but rather have a constant eye on the future. We look to the past for lessons, envision and anticipate the future we want, and then strive to create it, no, let's go *realize* it. How about coining a new word: *futurealists* (pronounced future-realists),

> **Work to Become a *"Futurealist"***

meaning those who anticipate and realize their futures. Really successful managers and CEOs do this almost routinely.

Planning for the future involves three basic steps. First, create a vision that your stakeholders buy into. The key is to make it an exciting, living, breathing vision that has relevance for everyone in the organization. Many years ago as the corporate planner for a

> ***Future* Step 1:
> A Vision Fully
> Accepted**

Fortune 500 company, my role dictated the creation of a massive 158-page business plan. No sooner had we finished, than we affectionately dubbed it "The Dust-Gatherer." No need telling you where that business plan ended up or how often we actually referred to it. *Approximately never* comes to mind. So make your vision short, to the point, keep it alive and a bit flexible. With your key players' involvement, write a one-page business plan to capture the vision. Put it in the hands of every employee and every stakeholder.

Yes, share your plan with customers and they'll help you realize the plan. Susan Rockrise at *Esprit* gave us a $900,000 print job in one of

our slower months, after she saw our one-page business plan and our publicly announced goal to become a $100-million-a-year printer so that we could buy the best printing presses in the industry. She understood our strategy and how it helped her company as well as all our constituencies.

A second step for future anticipation and realization involves creating an annual budget that's reaching yet reasonable, broken down

| *Future* Step 2: A Reaching Yet Reasonable Budget |

into one-month increments. As a benchmark, it's a good idea to have the budget finished no later than the first week of the year. Finished means accepted and bought into by everyone and fully documented. Otherwise, it's too easy to get off track before you even get started. It is a lot easier to stay on budget than it is to try catching up.

Once you have the budget in place, use it. Too many companies treat their budgets like their dust-gathering business plan

| Track Actual Results vs. Budget |

counterparts. They put enormous amounts of time and effort into creating them and then never really use them again. But the budget is more than a stodgy document. It's a critical management tool that plays a major role in keeping cash flow under control and profitability on course.

In particular, track your expenditures and expenses on a monthly basis and compare actual against projected. How about a

| T12M Charts Will Anticipate Cash & Profit Challenges |

regular monthly chart that shows whether you're a cash generator or cash user, and by how much on a T12M chart over time? Try tracking operating expenses – sometimes called selling, general & administrative – as a percent of sales using the 12MMA chart from chapter three. You will be astonished at what you see and what this tells you.

Here's an extraordinarily easy-to-interpret example from one very well run company over five years:

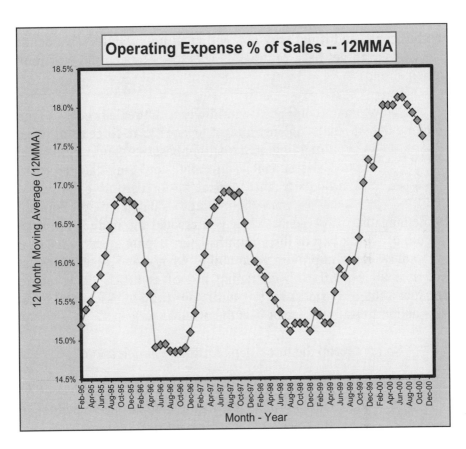

Operating Expense % of Sales -- 12MMA

What is going on here? It's *business bulimia*, a binge-and-purge pattern of running up expenses every time the company gets successful for a while. No doubt this pattern is repeated by thousands of companies all across America, yet they don't see it because they don't have T12M or 12MMA charts. After seeing this, the company's management instituted a limit line at 15 percent and at 16.5 percent and agreed to track monthly to assure they weren't exceeding either limit. Their profit and positive cash flow skyrocketed! Even better, they learned how to grow consistently, rather than just when they were doing exceedingly well.

Perhaps the most important thought about the budget: most folks review line item detail and that's good, but great would be to see how it looks from 30,000 feet up. Remember the best monthly financial format tool from chapter three? To wit, are we tracking to the big goals, and if not why not, and most importantly, what actions can we take to get back on track? This leads to step three of future anticipation.

Third in becoming a world-class futurealist goes beyond tracking actual results against budget, it goes to re-forecasting where you're going on a monthly basis. Again, we hike back

| *Future* Step 3: |
| Re-Forecast |
| Religiously! |

to best financial format tool in chapter three, particularly that annual re-forecasting column. In today's markets, things change very quickly. Something that made sense when you created the budget can easily get out of whack two or three months later. Doing a new forecast on a monthly basis improves your ability to respond to changes and keeps small brushfires from raging out of control. Each quarter, conduct a major business review with your team to assess and accept new action steps to realize or beat the original budget.

So let's recap the three steps for future anticipation:

1. Preach a vision that's fully accepted,
2. Get buy-in on a reaching but reasonable budget,
3. Re-forecast your entire financial
   statement regularly.

Future anticipation is the catalyst that takes us from plan to realization. It uses tracking to ascertain progress along the way against our goals. It uses early warning systems, like T12M charts, to foresee the future. It's all about looking ahead to see how better to achieve our goals. Remember that goals don't exist in a vacuum. Instead, goal setting is part of a continuing process, a cycle. The cycle is the seven-step management process, containing feedback loops that self-correct the process as we go along. Take a look at the following graphical depiction of the seven-step management process:

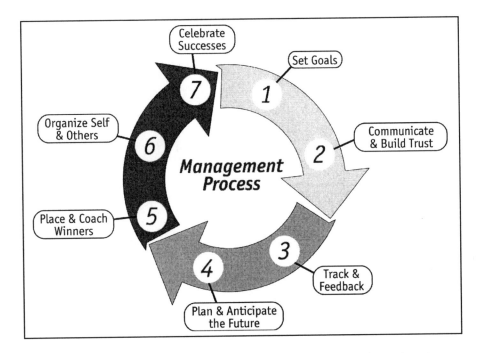

The figure shows a circular "Management Process" diagram with seven numbered steps: 1 Set Goals, 2 Communicate & Build Trust, 3 Track & Feedback, 4 Plan & Anticipate the Future, 5 Place & Coach Winners, 6 Organize Self & Others, 7 Celebrate Successes.

There's a feedback loop from step four involving planning to step one where goals are set. Future anticipation is an integral part of any good goal-setting process. Running a business without planning and continual re-forecasting is like driving your car with the windshield papered over. You only see where you've been in the rear-view mirrors from your accounting reports and you'll run into something unfortunate – very soon indeed. So try a few of the following tools with the seven-step process to accelerate your business to the speed that you want to drive it.

Another thought about planning and action: many CEOs and managers have a short horizon, say three months to maybe a year or so. They will still be looking at that one to two year picture five years from now because they didn't take action even though they prepared plans. Change that! Do the things you need to do in the short-term now to get where you keep saying you want to be in two-three years. If you can't do it yourself, hire some people to work for you that can do it and then let them do it.

Turning Your Business Plans Into Action

Depending on the size, complexity and nature of your business, you may want up to seven different types of plans. Pogo,

the lovable Walt Kelly opossum cartoon character, opined, "we are confronted with insurmountable opportunities." Hopefully the following choices and explanations will resolve most of those over-powering opportunities for you:

- **Strategic plan.** This typically covers the vision, long-term direction and evolution of the market. It identifies multiple opportunities and how the company will pursue them.

- **Marketing plan.** This identifies how the company will position itself in its markets and gain market share over time. It spells out the specifics of growth and market penetration.

- **Sales plan.** This lays out strategies and tactics for growing the company's revenues profitably on a day-in-day-out basis.

- **Business plan.** This describes the direction, market and resources of your business and how the goals will be achieved this year, including action steps.

- **Succession plan.** How will the business continue to run should you die prematurely or become disabled? This plan is especially critical for single-owner and family-owned businesses.

- **Estate plan.** This identifies reaping and keeping your hard-earned wealth.

- **Exit plan.** This identifies how you'll pass the business on to the next stewards when it's time. This happens to everyone and sneaks up on us too soon.

Any of these plans can be documented on a single page and laid out very similarly to your one-page business plan. And while plans are great, they have no value unless and until you and your people implement them. What if you created a one-page action plan for turning any of these seven business plans into reality? Here's a straightforward formula for doing that:

One-Page
Action
Plan

1. Have a meeting with everyone involved. Use a flip chart broken down into four columns:
   - *Action step*
   - *Target date (When)*
   - *Who is responsible (Who)*
   - *Who will hold him/her accountable (WHA)*

2. With the help of those involved at the meeting, write the action steps. Each action step must specifically identify all four points from above.

3. As a group, conduct weekly or monthly meetings to review progress.

4. Update and add new action steps over time.

5. Repeat the entire process on an annual basis.

Action Step	When	Who	WHA
1.			
2.			
3.			
4.			
5.			

The Power of Written Tactics

Although one-page business plans do a good job of keeping people focused on the major organizational goals, they don't provide a lot of detail. To provide more specific direction for your management team, consider using *1-page tactical plans* that you'll subsequently turn into action plans. Here's an example of a one-page tactical plan that we used successfully at the printing company:

Business Strategies → Tactics

1. **Increase the ratio of sheet-fed to web business.** Increase sheet-fed printing volume throughout the coming year to improve overall gross margin while increasing utilization of prep and finishing assets. This will simultaneously improve sales capability in future years. Specific actions next year will include hiring additional sheet-fed salespeople in Portland, San Francisco and Los Angeles.
2. **Implement cost-monitoring systems for improved cost control.** Implement an enhanced war-on-waste (WOW) program to reduce spoilage, with paper and ink as the primary targets. Reduce job-related spoilage by use of better measuring sticks.
3. **Reduce overhead going into the slack months.** Effect overhead reductions prior to April 15th to minimize the impact of very slow second quarter months, and by October 15th for slow fourth quarter months.
4. **Improve volume in slack months via sheet-fed sales.** Implement highly leveraged promotional programs at reduced pricing to improve sheet-fed capture ratios during slower months.
5. **Improve management-to-salesforce communications.** Increased emphasis on solving sales problems as they relate to plant activities via regional managers direct to division managers. Greater customer care throughout. National sales meeting and quarterly sales management meetings. Improve daily communications and approach of scheduling and production with the sales force.
6. **Greater focus of selling efforts in GAC's "best" markets.** Emphasis will be placed on increasing the quantity and size of annual reports, especially in off-calendar yearends. Quarterlies and other commercial work will also be sought, as will off-peak month catalog sales. Sales personnel for web (mainly commercial) will be added in Chicago, New York and Los Angeles.

Each of these six tactical directions should then be turned into action steps. Specifically, sit down with the people who need to be involved and draw up the one-page action plan for each sub-element of each of the six items. Let's take an example: the one-page business plan above spoke about dramatically increasing sheet-fed sales. Tactics one and four then become a bit more specific about what that means. Within tactic one, then, we outline action steps, which involve when we would have SPIFs and promotions and bonuses and customer involvement to increase sheet-fed sales. Here's an example of one action step: every customer – including those over 3,000 miles away in New York – would be asked to give us at least one sheet-fed printing job this month. This was handled through GAC's salespeople, who were then asked the specifics of their conversations with customers this week and every week regarding sheet-fed. The salesperson's immediate sales manager asked, the VP of sales asked, and yes, the CEO asked. Perhaps not too amazingly, sheet-fed sales took off.

> **Turn Strategy Into Tactics, And Then Into Action Steps**

The thing is, this usually doesn't happen, unless of course you have specific written action steps, just like these, which you implement and continue to ask about in a positive, reinforcing way. People in the industry would tell you that a sheet-fed job of less than $20,000 should never be printed clear on the other side of the U.S., but in fact New Yorkers gave us lots of such jobs to print in Oregon just because we asked, we asked first, and we asked often.

Another specific action step was to hire three new salespeople, dedicated to sheet-fed, one each in Portland, San Francisco, and Los Angeles. My job as CEO involved holding Bill Barnes, Ken Clark, and Dan Freedland accountable, respectively, for doing that in each of their sales regions. I did, they did, and sheet-fed soared. "Sheet-fed travels well" became one of the prevalent slogans at GAC. We all talked sheet-fed all the time. One tool being used here is breaking down goals into specific actions that individuals can act upon. A second tool is repetitive communication, that is, communicate again and again the imperative, the direction, the cause, the flag everyone on the team will rally 'round.

> **Break Goals Into Specific Actions**

> **Repetitive Communication**

125

This kind of thing has to come from the manager in charge, and that might be the CEO or any other manager who shows passion and commitment. Anticipate the future: figure out what alternative scenarios we'll encounter and what things we'll need to react to or pro-act about. Be ready to change course. Listen mightily to what your people are saying, but add savvy judgment to that negative or neutral input from naysayers. Tom Peters, well-known author, speaker and management guru, has a great saying, "test fast, fail fast, adjust fast." But in the midst of it all, find a way to stay the course within bounds of your best business intelligence. Find ways to know when to get more information.

The Right Growth Rate

Over 99 percent of all businesses have a limit on how fast they can grow without running out of cash. It's different for every company. Some refer to this limit as the "maximum sustainable rate of growth without running out of cash." Let's take it a step further to the *right growth rate*. Because so many factors are involved and it differs for every business, we need to know how fast we should grow. Regardless of how the numbers turn out, the process of determining your right growth rate – and then managing your business by it – will provide a very effective tool for anticipating your future.

Don't Run Out
of Cash: Right
Growth Rate

CEO Tool
Right

Many CEOs and managers consider the income statement, balance sheet, and cash flow statements as separate entities. In reality, they all form one comprehensive financial management package, and a change in one line item on any one statement usually causes something to change on the other two. In an integrated computer model, these three statements can determine your company's ideal growth rate. For example, suppose you want to determine how fast your business can grow over the next five years without running out of cash. Here's how it works.

126

First, build an integrated income statement, balance sheet and cash flow model. You can try this in Excel or Lotus or some other spreadsheet, but you'll go crazy keeping the equations straight and it takes at least 20 fully-interactive spreadsheet pages filled with numbers. Even the best spreadsheet models run by the best numbers-people make huge errors. Instead, try one of the great software packages that do this – they typically cost less than $500 to buy and work in Microsoft™ Windows® environments. One nifty software package is recommended in the appendix and is directly accessible via the Internet using the CD/Desktop helper associated with this book.

Use your model to project five years' growth. Be sure to include some realistic assumptions about your firm's borrowing capacity. Next, run the model using different growth rates. Start out with 10 percent growth a year, then try 20 percent, 30 percent, and so on. After each iteration pay close attention to your balance sheet. When it goes *tilt,* meaning the cash account goes negative and the line-of-credit exceeds its banks – pun fully intended – back up a little bit until the balance sheet is in bounds. The rate of growth at this point represents your maximum growth rate without running out of cash, your equilibrium growth rate. Now back down from that rate by two or three percentage points to give yourself a safety margin, and that's your right growth rate. The backing off of about three points gives you just enough cushion between right growth rate and equilibrium so that if you accidentally grow a little too fast, you won't tick off your bank or lender.

Now your challenge becomes figuring out how to grow at this rate. Knowing what the rate is helps a lot, since it gets you thinking about the possibilities.

At GAC, our right growth rate model went tilt at 25 percent. We backed up one percent at a time before determining that 23 percent represented the maximum rate we could grow without running out of cash. We then arbitrarily decided that about 20 percent was our right growth rate, giving us a three-point safety cushion. Now, admittedly we got lucky turning this growth into a month-after-month, year-after-year sales

> **What's Your "Right" Growth Rate?**

trend-line. That straight-line sales growth propelled us to where we were virtually minting money.

We did indeed get lucky to have that sales curve be such a straight line for so many years in a row. A big part of that so-called luck came from the tools we're looking at throughout this book – getting goals down to actions that were understood by each individual – repetitive communication of exactly what we were aiming for – then tracking results, giving our people regular feedback – and finally but most important, recognizing everyone as they hit or came close to their marks.

Some thoughts about applying the right growth rate in your business situation might be of interest:

1. Never try to determine your maximum growth rate just by running the business. It's a sure way to run into the out-of-cash wall.
2. The closer you get to your maximum growth rate, the greater the risk. Leave yourself plenty of cushion, but not so big that you leave a lot of money on the table. And track your company's performance, especially cash flow, carefully.
3. Re-run the model every two or three years. Your right growth rate will change over time, especially with margin and debt-to-equity ratio changes.

Asking *What If?*

Every company has its share of negative folks, people who seem to take real delight in quashing an idea before anyone really gets a chance to look at it. You know who they are – the ones who, when someone proposes a new idea or way of thinking, chime in immediately with "that's impossible" or "that won't work!" They're not bad people, they just have a tendency to focus on the negative and pass judgment before allowing a seed to sprout and blossom. If no one stands up to them, they will suck all the creativity out of the organization. Too many companies have become complacent through quashed creativity.

One simple yet powerful technique for overcoming these purveyors of doom and gloom and keeping ideas alive involves asking "what if?" Whenever someone tries to kill an idea without giving it a chance, simply intervene and ask, "what if it *were* possible? Suppose we could make it work.

> Try Out the "What If?" Tool

What would it look like and what would be the outcome?" Once you get people focusing on possibilities rather than negative assumptions, they will come up with some very creative, often brilliant, ideas. The following example illustrates how asking *what if?* led to millions of dollars in profits for Snapper lawnmower.

Back in the '90s at Snapper lawnmowers, we developed a new mulching blade that attached to standard lawnmowers. The blade was superb, easily outclassing every other blade in the industry. It totally mulched any and all grass it encountered. When I saw how well the finished product worked, I had visions of dollar signs dancing in my head. However, with infinite wisdom our outside advertising people gave it a horribly unwieldy name like the "bi-level, six-edged mulch-everything blade." It probably sounded good to some folks, but in my wildest dreams customers wouldn't go into a retail outlet and ask for this lawnmower blade by that name. If we wanted to set the world on fire with this product, we needed to come up with a catchier name, something simple to ignite the buying public's interest.

As we pondered the cumbersome nom de plume during a management meeting, someone happened to mention that the blade looked kind of "Ninja." He probably meant it looked like a shuriken, one of those star-shaped weapons that the Japanese samurai threw in relatively close combat. Another manager suggested we call our mulcher the "Ninja blade." No sooner were the words out of his mouth, someone else piped up, "we can't do that. It's already taken, it's someone else's trademark." The idea of a Ninja blade caught our imagination and we asked, "well, what if it wasn't trademarked already? What would happen if we called it the Ninja?" Of course nobody knew, but because we asked what if, everyone was now considering the possibilities rather than rejecting the idea outright.

We asked our attorneys to look into it and they discovered that, although trademarked in some applications, the term Ninja had never been used in the outdoor power equipment field, which gave us license to use it for our purposes. We trademarked it for our industry and put the blade out under the Ninja name. The fact that the *Mutant*

Try Playing On
Current Themes

Ninja Turtles TV show had been popular at the time didn't seem to have an adverse effect on our effort either. We sold hundreds of thousands of the Ninjas the first year alone and at rather substantial margins. This was not so amazing when you consider that there are over five million Snapper lawnmowers actively cutting grass out there, coupled with the fact that the world was trying to do something about landfills at the time. By introducing an environmentally sound adjunct product and not letting "it's already taken" stop our strategic thinking, we became the leader in mulching overnight, and coincidentally made a ton of money in the process.

All that because we asked *what if?* A funny sidelight: Tanaka-san, my counterpart and friend at Honda Lawnmowers, laughed with us when I told him about the name. I'm not sure he wasn't envious but perhaps dubious of it as a name because of its historical or cultural implications.

The next time the nabobs of negativity rise up to kill an idea in your organization, put them right by asking *what if?*" Obviously not every idea will turn out as well as the Ninja blade. But who knows how many millions of dollars you may have already lost because some bonehead said, "that's impossible" and everyone believed him.

According to the frequently told tale, Fred Smith was apparently in his senior year in college when his thesis advisors called him in to say, "Fred, we've looked at this thesis topic of yours and determined it just won't work. Your idea of delivering packages to people anywhere in the continental U.S. by 10 a.m. the day after you get those packages just can't be done. We're convinced it's *absolutely, positively* impossible."

Well, by now you probably recognize Mr. Smith as the founder and great leader of FedEx. An early advertising campaign proclaimed, "when it *absolutely, positively* has to be there." But what if Mr. Smith had listened to the naysayers? You know, it's impossible so let's not even try it. Thank goodness Fred Smith had the audacity to ask: *What if?* Nowadays FedEx does over $17 billion, with a B, in sales and around $700 million in after-tax profits. But it must not exist because it's impossible. FedEx is often the single largest shipper of packages every single day in the world. But, you know, it just can't be true because it's impossible. Fred Smith, thank you for trying and then doing the impossible. We love what you and your company have done and continue to do.

As a postscript, a gentleman who worked directly with Fred Smith put me straight on the fable, since it has been modified more than a little with the telling and re-telling over the years. Apparently Mr. Smith's anecdote was focused around a paper for an undergraduate class, and the idea or subject was the transfer of Federal Reserve funds overnight from facility-to-facility around the country. Nevertheless, that too was considered impossible back then.

That great creator and leader of FedEx wasn't alone with his insight. Albert Einstein interpreted the impossible this way: *Imagination is more important than knowledge.* Always take a moment to inquire, what if? Always.

Sometimes bumper stickers say it so well. Here's one we recently saw in a delightful diner in St. Michaels, Maryland that catches the anticipatory nature of this chapter:

> *Poor PLANNING on your part*
> *does not constitute*
> *an EMERGENCY on mine!*
>
> **PLAN THE FUTURE, THEN GRAB IT!**

The Top Ten Planning Tools

1. Listen mightily to employees. Employees always know the solutions to a lack of growth, how to turn the company around and where the opportunities lie. Involve your people in developing your plans. Walk the four corners of your company and ask your people how to improve the business.

2. "Tell me what your company does." When asked this question, most employees and CEOs give a very generic answer. Pursue a niched, differentiating answer to this question. You'll then have your definitive vision and mission.

3. Lawnmowers vs. beautiful lawns. Know what your business really sells or does best. This is your unique business proposition (UBP) and will differentiate you from everyone else in the world. Example: Snapper is the #1 brand of lawnmowers sold through servicing dealers in America.

4. 1-Page business plan. Create a one-page plan to plug all employees into a common direction. Let it shout out your unique business proposition and your goals, purpose and strategy. Give it to everyone and reinforce its message regularly.

5. The "right" growth rate. Every company has a right growth rate. Steady up your growth rate, instead of growing erratically, and watch more profits and easier cash management materialize.

6. Just plan it! Seventy-five percent of companies have no plan, yet believe they should. Why not draft your 1-page business plan today? UBP + goals + purpose + strategy = a great plan.

7. Watch *Hoosiers*. This movie isn't about planning, but its management message will put your team in an open, brainstorming mood for planning. Watch the movie with Cokes™ and popcorn, then at the end capture the take-away messages on a flip chart. You'll be amazed at how well this sets your team up for the planning effort.

8. Passion and commitment. Conviction & company evangelist wanted: apply here! Exude passion and get commitment from your people.

9. Timing is everything. All things go in cycles, so study the cycles of your industry and company. Set up a system to track an "industry composite" of competitors.

10. "So what?" Ask *so what?* about any goal, strategy, tactic or action step you're considering. What will really happen if you implement it? Will it really work? Many thanks to Dan Wertenberg, CEO and CEO Coach, for this insight.

Top Ten Business Strategy Tools

1. Play "what if?" The two most powerful words in any language are *what if?* These words spark the imagination and lead to greatness. Test what could go wrong – or right – by asking *what if?* on a regular basis. Go after the impossible.

2. Fill valleys, *then* clip peaks. First find new customers, then cut marginal volume. Don't make the mistake of weeding your customer garden before planting. We did at a Fortune 500 company and almost took it into Chapter 11. At GAC printing, success came quickly when we reversed the order.

3. The S-W-O-T-P-I-C-Ks approach. Most companies analyze their **S**trengths, **W**eaknesses, **O**pportunities and **T**hreats. Add **P**roblems, **I**ssues, **C**oncerns and **K**eys to **S**uccess as part of your strategic analytical review.

4. Price + mix + volume formula. Tweak these variables to maximize market share and drive competitors crazy. Try increasing your effective price by changing your mix, bundling or un-bundling to improve price-mix, or trading price for volume.

5. Write down and then test all assumptions. We make assumptions without even thinking. Write all assumptions down. Then test them to death. You'll find glaring mistakes and big holes in your strategies. Test them again as you're rolling along.

6. Understand your sweet spots. Every business has sweet spots – points in volume, size or time where everything seems to go well. Figure out why this is so and you'll have powerful clues for future strategic direction.

7. Vertical→horizontal→outside. Look at what Wall Street does to create new products, e.g., the LBO led to the roll-up. Try thinking totally outside the box.

134

8. Anticipate strategy changes. Study how your business must change and how it will change over time, even without your doing anything. Try modeling different strategic scenarios. Watch technology closely – this is re-making entire industries.

9. Create dreamtime. Dreaming, imagining, visioning, what-iffing – whatever you call it, take time for this every week. Tell your managers, "take an hour each day to put your feet on the desk and just think. We pay you much too much just to do!"

10. The 1-page *action* plan. Get everyone who can make a goal happen into a room and identify all the action steps to achieve the goal. On flip charts, write who will achieve each step, on what date and who will hold that person accountable. Every few weeks, gather the group to review progress and set new action steps. This is only #2 behind QPM as the best management tool ever.

> **"People don't dislike change, they dislike *being* changed."**
> Michael Basch

Chapter 5 – Get, Coach and Keep Winners

What are the three or four *key customer-impacting jobs* in your company? These would be the main job positions that make it or break it with customers and prospects. Once identified, how do we get those jobs *exactly right*, meaning how do we assure the people in those positions are winners, have the right tools, know how to use them and are highly motivated to apply them? This is a flashback to our Cuisinart® and electric screwdriver analogy in chapter one: it's all about having the right tool for the job.

The key customer-impacting job is perhaps the most powerful tool on the people side of any business for increasing sales. So, what does this tool have to do with getting, coaching and keeping winners? In my experience, almost everything.

Key Customer-Impacting Jobs

Winners like to know they're doing meaningful work, going for those meaningful goals from chapter one. So our task as manager is to place winners in the key jobs that count the most and show them why their work is meaningful. Let's identify *the top five customer-impacting jobs* in your company and get them exactly right. Put superstars in those front-line positions and give them whatever they need to be successful. How do you identify the top five customer-related positions? Try brainstorming this with your management team. Ask them, "which jobs have the most impact on the customer? Which jobs really make the difference for the customer in this company?" Then go back and forth in a series of meetings to agree on the five positions that really should be focused on the customer. Typically

> **Key Customer-Impacting Jobs**

these involve anyone who communicates directly with, supports or services the customer. Of course, you can make the case that everyone in the company serves the customer. But without question, some have more direct involvement, more impact than others. In this instance, we're talking about positions like salesperson, service rep, technical or customer support staff, or even the shipping clerk. It's anyone who directly touches the customer.

Sometimes, getting the job exactly right requires a major overhaul of the position. Other times, it just takes a little twist. For example, most shipping clerks, and even mail clerks in service companies, work an 8:00 to 5:00 shift. Typically, they

| Get Key Jobs Exactly Right |

do very little productive work for the first two hours – there's nothing yet to ship or mail. But let's say a package arrives on the outgoing shipping dock at 5:01 p.m. If the shipping clerk stays an extra five minutes to send the package, it can get to the customer a whole day sooner. In today's world, that whole day can easily mean the difference between a satisfied customer and a lost account.

But who wants to badger their shipping clerk into staying an extra five or ten minutes every day? That creates headaches for you and the shipping clerk ends up feeling used, even abused, rather than motivated. Why not try this instead: change the schedule to fit the job. Bring shipping clerks – or mail clerks in service companies – in at ten in the morning and keep them doing great things for the customer until 7:00 p.m. – which is almost certainly why UPS™ and FedEx™ have chosen to make this their last pickup of the day. This allows you to take much better care of the customer without pressuring or eventually antagonizing your staff. Isn't this what getting jobs exactly right is all about?

In most companies, the receptionist definitely qualifies as one of the key customer-impacting jobs. But very few managers recognize that, thinking the receptionist is an entry-level position. Fewer still take the extra little effort and time to get the receptionist job exactly right. Most managers view the receptionist as a "pass-through" or "low-impact" position, meaning people only take the job on their way to something else. And yet there is such a thing as a career receptionist. Great receptionists are worth their weight in rubies, and a great many of them want only to be receptionist.

How do you get the job of receptionist exactly right? First, let receptionists know how much you value the job and their talents. One visible way of demonstrating this is to give your receptionist a business card that says something like "Director of First Impressions" (DOFI). After all, isn't that what they do – create the first impression for everyone,

> **Receptionist Title Should Be: *DOFI!***

especially prospects and customers? And can you think of anything more important than creating a great first impression with customers and prospects as well as with everyone else contacting your firm?

Next, train your DOFI to represent your company in the manner you want. Receptionists usually already know how to answer the phone, but if they don't, teach them your way of greeting callers. What receptionists usually don't know at all is who you are as a business, what you do differently for customers, what products and services you produce and how they're special, who to hand certain calls off to…and so on. Make sure your receptionist understands the vision, mission and values of the company, especially as they relate to customers and prospects. Make a list of the most difficult types of calls that come in and give your receptionist specific training on how to handle each one – a difficult-calls list for the front desk. Write them down, so that

> **"Difficult Calls" List at the Front Desk**

when temps fill in, they will also know how to handle those calls. That's the kind of training that will turn an average receptionist into a superstar and make you look like the supreme supplier to your customers. Once again you'll have made sure you have the position exactly right.

To retain superb receptionists, give them plenty of personal growth opportunities. More important, give them lots of recognition and praise. In many ways, they have the hardest job in the company. Receptionists have to put up with all kinds of stressful and difficult situations, and they have to do it in a cool, calm and collected manner while being positive and warm. That even sounds contradictory, and it is tough to do. This is almost certainly the toughest job in any company. Yet, often receptionists are the least appreciated and most maligned employee on the entire staff. Say "thank you" to them often, publicly recognize their outstanding performance with praise, and constantly let them know how much you appreciate the job they do for the company. After all, this position is your front door to the world.

Many of the top five customer-impacting jobs are like the receptionist. These are career positions, not stepping-stones on a career path. They need a different approach, not just

> **Identify Your Career Positions**

as described above, but also in compensation. Two mid-sized, very successful businesses pay their DOFIs $54K per year and $80K per year respectively. Yep, you guessed it right, these two special people make millions for their firms each year.

Want to talk to one of the best DOFIs? Call (503) 224-7777 and Joanne Bechtold will probably answer the phone and charm you. She might even get you to buy printing from GAC. She's been at Graphic Arts Center printing in Portland for over 15 years, doing a wonderful job. Incidentally, you can't hire her away. If her employer ever ruffles her feathers, we have a deal that she calls me and I will do a current client and her the biggest favors in the world by matching them up.

Ultimately, your receptionist serves as the storefront that showcases your company's uniqueness. Take the time to get this position exactly right and it will pay dramatic dividends. Sometimes it's the simplest things that make the difference. The other day a receptionist responded to my request to speak to Todd, the president, by saying "I'll see if he's in for you." What she must have meant was "I'll see for you if he's in his office," and what she really should have said was "He's in but he's on another call; would you like to wait a few moments or shall I ask him to call you right back?" Getting the receptionist job exactly right takes but a bit of coaching in how to say what you want to portray.

Weeding Your Employee Garden

What about getting poor performers out of key jobs? Let's describe someone who's now in your business or was in the recent past. This person has very high performance but very lousy and low attitude...I'll bet you know who I'm talking about. You *will* fire this person someday, and what will everyone in the company say on that day? You guessed it – "it's about time" or "what took you so long?" or "thank goodness!" If you know that's the answer now, why not put a plan in place today to replace that bad-attitude person during the next six weeks? Get the performance taken care of by someone else, and then get the bad actor out. Make him or her available to industry. Your culture just can't stand leaving these kinds of folks in place.

> Outplace Those Poor Performers!

The really tough outplacements are the near-mediocre performers with really nice attitudes. Even here, we've got to move along if we want a successful business, because if you tolerate even one, how many more will you tolerate? A subsidiary CEO who worked for me at one point had a problem with his brother who also worked for the division. This younger sibling was a delight but didn't perform at all in his sales job no matter what we tried. Finally we engineered a competitive firm across town hiring him away from us. Now look, you have to do this kind of outplacement your own way, and many would be more direct with the family-member, but this is the way our CEO wanted to handle it. Don't judge the how of it, just find your own way to do it, but then do it.

Hire Winners and Put Them in Their Best Jobs

Once we identify *the key customer-impacting jobs*, let's put winners in those and other key positions. Start by identifying superb performance in that position for the customer. This will be the meaningful goal for this job. Sit down with employees and ask point-blank, "what's superb performance for the customer in your job?" Engage in a give-and-take discussion on the subject. Chances are you won't reach agreement

> Define "Superb Performance"

right away. It may take two or three conversations. Yet pretty soon you will reach a consensus on what superb performance for the customer looks like in that position. For example, superb performance for the receptionist position could be defined as handling the transfer of each call to exactly the right person in the nicest possible way, quickly. Thanks to Michael Basch, the speaker-author, for his wonderful wisdom: *People don't dislike change, they dislike being changed.* What a great example: the setting of superb performance with our people, not for them.

Next, quantify your definition. This typically proves harder for some positions than others, but my belief is that every position can be measured. For example, superb performance for a payroll clerk could be defined as six perfect payrolls in a row. Even receptionist performance can be quantified, such as X number of calls transferred without error, or three unsolicited customer compliments per month. You could also have an outside associate call in blind to throw a few curveballs at your receptionists to help them learn how to handle difficult callers. If so, be sure to tell receptionists in advance that you intend to use mystery callers. Position it in a way that helps them improve their performance and grow, never as criticism. If you present it properly and get their involvement, they will enthusiastically go along with this ongoing learning process. Like everyone else, receptionists want to grow and get better. We all want to please those around us.

Every Job Can Be Measured

After defining and quantifying superb performance, do three simple things to support employees in achieving that performance:

1. A compensation system where when they do well, employees know they will get a bonus or SPIF (special performance incentive fee). Payouts should be frequent, monthly or quarterly, so employees can link the bonus to their own current performance.

All Key Players Need: Incentive $...

2. A recognition system where the employee receives regular pats on the back for superb results (recognition = praise for performance).

...Recognition

144

3. The training and tools to do superb performance. Training for receptionists might include an intensive two days on who we are, what we do, and how we do it. For tools, a list at the reception station might identify the top ten most difficult calls and how to handle them, plus a page of directions to your place of business. Finally add the ability to fax or Email them from that desk.

> ...Training & Tools

With systems like this in place, superb performance shines in every job. Start with the jobs that have the most impact on customers and make sure you have winners in those jobs. Sit down with those winners and discuss what superb performance for the customer looks like. Get agreement with each employee on what superb performance is, and write it down in quantifiable, measurable terms. Align your compensation and recognition systems with the performance criteria so that every time employees hit the target, they get pats on the back and small bonuses. Once you have the key customer-impacting jobs squared away, move on to the other important jobs in the company. This process doesn't happen overnight, but in about six months, you can dramatically improve the performance of individual employees and the company as a whole. Try it. It really works.

> Get Everyone's Job Exactly Right

Getting and Coaching Winners

Doesn't it all start with getting, placing and then coaching talented, motivated people? Not just hiring them, but rather getting them into the right jobs, getting them to see the outcomes needed from their work and getting them to feel appreciated for what they do.

> Get Them Committed to Outcomes

Critics say that my performance as CEO could have been better by changing management around more, meaning firing-hiring-reassigning. But by-and-large most companies already have really good people in solid positions. The problem is that these good people haven't been given challenges, haven't committed themselves to outcomes, and haven't been recognized or rewarded for getting results. At Snapper

> Get Them To Grab Challenges

lawnmowers, we turned a $54 million pretax loss in one year into a $13 million profit the very next year using the existing management team. At GAC printers, we outgrew our competitors multifold, becoming the undisputed industry leader – and again, we used the existing management team, but for one dropout. At the tiny Courtesy Coffee business, years of breakeven and loss performance became profitable thanks to the existing staff.

> **Recognize and Reward Them!**

What if you had the tools for placing and coaching people in your own business to accomplish these same kinds of results? Incidentally, the lawnmower industry continued to decline in the year we did the turnaround, while the printing industry was healthy yet growing at only single-digit rates per year. The point is that the industry and economy don't matter much. The tools for placing and coaching people work every time, everywhere. It's our people and their motivation that make it work.

> **They're having a recession and we decided not to participate!**

No matter what kind of business we manage, we can't do it alone. Moreover, we can't do it with mediocre or even average performers. Not many years back, companies could get by having a workforce where people sort of checked their brains at the door in the morning and picked them up again at quitting time. Astonishingly, many managers allow their companies or departments to do this today. In the turbo-changing markets we now live in, that simply won't do. We need people with the energy, drive, motivation, creativity and smarts to get the job done. So the first step in building a successful business involves dedicating yourself to hiring, placing and coaching winners with well-defined job expectations.

Experience teaches that winning in the people arena comes down to knowing what you want and having a system that helps you identify the attitude and performance traits needed to succeed on the job. Whether you hire, promote from within, move them around, or simply make-do with the winners you have, the steps to success are pretty straightforward.

Try these three steps to improve your score in the people performance arena:

1) identify the outcomes you want with each key person,

2) give them the tools and training to do the job, and

3) support them by cheering them on and praising them for performing, recognizing them for results.

The last step ensures repeat performance with very little additional managerial input from you. And that last step is so important that it cries for commitment on your part. Practice makes permanent, not perfect. Perfect practice makes perfect. And perfect practice is to praise people for performing, recognize them for results. A headline in the Wall Street Journal, lauding Jack Welch's long-lived superlative successes at GE says it all: *Raises and Praise(s) Or Out the Door!* The formula is clearly both compensation and recognition as reward for results. It creates permanent perfect performance.

> Recognize for Results

> Praise for Performance

We succeeded in turning Snapper lawnmower around using the same three steps. My predecessor had moved around the senior staff just before I was brought in as CEO. He had taken the VP of sales and made him VP of manufacturing. He took the VP of manufacturing and made him VP of engineering. And he had just hired a VP of marketing and sales. Wild, huh? Despite their huge inexperience in those jobs, my decision was to leave those folks right where they had been put. By working with them to identify the outcomes we wanted, then cheering them on and supporting them, this team grew Snapper from $165 million in sales to $248 million in just one year, a growth of 50 percent…in an industry that continued to decline. Much praise for performance accompanied and augmented the success of Snapper's people every step of the way. What follows is the actual application of these tools for hiring, placing and coaching winners.

Spotting Winners

Before putting winners in jobs, you usually have to find them. In today's workforce, there is no shortage of talented people, although almost every one of them is already employed. And with Internet job-matching sites like monster.com®, it has become increasingly easy to locate top talent. Again, the challenge is that there are more jobs than qualified people to fill them. We're usually in technical over-employment as a nation. As a result, employers face a two-fold challenge. To start, you have to find the talent and then match it to your specific jobs. Then you have to entice those people into working for your company rather than someone else's.

To identify what you need in a particular job, write a job specification – not a job description. The job spec does two things. First, it outlines the environment surrounding the position and identifies what the candidate must have to succeed at the job. Try to limit your must-haves to three or four factual or experience points, else you'll eliminate the entire universe of candidates. Second, the job specification identifies the person's responsibilities and authority. In this manner, the job specification paints a clear, comprehensive picture of the position so that you know exactly what to look for when interviewing job applicants. If you use search firms, it also makes their job easier because it provides focus for their search. Once you

> **Try Einstein's "Job Spec" Tool**

have the job specification, then you can begin looking for good candidates. My great, late mentor and friend, Kurt Einstein, taught us this technique in the '80s. His sage advice has resulted in over 100 key placement successes for me alone during the past twenty years.

Using all the tools available – job ads, employee referrals, online recruiting, networking – develop a pool of qualified candidates and narrow the field down to a manageable number. Get to know

> **Use Personality Assessments**

your candidates better by having each one complete a background information questionnaire. After reviewing the candidates' qualifications, conduct screening interviews to narrow the list down to three finalists. Test the candidates, using whatever personality or psychological

148

assessment tools you feel most comfortable with. My favorite personality assessment tool is InSight™ from Xyte, Inc. Compare the results with your impression of the candidates based on the screening interviews. During the testing, check references for each candidate thoroughly. You can outsource this reference checking and probably should. To get a more rounded picture of each candidate, conduct a social interview, such as taking the candidate and spouse or significant other to dinner. This often uncovers amazing discrepancies in factors and distractions relating to job-performance. To illustrate, a 2001 article in *The Orange County Register*, by writer Jennifer Hieger, quotes Bill Coleman of Salary.com: "Having a spouse in an insane asylum is better than having a spouse that should be." Your last step will be to have a final one-to-one interview at which you hire the superior candidate.

Once you have identified the traits and found the person you want, you still have to sell that candidate on coming to work for you. Here are five tools that make it easier to accomplish this goal in that final one-to-one interview:

- Have a great story to tell about your company,
- Have a compensation scheme better than your industry,
- Offer ongoing coaching (not annual reviews) as part of your culture (see Gary Markle's book in the bibliography),
- Offer challenge plus opportunity for personal growth, and
- Offer praise and non-monetary rewards for repeat results.

By proffering these items in that final interview, you can effectively close on this hire. Include communication, trust, feedback and openness as an integral part of your culture. Be a great company culturally and you will become a talent magnet. Be a place where people want to work and you will repeatedly win the recruiting wars.

We'll offer much more on what people want in their jobs and making your workplace desirable in chapter seven; this will make attracting, landing and retaining winners a slam-dunk.

Hiring Great Managers

As senior executives of what quickly became a billion dollar conglomerate back in the '80s, we hired lots of division CEOs and senior managers. Given our track record with the companies we bought and owned, we did a pretty good job once we put the right tools in place. Prior to this we made mind-boggling mistakes. We once hired a president to run a retail garden shop chain who had no retail experience and no green-goods experience. It failed miserably. Here's our solution to the hiring challenge:

MANAGERIAL SUCCESS TRAITS (MST)

Personal Motivation
Self -Discipline
Mentorship
Risk-Taking
Energy
Expectation of Success
Self-Confidence
Healthy Respect for Authority
Emotional Stability
Green & Growing
Enthusiasm
Introspection

Influence
Leadership
Communication
Organizes Self & Others
Human Sensitivity
Good Listener
Vision
Goal Setter
Trust Builder

Business Skills
Finance
Marketing
Relevant Business Experience
People-Selection Skills
Luck
Track Results
Focus on Customer

Intelligence
Common Sense
Street Smarts
Judgement
Academic Rigor
Conceptual Grasp

Decision Making / Professionalism
Intuitive Deduction
Problem-Solving Approach
Abstract Conceptualization
Balancing Results vs People Orientations

Problem & Analytical Skills
Asks the Right Questions

Memory
Long Term
Critical Detail

Score Candidates 1 - 10 on Each

Having made so many hiring mistakes, we finally got serious about devising a system for hiring managers. This has become one of the very best tools in that system. We've labeled it simply *managerial success traits* (MST). It's a list of personality traits and abilities that correlate very highly with success at the supervisor through middle-manager through CEO level.

The beauty of this tool lies in its simplicity and ease of use. The next time you're hiring key managers, use the short MST scorecard to select candidates using a scale of one to ten for each trait (see the CD/Desktop tool kit). Then review your rankings to discuss with candidates their weaknesses with them, preferably before you hire them. They will either sell you on their ability to overcome their weaknesses or you won't hire them. You know you have winners when candidates want to talk about their weaknesses. Winners don't pretend to be perfect. Instead, they acknowledge their shortcomings and tell you how they're working on them.

The MST scorecard is also great for managerial promotion decisions, or to guide you in managerial development; check out the Executive Development Planner tool in the last chapter. Give the MST list to each of your direct reports so they can score themselves. After a short discussion about their weak spots, give each one a $50-bill and say, "go to the bookstore and get some books on these topics. Work on these a bit so you will keep growing."

Also, encourage people to work on their strengths as well as their weaknesses. Just because something is a strength doesn't mean you can't improve it. And after all, in tough times we go to our strengths, not our slightly improved weaknesses.

To sum up, encourage your people to shore up their weak areas and reinforce their strengths. Handled properly, people love this kind of personal attention and development.

Pre-Employment and In-the-Job Testing

In order to hire, place or promote someone, you really only need to know two pieces of information: will they get the job done (performance), and will they have a good time while doing it (attitude)? Performance and attitude are all that matter about people in business. Good interviewing skills can uncover this information. And testing for aptitudes, motivations, work styles and learning preferences answers those critical questions with much greater accuracy. Plus, once you bring someone aboard, that kind of information can play an important role in coaching and guiding managerial and promotion decisions. For these reasons, pre-employment and, more importantly, in-the-job testing is paramount.

In the past, we've had great success with assessment tools such as the Motivation Analysis Profile, the Self-Descriptive Index and the Learning Style Inventory. The drawback to these earlier tools and many that are available today is that you have to become an expert on the nuances and uses of the tools. Recently, there's a tool that works much more easily. It's called Insight™ from Xyte, Inc. It blows the older models out of the water. This assessment system offers several layers of testing and evaluation, all of which can be used on the Internet by managers themselves with instant feedback. After the initial setup, you probably won't need those high-priced consultants to help you with this, or you can use them for what they're best at, namely coaching.

The first layer measures three things: how a person's behaviors manifest themselves in the work world, the person's general approach to work, and how to apply their behaviors for success on the job. A second level measures leadership traits, teaching and learning behaviors, interpersonal and team behaviors, compatibility with others, and creative behaviors. The feedback facilitates understanding of the strengths of individual job candidates so you can place them in their right positions, and once there, help them realize their full potential.

152

In addition to making better hiring decisions, the information gained from these tests can also be used to improve communications, build stronger teams, increase retention rates, and most important, increase productivity. So find an assessment tool or two that you like, apply it consistently across the board, and use the information to improve your placement and management batting average. One word of caution with testing – never make a hiring, placement, or promotional decision based solely on test results. What testing does is add an extra piece of information to the people placement puzzle, and it just might be the Rosetta Stone to your firm's success.

Breaking Through Invisible Ceilings

Here's an anecdote that illustrates the awesome power of putting winners in their right jobs and getting the jobs exactly right. GAC was the leading fine-color commercial printer in America, out-growing everyone in fine color commercial printing. But without warning we hit an invisible ceiling at $90 million in sales one year. We had suddenly stopped growing after several years of consistent 20 percent per year growth. No matter how hard we worked or what we tried, we couldn't bust through that invisible barrier.

Invisible ceilings are not caused by people but rather by structure and systems. They occur when a company hits sales of $1 million, $10 million, $100 million and so on. Well, of course not exactly $10 million, but somewhere in between $6 and $16 million – different for every business and every industry. Suddenly we're squashed up against an invisible ceiling and growth stops. Dead in its tracks! You can throw cash and people at it, but nothing seems to help. What's needed is a new look at how we're doing things.

> Invisible Ceilings Demand a New Look

At GAC our VP of sales left about then to go to another venture just before we hit our $90 million invisible ceiling. Since his position represented one of our key customer-impacting jobs, we needed to find a replacement right away. Our Portland regional VP of sales, J. Droge – pronounced "Jay" – had a solid track record of success. Because of that and because he already worked out of our corporate offices, it occurred to me he might fit the bill. At lunch one day I said, "J., we need a new VP of sales."

"Thanks, but no thanks," he replied. "I'm not interested in the job."

"Hold on," I countered. "I'm not necessarily offering you the job but of course you're fully qualified to be a candidate. In fact, with your experience and background, you are the most likely candidate."

After pausing to take a bite, I asked the question that would forever change the direction of the company. Managerial success sometimes happens by design. More often, however, it happens by

| Put People In Their "Best Jobs" |

luck. Take luck over skill anytime you can. In this case, it's not clear why the question came to mind. And despite his initial reluctance, it just seemed appropriate to me to get him to talk about himself. Either way, it just seemed like the right thing to do at the time. "J.," I queried, "what would you consider to be your best job? What do you do better than anyone else in the world?"

Without hesitation he looked me straight in the eye and replied, "I am the best printing sales administration manager you ever met! I'm the best in the world."

"What does that mean?" I asked. "We don't have that job in our company."

"Well, it involves just about everything but the printing itself: getting the job sold, getting it printed and getting it out the door. Taking care of the customer before, during and after the sale. It includes things like marketing, estimating, pricing, selling, credit and collections, customer service and the production planning part of the job."

"But some of those are manufacturing processes," I countered.

154

"I know," he replied, "but here's the deal. In order for us to do the best job for the customer and run the plant efficiently, all those things have to be coordinated."

"Okay, so how do you know how to coordinate all of those jobs?"

"Well, not only did I work in each of those jobs as I was learning the business here at GAC," he said with more than a little well-deserved pride, "but at one time or another I also managed every single one of those activities."

"Wow! You really are the 'Superman' of printing sales administration," I exclaimed.

In earlier times, my response might have been, "too bad we don't have a job like that," and let it go at that. But having seen what it takes to get the job exactly right, my suggestion was: "J., what if we make you VP of sales administration and you help me to learn how to handle the other half of the sales management job? We'll be in and out of each other's office every day doing sales management. How does that sound to you?"

A big smile spread across his face. "That might really work," he replied.

"Great! Let's go talk to everyone and see if we can't put it together." We did, and we hit not just a home run, but a bases-loaded, out-of-the park, grand slam in the 9th inning that took GAC to a whole new level. That year we grew from $90 million in sales to $120 million while our industry grew at a low single-digit rate.

And we solved the invisible ceiling that happens to most commercial printers at around $90 million annual sales. In fact, if you looked at an industry listing of printing companies back then, you'd find most of them get stuck at $90 million and go no further. For a | **Bust Through Invisible Ceilings** |
variety of reasons, once a printer reaches that magic number, internal bottlenecks develop that prevent the company from going any higher.

One of those bottlenecks was the need for J.'s sales administration, because there's just too much to do without an expert at coordinating all those functions that aren't directly sales related. Growth and the resultant invisible ceilings demand looking for new ways of doing old things.

Another bottleneck is the production planning function, which is one of the most critical in printing as it shepherds each print job through the entire process over several days or even weeks and months. It bottlenecks because all the decisions have to go through a single manager who has 30 people or more bringing a myriad of details every day. Line up ten new good-sized printing jobs a day – every day – and that person quickly maxes out at just about $90 million in sales.

Frank Stammers, GAC's VP of manufacturing at the time, recognized this, and with J. in his new position, brainstormed a radical, unheard of structure: the 30 production planners would group into teams of about four to five each, both physically and organizationally, and would report directly to each of our seven sales regions. What had always been a manufacturing function would now become a sales-directed function. In any other printing company, this would be considered heresy. Even at GAC, it was initially a tough sell but Frank was a strong manager. Since the people would still be physically located in manufacturing in the plant, a bi-modal functionality would develop. Well, it worked. And it never would have without J. being in his "best job" and Frank being in his. Both were winners, both in the right places, and both doing the right things.

> **Growth Means New Ways of Doing Things**

In his new position as sales administration VP, J. proved to be the key to unblocking our invisible ceiling as well as many other bottlenecks. As a result, we shot through $90 million in sales and kept right on going. Had we adhered to the traditional organization structure and said, "sorry J., we don't have that job at GAC," we might never have broken through the invisible ceiling. Instead, by getting a key customer-impacting job exactly right, we shattered the ceiling and eventually grew to nearly $200 million annual sales.

A thought on putting winners in best jobs – do this for only a few people in the company, not for most or all managers. Otherwise you will end up with perfect square pegs in perfect square holes that you can never replace because those employees are over-specialized for jobs that you designed around them. So my recommendation is use this tool with a maximum of one percent of the key people in a business. When you get those few positions exactly right, it's like having homerun champions Mark McGuire or Sammy Sosa on your baseball team. It genuinely changes the whole ballgame.

What does your industry look like with respect to invisible ceilings? How can you be ready to bust through them by getting your superstars ready and exactly right? Are you prepared to challenge conventional industry norms about organization structure? Answers to these questions can help keep your company from being "industry average" – one of the most dangerous phrases in all of business.

Top Ten Customer Tools

This chapter's been about people in business – winners – and effective tools for getting, coaching and keeping them. Perhaps the biggest and best tool of all in this area is simply to focus your people on the customer. You may have noticed that most of the tools in this chapter have pointed toward helping winners exceed customer expectations. Here's hoping the top ten tools on the following page will add more happy customers, and happy employees, to your business.

Focus Your People on Customers

FOCUS ON WINNERS!

The Top Ten Customer Tools

1. Key customer-impacting jobs. Find the key jobs affecting customers, put the right people in those jobs, and then really support them.

2. Customer care concept. Walk in your customers' shoes – step through each move in their process to simplify and ease getting their job done. Anticipate their every need, even if it's not what you do. Make your customer's life easy. Teach and re-teach customer care. Be the pacesetter on customer care.

3. Help your customers help *their* customers. Look way beyond the immediate. Find out what might be done to help your customers succeed with their customers. Then go do it.

4. The CEO should be the "CCO." Every CEO or manager in charge of an operation should be the Chief *Customer* Officer. This doesn't mean top salesperson or even sales manager. It does mean leading the team in precedent-setting customer care.

5. Treat older customers better. Yes, practice age-discrimination with customers who've been with you longer! Give them better service, better prices, better care. Don't ever start to think they're an annuity you're due.

6. Feed your customer garden. Jim Cecil, the marketing guru of this millennium, teaches us nurture marketing and Top-of-Mind-Awareness with prospects. But we forget to ask "what have I done today for my *customer*?" Top-of-mind-awareness must apply to every manager, so teach everyone to do something special for each customer, every single day.

7. Create a "customer calendar." Why not put together a calendar of key events related to what you do with and for your customers and give it to every employee? Cover the next twelve months and keep it updated so everyone's plugged in.

8. Serve your customers T-O-M-A. Top of Mind Awareness (T-O-M-A) is a marketing technique. Serve it to your customers and magic happens. Give your customers free product and service and watch them buy even more from you.

9. Weed your customer garden. There are a few folks that just shouldn't be customers. They want things you just can't do. Gently weed them out. This will give you more time to spend with real customers.

10. 100:100 (Help me help you). Join with your customers in a 100:100 partnership. We've seen that 50:50 deals never work in the long run. Be willing to make it work, no matter what it takes, but only with real customers.

Top 10 Tools to *Get, Keep, Excite* Winners

1. Create an *exciting* workplace. People want to have fun on the job. They also want to learn, be challenged and receive recognition for a job well done. If you don't provide these things, your employees will gravitate to companies that will.

2. Parallel your product-marketing with *people*-marketing. Set up a Marketing Program to attract employees the same way you attract customers. With a similar budget, status, and directive. Savvy companies are now hiring *product* brand managers to be *people* brand managers.

3. Look for talent in unusual places. Retirees, interns, college students, part-timers, parents-at-home and even former prisoners represent a rapidly increasing segment of the workforce. What are you doing to appropriately utilize these kinds of employees?

4. Hire a full-time, on-staff recruiter. Finding and hiring employees has become a full-time job for many companies. Consider recruiting 52 weeks per year. Most IT firms during the 2000 crunch had a full-time recruiter for every 15 or 20 techies.

5. Install the top eight "job-need" tools. Give people eight things in their jobs: compensation, recognition, fun, personal growth, challenge, convenience, security, and communication. Just watch your hiring and retention problems virtually vanish.

6. Become a student of recruiting. Make a commitment to become an expert at recruiting. Brainstorm new approaches with different groups each month (such as TEC, industry peer groups, chambers of commerce, Rotary clubs).

7. Hire consultants instead of employees. It's amazing how many boards of directors/advisors work for almost no pay, relatively speaking. A title often means more than money. Try putting experts like consultants on your board. It works.

8. Think *totally* outside the box. Many forward-looking businesses are acquiring other companies for the sole purpose of acquiring their people. Still others are hiring people from Chicago or Maine into Southern California or into Georgia in the dead of winter. Don't let mental or geographic boundaries limit your search for talent.

9. Outsource everything. Consider becoming a virtual, or virtually virtual, company. Ask yourself, why are *we* doing this? Aren't others better at it?

10. Be a *different* employer. One business pays more than anyone else in its industry and has no hire/motivate/keep people problems. Another offers fabulous fun, reward, recognition and "help me help you" programs; it, too, has watched its find/grow/retain problems disappear. How can *you* stand out from the crowd?

Chapter 6 – Get *Organized* to Get Results

Can you be a good manager if you can't manage yourself? It might seem obvious at first, but many managers and CEOs spend their time focusing just on business matters, yet neglect applying time to managing themselves. Occasionally we meet a pretty good leader who is not overly organized, but it's pretty rare we find an effective manager who's not organized. All managers and CEOs should dedicate themselves to ongoing growth of their leadership as well as managerial skills. *Organizing self and others* is probably the most significant mutual skill.

Organize Self First...

An organized company or department runs much more efficiently and effectively than a disorganized or unorganized one, plus it's really rough organizing others when we're the ones who are out of control. After all, who around us will bring order to chaos if we show no interest in orderly, consistent performance?

...which in turn Organizes Others

Here's substantiation: one of my very best CFOs (chief financial officers) was super-*un*organized when it came to storing and retrieving documents. He just couldn't find stuff! When he did, it often took hours – no exaggeration. And yet, he was the second best performing CFO out of several score in my experience. When he finally adopted the C-drawer tool described later in this chapter, he suddenly could find documents immediately and discovered that he had bought back about half-a-day per day of time for himself. It was great to see him playing golf each week on one of those free afternoons he had organized for himself. And even more to the point, everyone in his two departments became more organized, produced more, and improved our profitability. Financial reports now came out on the fourth business day each month, receivables rolled in faster, and his small operations support group started challenging the main operations division to keep up. Getting organized pays off for individuals and companies both.

When you get organized and help your people do the same, productivity and morale soar. That's because you're

| Set the Example |

setting the example and you are recognizing and rewarding employees for organized results. Flash back and forward to chapters one and seven. As we all know, happy employees mean happy customers and a much happier bottom-line. How has Herb Kelliher at Southwest Airlines been so successful? By focusing fiercely on making employees happy. In turn, those cheerful employees are more helpful and considerate than any of Southwest's competitors.

Some people have a knack for personal organization. Maybe it's genetic, maybe it's personality, or maybe just orientation to the world. Probably it's a little of each. For whatever reason, some people just seem to keep everything in order and never break a sweat. Others have to work a bit harder to keep a cover on the chaos. If

| Get A Great Admin Assistant |

you're not the organized type, get help! Don't try to go it alone. Start by hiring a top-notch administrative assistant. Personal experience taught me that a great one literally changes your life. This requires someone who not only has good organizational skills but, serving as your liaison to the world, must also have excellent people and decision-making skills.

| Tools to Buy Back Time |

Your admin should also be great at spreadsheets, list management and follow-up. When you find a great one, pay well, provide plenty of praise and show you appreciate the work done for you. Good admins are worth their weight in diamonds!

Continuing from our admin example, getting organized involves putting in place the people, tools and techniques that buy you back some time. So why not start with a time audit to benchmark yourself against other successful CEOs and managers?

Time Audit

Few things have more impact on your company's performance than how you spend your time. Try an annual CEO/manager time audit – a great tool for seeing where you spend your time and how you can use time more effectively in the future.

Periodic Time Audit

Take a Moment for a "TIME AUDIT"

PLEASE TAKE 5 MINUTES TO FILL IN BOTH

Step 1: Three Quick Cuts at How You Now Spend Your Time as a Business Person:

Step 2: Plan How You Would LIKE to Spend Your Time:

	NOW % of Time	6-Months % of Time
Customers	_____	_____
Marketing	_____	_____
Finance	_____	_____
Company Operations	_____	_____
Suppliers	_____	_____
Tracking Results	_____	_____
People/Communication	_____	_____
Strategy, Vision, Values	_____	_____
Reactive Problem	_____	_____
Administrivia	_____	_____
Total %	**100%**	**100%**
Managing	_____	_____
Leading	_____	_____
Doing	_____	_____
Total %	**100%**	**100%**
Hours per Week	_____	_____

Step 3: Decide HOW to Change Your Use of Time Over the Next Six Months. Specific Action Steps Will Help You Get There.

The time audit involves three simple steps. First, use the initial column of the worksheet to identify how much time you

167

currently spend in each category – either hours per week or percentage of your time. Make the percents add to 100 percent.

Then as a second step, project out six months into the future, identify how much time you would like to spend in each category, and

make those entries add up to 100 percent as well. Review your tabulation in the two columns and note the gaps between *Now* and *6-Months Out*. Finally in step three, write down some specific action steps to close the gaps between the two columns over the next six months. This could be anything from delegating certain tasks to taking a time management workshop to simply not doing some of the things you've formerly done. Sign and date your action steps. Ask someone – like a trusted advisor, mentor or spouse – to hold you accountable at one-month intervals for completing them. Both of you should schedule a lunch each month to review progress. Follow through on this and it will buy you back some time.

A different cut at the time audit involves three broader categories: leading, managing and doing. Repeat the process as described above, identifying the time currently spent in each category, the time you would like to spend and the action steps you will take to make the desired changes.

You'll get different answers when asking what's ideal in time allocation, but in general, really effective CEOs and managers spend their time about as follows:

	CEOs	**Managers**
Leading	45 percent to 60 percent	25 percent to 40 percent
Managing	20 percent to 35 percent	35 percent to 45 percent
Doing	10 percent to 20 percent	20 percent to 30 percent

Here are some tools for much more leading, more managing and less doing:

Leading	W4C	CEO MoLtr	Recognition Tools	
Managing	QPM	WGMGD	T12M	BAG
Doing	Time Audit	CoCal	1st Things 1st	

The appendix to this book contains a Tool Finder with page references for abbreviations used here.

If you're spending too much time doing, who will attend to the critical management and leadership functions of your role? Remember, you're the only manager of your group, the only CEO in your company. If you neglect or fail to recognize the key elements of your role because you're too busy doing someone else's job, those functions won't get done and your company won't attain its potential because of it.

Another thought about getting more organized with time: It seems like our entrepreneurial side gets us fully immersed in our businesses. Regardless of how we allocate our time among different areas, we still spend nearly 100 percent of our time on the job – not necessarily in the job. We just can't get away from it, and it occupies our every waking moment, plus much of our dream time. For our own sanity as well as the health of the business, we need to buy back some time for our family, friends and for ourselves. We also need to step back and look at the bigger picture. A fun tool that helps with this is to stand there at 5'10" every day but then zoom up to 30,000 feet for half-an-hour. Take a look down, and then return to 5'10" to tell everyone what you saw. Find your own style for doing this big picture stuff.

> Zoom Up To 30,000'
> Every Day

Along the same lines, my friend Walt Sutton, the internationally known business leader, speaker and writer, recommends a personal "CEO/Manager Retreat." Once a year, go off by yourself to a nice secluded spot where you can just sit and think. It could be a mountaintop, a train ride, a wide sandy beach, or a favorite park bench – anywhere you can spend a day or so thinking without

> Walt Sutton's CEO/Manager Retreat

distractions. Determine how to get some time back for yourself and re-focus on what's important in your future.

When we surveyed over 400 CEOs, we found the following patterns and trends in their use of time:

"TIME AUDIT" Survey Results

Actual results from a survey in 1998-99 of over 400 CEOs of American mid-sized companies.

	NOW		TREND	6-Months Out	
	% of Time	Range		% of Time	Range
Customers	25%	5% - 70%	up -->	28%	10% - 50%
Marketing	6%	5% - 10%	up -->	10%	0% - 20%
Finance	6%	0% - 20%	down -->	4%	0% - 10%
Company Operations	14%	3% - 40%	down -->	9%	0% - 30%
Suppliers	2%	0% - 5%	down -->	1%	0% - 5%
Tracking Results	4%	0% - 10%	up -->	8%	0% - 20%
People/Communication	9%	0% - 30%	up -->	14%	0% - 40%
Strategy, Vision, Values	7%	0% - 20%	up -->	19%	10% - 30%
Reactive Problem Solving	20%	5% - 50%	down -->	5%	0% - 10%
Administrivia	4%	0% - 20%	same -->	3%	0% - 10%
	100%			100%	
Managing	33%	10% - 50%		36%	20% - 50%
Leading	28%	10% - 42%		43%	20% - 60%
Doing	39%	10% - 80%		22%	5% - 35%
	100%			100%	
Hours per Week	55	40 - 70		45	30 - 63

Of course, one way to regain some of your precious time is to delegate more activities or simply stop doing them – deliberate

| Deletion |
| Rather Than |
| Delegation |

deletion. After all, we all do some things that are easy for us to do or that we like to do but that someone else in the company could do just as well, if not better. Some of these things just don't even need to be done. One really good solution is to take the time regularly to re-prioritize and let go of lesser activities that are taking up the best and highest use of our time. Sort of *first things first, second things never.* We pay people a lot of money to work for us. When we stop doing their jobs for them and delegate the tasks that don't belong to us, we can free up a lot of time to do our own jobs that much better.

> **Regularly Re-Prioritize**

Keep in mind that delegation does not mean dumping. In fact, probably the biggest reason most entrepreneurial CEOs and managers don't delegate is that they try it once or twice, get burned by delegatees not succeeding, and then vow never to try it again. The problem is often the way they're delegating. When delegating, be very specific about what and when, and in some cases, how. Choose your "delegatee" carefully, and make sure to delegate the authority to accomplish the task. Delegation carries with it an obligation on your part to follow up regularly, monitor the person's progress and give constructive, encouraging feedback. If we don't do these things, we're just dumping activities and tasks. It's not fair to us or to the delegatees.

Delegation also requires properly trained employees with proper tools. If an employee doesn't exhibit any clues about how to accomplish the task or doesn't have the tools, skills and/or training to do it, don't expect success. So choose the person carefully, provide plenty of details on what and when, monitor progress and measure results. Manage the process; lead the people. Remember you really can't manage people; they usually will manage themselves well if we just give them the training and tools for getting organized.

Alan Lakein's Wonderful *C-Drawer*

Let's hike back to the late '80s and '90s when computer experts predicted the paperless office. Well, it hasn't happened yet and it doesn't look like processed tree pulp is going away any time soon. The paperless office is pretty much a fiction. Using your time and attention most effectively requires managing the incessant flow of physical paper and digital paper (Email) that comes across your desktop. It's about managing

> **The Great "C-Drawer" Organizer**

information and not data. One of the best tools for managing paper flows of both kinds is the wonderful "C-drawer," from Alan Lakein, the granddaddy of time management. Over the years we've modified his approach somewhat.

In general, five categories of paper come into your office every day: A, B, D, R and C. To start the paper management process, put all the documents in a pile in front of you and begin sorting, one by one. Category "A" documents have to do with growth, profit, customers, and your people. They are important to the success of your business. Put these in the center of your clean desk and move on to the next document in the pile.

Category "B" documents involve tasks and activities you can delegate. Do not let them pile up on your desk. Get them gone – delegated or done – as soon as they come in so you only handle them once.

Category "D" documents are trash. Throw them in the trashcan immediately. The fourth category of paper, "R," involves material that you would like to read at some point in time. Put these on your reading shelf or in your briefcase to read at home, on the train, in the airport or whenever you have time.

Believe it or not, about half of all the paper that comes into your office falls into Category "C" and it's still sitting there in your in-basket, or Email inbox. You don't know exactly what these documents are or why you need to see them, but you can't throw them away because they might be important. You can't delegate them because you don't understand them. Please don't delegate stuff you don't understand – that tends to be dumping rather than delegating.

Here's where the C-drawer flexes its "getting organized" muscle. Open your C-drawer, preferably at least a double-size drawer in your desk, put all the C documents inside and close the drawer. Just like that, you are done with them. Really done, kaput, finee, ces't tu! You can now go about your

Do 1st
Things 1st

day with an uncluttered mind. More important, this clears your desk so you can focus only on those genuine A documents that demand immediate attention. It's a simple business philosophy: first things first, second things never. Always find ways to put top things on top.

Because C documents have a tendency to pile up very quickly, make sure your C-drawer has a large capacity. Even with a large drawer, however, you will be amazed at how quickly it fills up. Here's the secret to the C-drawer system. When the drawer starts to overflow, remove the entire stack of documents from the drawer and lay it carefully on your desk in front of you. Take the top half of the pile and put it back into the C-drawer. Then grab the remaining bottom half and, in one smooth uninterrupted motion, dump it in the trash. Don't even slow down, just dump it. Like magic, you have just cut your C-pile in half. This gives you another 30 to 45 days of breathing room to refill the C-drawer, allowing you to go forward in an organized manner with your first things first.

But wait, you say. How will you know if you're throwing out something important? Don't worry. There really is not anything of importance there. So, when you get ready to discard that bottom half of the C-drawer, just close your eyes and do it. Otherwise you may find it difficult, if not impossible, to throw it away. Remember the ancient Greek goddess, Medusa, who had snakes for hair? Sailors who set their eyes upon her immediately turned to stone. C-drawer documents have that same power. If you cast your open eyes upon the C-drawer documents you're trying to discard, three or four snakes will stick up their heads and cry out, "save me, save me, save me!" You will then spend the next two hours frozen at your desk, sorting through the pile, wondering whether or not to keep or trash the various documents. Don't do it!

> **Don't Ever Sort Your C-Drawer**

Your time is probably far too valuable to waste being a human document sorter. Instead, keep your eyes closed and throw that junk out. Let the C-drawer manage your paper flow, stop letting the onslaught of data manage you, and you'll buy back time for yourself. Thank you, Alan Lakein, for teaching us this technique over a quarter century ago. It still works now and we highly recommend Alan's book, *How to Get Control of Your Time and Your Life*.

Roles-at-the-Top

Why not take a cut each year at re-setting the roles of the top five people in your company or your group? One of my clients in the construction industry does this every year and has grown very profitably from about $30 million to over $130 million annually in

| Set Yearly "Roles at Top" |

just over four years. We all know construction companies just don't grow that successfully or that fast. My client's ongoing success comes from the re-setting of roles annually, a constant vigilance against complacency in everything they do, the use of a bunch of CEO / manager tools – like T12M charts and other timely tracking tools – plus an adherence to core values with an approach of evolving toward being better organized as they grow. It's this *evolutionary organizing* that's their key to supremely successful, phenomenally fast growth.

What are the elements of getting the top roles right? Begin by identifying what's really important in your business,

| Match Important Things to Exec Roles |

things like customers, growth, profit, and your people – just a bit of déjà-vu from the C-Drawer. Then take a look at your organization, usually consisting of a CEO, Chief Operations Executive, Chief Financial Executive, and others. Suddenly it may dawn on us that the things that are important in a business don't usually have a champion, that we're organized in a functional way that's very unrelated to what's really needed! So simply divide up these important things among your executives and make sure you're tracking and managing these and not just the normal functional areas. Try to reset these roles-at-the-top each year as you grow.

It might surprise you to learn that my view of CEO is Chief *Everything* Officer, but certainly not all at once or for very long. The

| Chief Everything Officer |

CEO and manager should move from area to area, helping to align, fix, support, and get everything in that area going just right for the long-term, then move on to the next area. The following list of roles might help with getting hold of this concept. Who's watching after these things in *your* company?

CEO = *Chief Executive* or *Everything Officer?*

CCO	Customer	☐
CMO	Marketing	☐
CSO	Sales	☐
CSO	Strategy	☐
CVO	Vision	☐
CPO	Planning	☐
CKO	Knowledge	☐
CIO	Information	☐
CTO	Technology	☐
CQO	Quality	☐
CPO	Profit	☐
CFO	Cash/Flow	☐
CFO	Financial	☐
CGO	Goals	☐
CTO	Tracking	☐
CDO	Direction	☐
CGO	Growth	☐
CCO	Culture	☐
CVO	Values	☐
CCO	Communication	☐
CCO	Cheerleading	☐
CRO	Recognition	☐
CSO	Support	☐
CPO	Passion	☐
CFO	Fun!	☐
CPO	People	☐
CAO	Administrative	☐
COO	Operations	☐

When asked, "who is watching these areas?" my audiences often answer *everyone* or *me*, indicating themselves as CEO and/or manager. The answer *everyone* means no one is watching that very important area.

> Who's Watching in Your Company?

And if the answer is *me*, then that's no one as well, since no single CEO or manager can watch all those areas at once or very well.

175

Roles-at-the-top is deciding what's to be done in each key area this year and then divvying up the responsibilities for getting them done. Try meeting once a month to challenge each other as to progress. Tick off the action items and set some new ones. Coach and help each other to re-assess on a continuing basis. Then reset these roles at least annually.

The Chief Everything Officer tool applies equally well to managers and CEOs. Get the managers in your group or company to

Score Your Company On 1-10 Scale

rate your performance on a one to ten scale on each of the everythings listed above, where one is the pits and we really should do something, while ten is great or almost perfect. Compile the results and see which ones need serious attention. Then get together and brainstorm fixing those weaker areas. As always, this exercise will yield remarkable results, since your people always know where the weak spots are and they do really know how to fix them. It's just that they usually don't have the time, the teamwork, or all the tools to fix them.

CEO Tool
CEO360

Organizing Others

The secret to organizing others is to help them develop *self-accountability*. Take another look at the discussion in

QPM Organizes Self & Others

chapter three regarding the quarterly priorities manager (QPM) tool – the very best self-accountability tool around. It's fun getting yourself organized as well as those around you.

If you don't use the QPM, use some system that sets goals with your direct reports, supports and checks in with them over time,

CEO Tool
QPM

and finally reviews and rewards success frequently and again as each goal is accomplished. Use daily lists or weekly lists and suggest them to those around you. Getting others organized isn't tough once you're organized. Remember that everyone in the organization is watching their bosses to see how they do it. They are really watching. Find ways to get yourself organized and in turn they'll get themselves organized. This will buy you back tons of time.

A Letter to Myself (*Monthly Operations Report*)

Think of the *Monthly Operations Report* (MOR) as a letter to yourself, a gift for your own current and future efficiency. Here's how it works: it's a one-page narrative after the end of each month, telling what happened during that month, what should have happened, and what we'll make happen in the month just starting. Include all the elements you know are important, like customer events, financial results, people progress, market penetration, new products or services, growth successes and competitive victories. Both positives and negatives should be identified.

Monthly Operations Report (MOR)

The MOR should change over the months that you write it, moving toward the accomplishment of your vision and big goals. Write it to an imaginary or real board of directors or chairman or boss, even if you're only writing it to yourself. Why? Simply, it's a *gift of better focus* on your business. The MOR is the focus ring on your management camera. This is why it's an organizing tool – it's about focus and prioritization. Here's a somewhat humbling lesson:

MOR: Focus-ring on Management's Camera

After starting my own consulting firm, Corporate Partners Inc. in the late '80s, the thought of writing the monthly operations report just never occurred to me. A couple of years went by when my old friend Larry King, the great nationally known speaker – not the "live" one on TV – addressed a presidents' group in Atlanta. Larry mentioned keeping a monthly journal of what happened in your business the past month, and suddenly my light bulb flashed on: his monthly journal was the same as my MOR. But even having used it and preached about it for years, it was not to be found in my own business. It's kind of like the cobbler who never gets around to repairing his own shoes. Immediately that month my first MOR was penned, and did it ever open up my eyes! Staring

Larry King's Monthly Journal

back from my mirror was a new person and a new business. In the next six months, my business doubled because that MOR refocused me on the right things. Here's that wonderful Winston Churchill wisdom again: *I'm always willing to learn, but not always ready to be taught.* Six years later my MOR still guides me month-to-month and year-to-year.

Picture, for a moment, someone else running your company, or division or functional area, and sending you only one narrative page each month as input on results. What would that page say? Wouldn't you want it to tell you everything really important that happened last month and what the ensuing month and year might look like? Wouldn't it be succinct, focused, and hard-hitting in just those areas that you really should know about? Wouldn't it contain just the salient statistics and facts? And wouldn't it provide fundamental insight to the solutions to making your company the greatest that ever existed? That's the MOR.

The first time you write an MOR, your eyes should pop open wide and you should feel that something's missing in the way you're running the business. Rest assured, that reaction is normal. The MOR is a mind-expanding exercise that reflects how your business should be run and jolts you into realization in those areas where you've gone off-track.

A belated benefit is that a year from now you'll look back at the same month last year as you write your MOR: what a remarkable,

| MOR as Rearview Mirror |

ready-reference it is, reflecting what really happened back then. This rearview mirror will dramatically re-direct your thinking and prod your progress toward your vision and big goals. An add-on tool: get your direct reports to give you their MORs each month. Over time, you can have your entire management team on track with this terrific tool.

Following is an example from one of my former companies, citing performance statistics for the month and detailing what happened, what should have happened and what we'll try to make happen next month:

XYZ Manufacturing Corporation

Board of Directors
XYZ Manufacturing Corporation
123 Main Street
Anyoldplace, State 11111

February 7, 2001

Monthly Operations Report:

XYZ had a good month in January, generating about $1.7 million in shipments, an increase of 25 percent over last January. Total A-product was $930K with B-product at $780K in January; fill levels were 98 percent. We are now working on key measures to add an indicator of customer satisfaction with these shipment levels.

Better yet was the growth in pretax income to $174K this month, surpassing January last year by 27 percent. As compared to budget, we're up 2 percent on revenues and 2.3 percent on pretax profit.

On the operating side of XYZ, the physical move and much of the reorganization were completed this month. The sales/customer service teams are in place with new monthly goals and incentive plan. Shipping has been moved to Building One, however their reorganization is not yet complete. Overall, a few files are still to be put away, but essentially the move is behind us and on budget. A new schedule for redecorating will be developed in February as we learn more about the arrival of materials.

Other key events in January were the new employee newsletter (printed), the issuance of an annual corporate calendar, the initiation of operations meetings, a change in receptionist hours to improve customer service, and the Customer Advisory Committee meeting scheduled for next month. Officers' priorities are nearly implemented at this writing, the aim of which is to improve self-accountability as well as overall teamwork and communication.

Personally, I have met with over half of XYZ's people and a dozen customers in one-on-one's and have learned a great deal about the culture and success factors of the company. I look forward to completing these input interviews in February and beginning the development of a marketing plan and the setting of the longer-term course for the company.

For February, our forecast is currently $2.1 million of shipments, which should be a major step up from February last year. The Employee Health Fair will take place on February 18th, with a great deal of enthusiasm currently being shown from all quarters.

It will be a pleasure to provide this operations report each month to the Board as well as the Officer group, and hopefully the scope and content will expand meaningfully over time with everyone's input.

With best regards,

Kraig

Kraig W. Kramers
President & CEO

Give People Road Maps *(Company Calendar)*

Here's another great organizing tool – the *company calendar* – that you'll find on the CD/Desktop tool kit as CoCal. It's easy to create, simple to use and very effective in keeping people on track with what's going on in the business. List the 12 months of the year across the top of a sheet of paper. Down the left side, list every event of importance that will take place in your company during the coming year and then fill in the specific due dates across the spreadsheet. Make copies of the calendar and give one to every employee.

[12-Month Company Calendar]

The company calendar accomplishes two important things. First, it helps to keep everyone on the same page. Second, it shows your employees that you respect and trust them enough to say, "here's when things are due. Get us ready for that trade show" or whatever the event or activity might be. Your people won't accidentally schedule vacations for the two weeks before the trade show because they now know they have to get you ready to be there.

The company calendar doesn't have to come directly from you to be effective. You can delegate it to just about anyone. To make it easily updateable, put the calendar in a spreadsheet format with each month as a column, and hand it out to employees at least every quarter. To update the calendar at the end of a quarter you can simply move the three months of the old quarter just ended and tack it on the right end of the sheet, add new dates, print it out and re-distribute to all employees. So it's a perpetual company calendar, from which employees will quickly learn to manage their own time, with just a little coaching from you. This, in turn, will buy you back some time through less involvement on your part in managing their time. All employees love this, since managing themselves makes them more self-actualized.

Here's an example of a company calendar. Normally, it would show all twelve months and the dates would be filled in the columns, but for display and readability here, we've left them out.

Employees love the company calendar because it makes a handy reference tool for tracking and knowing when they need to get things done. It tells them you trust them to manage their own time, which then in turn buys you back lots of time as you no longer have to

NAME OF YOUR COMPANY, INC. Company Calendar					New Release 01-15-02		
	Jan 02	Feb 02	Mar 02	=======>	Oct 02	Nov 02	Dec 02
Financial Month End							
Financials due							
Officers Meeting							
Financial Audit							
Annual Budget Process:							
Guidelines Issued							
Sales Plan Finalized							
Strategy Meeting							
Capital List Finalized							
Budget First Cut							
Final Budget Approved							
Marketing Calendar:							
New Marketing Plan							
Sales Meetings							
Other Meetings							
Trade Show Dates							
Other Conference							
Annual Customer Conference							
Monthly Customer Report							
Monthly Meeting							
Other Customer Dates							
Operations Calendar:							
Operations Meetings							
Reports Prepared							
Employees Calendar:							
Employee Reviews							
All Employee Meetings							
Company Holidays							
Christmas Party							
Attendance Bonds							
Wellness Program							
	Jan 02	Feb 02	Mar 02	=======>	Oct 02	Nov 02	Dec 02

Note: months of April through September would normally be included. They were left out here just to fit this on the page. Also, the page would normally be filled with due-dates in each month.

manage their time for them. Remember trust building from chapter two? Well here it is again, helping you help yourself with getting more organized.

Here's another road map for your organization. Why not try a 12-month *customer calendar,* just like the company calendar? You

> **Try a Customer Calendar**

can position the customer with all your people so that customers are the #1 focus. You will probably develop some new things to keep customers happy just by addressing the idea of a customer calendar.

As an adjunct to the company calendar, Email provides an effective method for sending monthly or periodic reminders of important upcoming calendar events. Get an Admin Assistant or some other well-organized person to manage your company's *company calendar.*

While touching on the subject of Email, this initially super-effective communication tool – *Email* – has turned into a data dump,

> **New Email Rules**

denying us much real information. Email has turned into an overwhelming mess for most. Overcome the Email pile-up in your company or group by effecting the following ground rules:

- The "To:" line is only to be used for addressees who are expected to take action. All other addressees go on the "cc:" line.

- Stop the use of "Everyone" as an addressable Email group (except in carefully proscribed instances).

- Establish a priority system using a letter in the "Subject:" space, like U for urgent, I for important, R for routine, F for FYI.

You may need to police the use of such a system for a few weeks, but it's well worth the extra effort to free your entire employee population from Email tyranny. Just think of how much more effective they'll be. All of a sudden, Email will again be that terrific tool that buys you back a bunch of time.

Quarterly Business Reviews

An easy and effective tool for most businesses is simply conducting regular half-day business reviews – with a formal agenda and outline – once each quarter, with a mini-version each month. Companies that do this just plain perform better. Get your financials completed by the fifth business day of each month, and on the seventh business day have a financial review, a market growth meeting, an operations and service/support assessment, a personnel performance report or anything else that needs attention. Call it a monthly or quarterly business review (QBR) or whatever you want, but just do it. It'll be the one meeting that has a real agenda triggered by the monthly financials or maybe your monthly operations report. Here's a possible agenda for your QBRs or monthly business reviews (MBRs):

> Quarterly Business Review (QBR)

1. Review key points in our 1-Page Business Plan.
2. Show our 1-Page Budget with emphasis on this month, year-to-date and T12M charts.
3. What our latest "MOR" says.
4. Explain our latest T12M Charts and Key Indicators.
5. What this month's "Re-Forecast" says about the near-term future and full year.
6. What our "Action Steps" are to realize or exceed the new re-forecast.

The review for each business unit should ideally take only 20 minutes, but if this is your whole operation, maybe it's an hour. Be sure to include re-forecasting in your QBR or MBR so that you're looking at the rest of the year and figuring out how to get back on budget or hopefully

> Monthly Reviews with Pre-Triggered Agendas

more common, stay ahead of budget. Identify actionable items – that's the ticket. They only come out of such formal QBRs or monthly reviews, coupled with a penchant for taking responsive, often anticipatory, action. Was that a flashback to chapter four? You bet! Tracking, review and anticipation all go hand-in-hand.

At most of the companies in my CEO career, these quarterly reviews were mandated by the parent company. We hated them! We loved them! But no matter your view of them, they are usually

| Anticipatory Action Steps |

effective in producing long-term bottom-line results when you focus on the actions needed to improve what you see just ahead of you. As a manager, maybe you want to try these monthly at first, just to perfect the format and flow.

Cultivating a Self-Consistent Organization

All companies have values, but few have a mission or vision understood, accepted and practiced by the people who work there.

| Create Self-Consistency |

Getting organized means getting all five of your constituencies – employees, customers, suppliers, owners and the community – in alignment with your company's mission, vision and values. Many great books and speakers cover the subject well, but my take in this area might surprise you.

In most businesses, these concepts are not aligned, meaning the opposite of a win-win-win-win-win with all five constituencies. In addition, the people in the constituencies don't know the mission-vision-values even if they are aligned to everyone's benefit. In the rare cases where they are aligned, lack of consistent communication means that the mission-vision-values don't get universally integrated into people's thinking and on-the-job behavior. Conversely, get well enough organized to assure alignment, awareness, communication and consistent application. You'll then turbo-charge your business success. Most everyone has heard how Ritz-Carlton does this, but if you haven't, just ask any one of their employees.

Here's how it can go wrong: At GAC printing in Portland, the values were aligned, everyone was subliminally aware of them and applied them pretty consistently, but we didn't communicate them

184

very often. We had most of the equation exactly right and it paid off in rapid, profitable growth far exceeding industry norms. Yet the values weren't verbally or visually communicated except in daily actual practice, which led to a few unfortunate incidents. Example: we had been executing a $900,000 print-job-and-mailing for *Esprit* with a definite "in-home" date, meaning the catalogs had to be in the homes of consumers on the Friday before a special in-store promotion and sale that weekend. On the Monday following that weekend, Susan Rockrise, vice president in charge of all advertising, promotion and printed materials for *Esprit*, called me to say store activity was not high over the weekend and could we please check on the actual in-home date. To my absolute horror, we had not only failed to complete the mailing in time, but a cover-up of preposterous proportions had taken place. Could this be the same company that always performed for customers?

As CEO, the responsibility was clearly mine. And so the phone call to tell Susan what had really happened was really mine, too. After filling Susan in on the debacle, a very long, painful pause ensued. After what seemed like an eternity lasting in reality less than 10 seconds, she said: "Kraig, we've been working with GAC for a very long time with great success and without any real problems. This one's huge, but our good history together is not for naught. Please get those books in the mail this week and we'll overlook the problem this time." She could hear and feel my mental sigh of relief 636 miles away, along with my verbal expression of appreciation. It took no time at all to correct the internal misdirection permanently and in all conceivable futures for all our constituencies, yet it took me many years to understand what we really learned. Namely, that values-vision-mission must be understood, accepted, re-communicated regularly and applied | Build a Self-Consistent Culture | consistently for a business to really do well. My name for this is *self-consistent organizational culture*.

Quite often contrast brings us to deeper understanding. At Snapper we had values all right, about five sets of them, all different and all pointed at something different in various parts of the extensive organization. This was evident during my tenure, but the full impact of the situation didn't dawn on me until a decade later. We managed

185

to reconcile much of the value-disconnect between manufacturing and the sales organization. This meant getting Snapper's manufacturing and marketing to march together with our 60 independent distributors and 10,000 retail servicing dealers. Even so, we didn't get full alignment and Snapper paid a price for it down the road.

After leaving Snapper, my replacement was required by the parent company to take Snapper directly into the mass merchants of America (e.g., Home Depot). Our team had studied this strategy and concluded that it would lead down an unhappy and very unprofitable road. The only possible way would require designing a totally different Snapper-manufactured line of products that had a different brand and cost for the mass merchant. But the parent company not only was adamant about going into the mass merchant market, it insisted on doing it now. My successor charged forward into that market and proceeded to lose about $100 million at the pretax line over the three years of his tenure. Along the way Home Depot stopped carrying Snapper lawnmowers and Snapper's president was removed. Had the values of the various constituents been aligned, the outcome almost certainly would have been very different.

We talked about values in chapters two and five; now we're talking about getting your people organized to practice the values, march to the mission and realize the vision. It's the *self-consistent organizational culture*. You'll need communication tools from chapter two plus recognition and reward tools from chapter seven to get there. When you realize your self-consistent organizational culture, you'll see that you're suddenly at the *we* culture discussed in depth earlier. Here's a tidbit from the past that portrays the point perfectly: when the great aviator Charles Lindberg returned from his world's-first solo transoceanic flight, he authored a book simply titled *We*. What a wonderful place to get to and be!

DON'T JUST ADD MORE STAFF: GET MORE *ORGANIZED!*

Top Ten Tools for *Getting Organized*

1. Time audit. Audit your time to get rid of comfort-zone things you do that aren't focused on customer, people or profit. Studies show that managers spend up to 40 percent of their time on reactive problem solving and administrivia. Get rid of these and refocus on results.

2. The "c-drawer." Many thanks to time-management guru Alan Lakein who helped us see what getting organized really entailed. The c-drawer and its many variations have put many of us on the right track.

3. Roles-at-the-top. Set roles to focus on what's really important in your business each year and put champions in charge of taking care of customers, growth, profit and people. Who are your VPs of customers, growth, profit and people?

4. Quarterly priorities manager (QPM). Encourage managers to share five individual quarterly goals with each other on a regular basis and then help each other achieve them. The quarterly look links the day-to-day out to the vision.

5. Monthly operations report (MOR). This is the manager's personal report card, building both track record and results. This is a monthly self-review of what you ought to be doing. By forcing yourself to write it, you force self-realization.

6. 12-month company calendar (CoCal). Show all key future events to all of your employees, creating coordinated results. This will surprise you. Each quarter, the months just ended are appended for next year, creating a perpetual calendar.

7. Organize self before others. It's really hard to be believable if you aren't organized. Take hold of this issue and become an organized executive. Take a seminar on getting organized, try some of the tools on this page, and then go teach them to those around you.

8. Quarterly & monthly business reviews (QBR). The perfect vehicle for applying tracking tools and anticipating the future. Turbo-charge your actions as managers.

9. Join a monthly CEO/manager learning group. Stay abreast of organizational initiatives by joining TEC (The Executive Committee) or a similar group that meets monthly to enhance the business success and lives of its members.

10. 15-minute daily meeting. Ritz-Carlton hotels probably invented this concept with their 10-minute stand-up review of what's important in service to the hotel's guests. Your 15-minute stand-up meeting could review yesterday's lessons and today's improvements with your key managers and players each day.

Chapter 7 – Celebrate *Every* Success!

Ever wondered why some goals continue to stay totally out of reach? Let's return for a moment to those meaningful goals from chapter two. The proof of meaningfulness for most people is some kind of reward or celebration, once the goal is achieved. *Celebration* confirms that the goals were indeed meaningful. Isn't it a hand-in-glove relationship? Without celebrating the successes, all goals soon become meaningless, | **Celebration Creates Meaning** | useless, and even dangerous in a really big hurry. Yes, dangerous because goals often become counter-productive in the absence of celebration.

Here's a case in point: my first time ever as CEO was at Courtesy Coffee Company in San Diego, where we set an annual sales goal to grow from the flat $1.2 million year-after-year performance to $2.5 million in two years. We accomplished just $2 million, a terrific 67 percent jump over the two years, but we didn't celebrate at all. You could feel employee morale palpably plummet going into the next year. Fortunately, the parent company decided to sell the coffee business before the consequences of de-motivation took hold, offering me a graceful and timely out. Three lessons leap from this experience: first, always celebrate in order to tee up the goal for the following year. Second, accept luck whenever it comes along. And third, keep a watchful eye on your parent company at all times ☺.

We've seen again and again that companies taking a little time to celebrate successes achieve far more than those that don't. It's an ongoing cycle where celebration and recognition of people for getting results leads to | **Celebration *Links* the Goal Cycle** | repeated results, which in turn leads to more celebration and recognition. So celebration becomes cumulative by creating even greater results. It's the linchpin that makes goals meaningful.

People want to come to work for a lot more than a paycheck. Sure, money's important. And sure, people want decent pay for a day's work. But people also want challenging work with opportunities to learn and grow, and most important, they want to know they're making a difference, indeed that their hard work is contributing to a meaningful outcome. This is why celebrating success is so important. It demonstrates that the CEO, executive, manager and especially peers appreciate the hard work and recognize (i.e., celebrate) each person's results. Celebration is vital for repeated individual results and paramount for team performance. Celebrating reinforces the notion that your people have contributed something of value to their company and to their community. Here, community especially means fellow employees. And when we celebrate, people can then let go of the goal they have just achieved. It's a mental "whew, we really did something here!" Then, and only then, are they ready to set new, more aggressive, more meaningful goals with greater excitement, energy and enthusiasm.

Serendipitously, celebrating near-miss situations also jumped into my tool kit at GAC printing. We undertook big audacious goals monthly and quarterly. We made the BAGs over 16 quarters in a row. Sometimes we missed the monthly BAGs, yet by reaching for them, we achieved so much more in total. So why not celebrate the improved results, even though technically we "failed?" Of course we did celebrate, and everyone learned that as long as we gave it our all, we would always celebrate the results. This helps keep the effort in high gear at any company while making it okay to fall somewhat short of BAGs. In the monthly superstars letter example in chapter three, you may have noticed that we recognized Richard Venner as our near-misser that month for being within six percent of his target. That might seem like a sizable miss, but please realize we said BIG Audacious Goals. For reasons having to do with the market at the time, Richard's performance was prodigious. Richard's results were as good as getting all the way there.

Celebrating success doesn't mean sending the whole team off to Las Vegas or Cabo San Lucas every time you attain a goal. At the same time, it should involve more than releasing a few balloons and shouting "hooray!" at employee meetings – although that's a good start. Celebrating success is an attitude, a philosophy, and an approach to doing business. It can become part of every company's culture so that when people do good things, the recognition and celebration happen automatically.

What's the best way to put celebration into your company? Do you suddenly have to be the funny, happy, life-of-the-party type? The good news is that you don't. You do need to get celebration started by appointing or convincing a few people to undertake the effort, and then you do need to support those who will do the fun, celebratory things and add happiness to your organization.

Checklist for Celebrating

Here's a solid checklist for celebrating in any organization. See if your company or group is offering something impactful and important to your people in each of the following eight celebration checkpoint areas:

1. **Compensation**
2. **Recognition**
3. **Fun**
4. **Personal Growth**
5. **Challenge**
6. **Convenience**
7. **Communication**
8. **Security**

These celebration areas are not listed above in any particular sequence other than an anecdotal order, which most managers seem to think is their relative importance. When asked – assuming compensation and security are competitive or at least solidly okay – employees order them as follows: communication, recognition, convenience, challenge, personal growth, fun, security, and compensation. These eight areas are not only for celebration – they are the things all employees want in their jobs. Are we giving them all eight in appropriate amounts?

Try scoring your company or group to see which areas might need some tuning up. The following example is pretty self-explanatory with one area needing further discussion.

8-Score: Management's Employee Satisfaction Index   EXAMPLE

Enter Each Manager's Name -->	John Doe	Sue Smith	Dick Brown	Gina Green	George Jones	Amy Black	Bobbie McGee	TOTAL SCORES
KEY CRITERIA:								
1-Communication	5	7	5	6	8	5	6	42
2-Recognition	7	6	5	7	8	6	7	46
3-Convenience	9	9	5	6	7	5	9	50
4-Challenge	4	6	5	8	7	6	5	41
5-Personal Growth	5	6	5	5	6	6	5	38
6-Fun	5	7	5	6	7	5	5	40
7-Security	8	8	7	9	9	6	7	54
8-Compensation	8	7	7	9	9	5	7	52
TOTAL SCORES =	51	56	44	56	61	44	51	6.5 ESI

INSTRUCTIONS:

Manager and Direct Reports score each criteria on 1 - 10 scale. Design action items to improve each area that needs upgrading. Re-score every quarter to measure improvement by area. Then track each on a Trailing 4-Quarter Chart to see if improvement is ongoing or at least maintained.

ESI: This box shows an Employee Satisfaction Index (ESI), as estimated by management. Re-score the ESI each quarter and track it on a Trailing 4-Quarter Chart to measure improvement in estimated employee satisfaction with the 8-Score Criteria. The ESI represents the combined average score on a 1 - 10 scale. The model corrects for the number of scorers and computes an average.

This model has built into it an automatic calculation of an Employee Satisfaction Index (ESI), determined from management's estimates on each of the eight key criteria – that is, the things people want in their jobs. Simply ask your managers to score their estimate of employees' satisfaction with the eight key things on a 1 – 10 scale. The model calculates an average in the ESI box. It's on the CD/Desktop helper as 8-Score for ease of use. Why not score your performance in the eight areas and track your ESI on a trailing four-quarters chart to see how you're really doing with your people? Here are tools to use once you've decided to seek improvement in one or all eight key things people want and need in their jobs:

1. Compensation. Every time we set new goals, let's make sure we align compensation with those goals. Nothing de-motivates employees quicker than working hard to achieve a big goal and then not getting financially rewarded for it. Even worse is when they know compensation isn't there from the get-go on a new goal, unless there's some other, perhaps more noble, reward coming at the end. Compensation has got to be there – it's sort of jacks-or-better in poker, an opener to get the game going. Too often, companies set new goals but forget about making sure the compensation plan is aligned. A great example of what works was the sales compensation program at the printing company, already in place upon my arrival. Simply, it was a 100-percent commission compensation plan, which was upward sweeping with volume and profitability while having no cap on potential individual earnings. It was perfectly aligned with an aggressive sales management, always pushing yet supporting ever-greater performance from every salesperson. Of course, salespeople need to also have the tools to get the results. In our case, that meant they had pricing authority and autonomy.

> Always Align Compensation with Goals

What had been missing before my arrival at GAC were monthly sales targets for each salesperson. We instituted joint sales targets and *voila!* The result was solid, ongoing results for the next five years because now compensation was perfectly aligned with everyone's growth goals.

Incidentally, how on earth would the need for sales targets ever come to my attention? It certainly wasn't my being that smart. It was that something had been well ingrained in me: namely, seek out people who might know more than me about producing profits in a particular situation, in this case in a printing firm. Back in chapter

| Take Your Predecessor To Lunch! | two, we talked about taking my presidential predecessor to lunch. Even though that predecessor knew of my direct involvement in his firing, he was |

appreciative and justifiably flattered that someone in the CEO job now would take the time to ask about things he had done several years back. He told me that the only time in its 95-year history that GAC made money in the first quarter was when he had instituted sales targets for each salesperson, which was not generally industry practice. Always take lessons on those business things you don't know about. For example, you may know your industry but are not an expert in finance or marketing or rapid growth acceleration. Get coaching, consulting, or at least input from your predecessors in those areas.

So, a couple of bonus tools pop up here. First, go a little outside your comfort zone and get information that may lead to

| Get to Know What You Don't Know! | surprising results. Always find a way to meet and ask your predecessors what worked and what didn't for them. Ask your people, too. |

Second, challenge industry practice, but do so carefully. Please don't do something that will lose you a bunch of customers, as happened in the case of a sporting goods distribution company that asked me to be CEO. Munson Sporting Goods was the leading wholesaler of hunting, fishing, camping and athletic gear in the West and my predecessor president decided to eliminate long-dating on

| Carefully Challenge Industry Ways | certain products, an established industry practice of nine-month delayed invoice collections from its retailer customers. The company immediately lost a |

huge number of its independent retailers and sought refuge by selling to a mass merchant to get more volume. Total sales volume remained flat during this period, but gross margin dropped from 22 percent to 8 percent on about $8 million of the company's total $40 million annual revenue. And the mass merchant demanded many more support services than the independent retail dealers. You can just imagine how much red ink resulted. How did this come to my attention? Simply by asking for a trailing twelve months (T12M) chart of sales – which was perfectly flat for four years. Now, dead flat for four years is almost impossible. So when asked about four-year flat sales, the story of the move to the mass merchant came tumbling out. Aha! The T12M chart again proves its value as a tool.

CEO Tool
T12M Chart

Another big compensation tool is to be sure your incentive comp pays off in sync with results being produced. Too many companies have annual bonuses, most employees and managers forget they even got the bonus within three months after receiving it. Incentives should be paid timely with performance. Monthly is great, weekly would be even better, and quarterly is okay. But annual incentives don't work most of the time, in my opinion.

Incentives Synched To Results

By now, this has probably gotten your attention big-time: do away with my own annual bonus? Kraig, are you nuts? It's just that incentives work best if they are frequent and timely. Once you accept this concept, it will then be okay to reinstate your annual bonus, only for very senior executives and only for three-year or five-year performances. This keeps us from sacrificing the future for current results, keeps us focused on the big picture. But nobody below the top four or five people should have this long-term bonus paid annually. Everyone else should be on a monthly or more frequent incentive.

Ban the Annual Bonus!

2. Recognition. As managers, we typically don't do a good job of providing recognition for the results our people create. Yet, nothing has more impact on great performance than recognition. It pays off at least 1000:1 over compensation. *Tell* folks they did a good job when they do, and they'll do a good job again and again. *Pay* folks for doing a good job, and they usually just want more money.

Recognition Pays 1000:1 Over Compensation

We're generally not good recognizers because most CEOs and many managers are moody. We CEOs and managers tend to be moody individuals because we spend 100 percent of our time on the job. All really good managers do this in their own ways. We drive ourselves crazy with responsibility. We're Atlases with the world on our shoulders. We have to make payroll, we have to get that new loan, we have to get results, we have to do this and we have to do that. And guess what? The constant pressure from all these "have to's" shows up in our interactions with others. Unfortunately, our inconsistency in mood also usually keeps us from being good recognizers. We're often too moody to stop and do the recognition at the moment the good performance is observed, which is when the praise is deserved and has the most mutual benefit. Miss the moment for praise, and it becomes makeshift and nearly ineffective later when we get to it.

So you think this moodiness concept is far-fetched? Let me assure you it is real beyond belief. My speaking career over the past 20 years has placed me in front of about 30,000 CEOs in audiences. Everything I've encountered both in speaking interactively with them and in consulting with them manifests this moodiness.

Here's a real-life example: One of my clients asked me to facilitate his strategic planning meeting. We went off to a quiet but very nice site, met as a group, did our S-W-O-T (strengths-weaknesses-opportunities-threats) analysis, our P-I-C-Ks (problems-issues-concerns-keys to success) exercise from chapter four, and identified all the issues facing the company. One issue that came out somewhat accidentally was that the CEO was moody. No, not just a little moody like most CEOs. He would pretty routinely come into the office and folks felt they couldn't let him get near employees, much less customers. What a challenge this was for me as strategic facilitator to face this issue within the first three hours of the meeting. You see, he wasn't just moody, he also didn't know he was moody. Not uncommon among strong leaders: we just can't see our own management backswing.

Together as a group, we came up with an elegant solution at this strategic meeting: any day this CEO came into the business in a bad mood, the first person seeing him would whisper "dark day" in his ear. This was the codeword for him to turn on his heels, go into his office, and not come out till he got positive or it was time to go home. Yes, it really worked! This company took off growing and making money after this episode. How proud we are of this CEO for being willing to deal with this, and his crew for handling it so well. Can't we all grow from hearing of such an experience?

Yes indeed, we CEOs and managers are moody, and it occurs to me that the moodiness may just be the reason we seldom see how powerful recognition is. Our introverted, sometimes selfish, down-moods fly right in the face of the more extroverted pats-on-the-backs to others for getting results. So let's set up recognition systems to generate that 1000:1 payoff from recognition we wouldn't otherwise be able to realize. Let's get those around us to implement the recognition system and use the tools.

> Recognition Systems to Overcome Moodiness

Incidentally, a good compensation system does not take care of recognition. You need both compensation and recognition; patting people on the back and saying "thank you, ya done good!" yields far greater returns than compensation alone ever will. You can't overestimate the importance of recognition for results, or if you prefer, praise for performance. To get repetitive results, recognition requires consistency. It's an ongoing cycle of perform → praise → perform → praise → perform.

Let's return to GAC printing for an example. Five years straight-up profitable growth, more than four times the industry, was possible only because it was directly tied to alignment of each key element: individual sales targets (*meaningful goals*), 100 percent commission (*compensation,* where you get what you earn) and regular weekly, monthly, and quarterly cheering of individual successes (*recognition*). That recognition took the form of a weekly call to each sales manager and to that week's sales stars by the CEO. Monthly the entire sales organization saw the monthly superstars letter celebrating success by recognizing, by name, those who made it happen. The quarterly recognition took the form of salespeople who achieved their sales targets receiving publicly a handsome award plaque to display at home or in their offices. Flash back for a moment to the Q1=$1.00 symbolism tool in chapter two.

3. Fun. Having fun really sets the great companies apart from all the rest by keeping the great people there, enjoying getting results.

| Appoint a CFO: Chief "Fun" Officer! |

Yet most companies don't have much fun. To make fun an integral part of your workplace, try appointing a "CFO" (chief fun officer). This probably shouldn't be the same person as your chief financial officer

| Bob Nelson's "1001 Ideas" |

unless you want creativity in your accounting! To get some fun ideas, read best-selling business author Bob Nelson's first two books, *1001 Ways to Reward Employees* and *1001 Ways to Energize Employees*.

Or try a few of these fun tools: One involved an unusual Employee-of-the-Month (EOM) program at Courtesy Coffee Company where we took off in search of the EOM with awards, cake,

| Employee of The Month *Can* Work! |

and camera in tow. Each month the senior staff toured different departments asking, "is this where the EOM lives? Come on along with us to find our EOM!" Each month the EOM received a $100 gift certificate, the best parking spot (even better than customers but by only one slot), direct recognition that day in person and on the public announcement system, a photo plaque at every employee entrance and a personal award plaque. If customers or suppliers were in the building, they too would be encouraged to participate in finding and celebrating the EOM.

Another recognition tool involved celebrating the achievement of our quarterly goal with the officers serving pizzas to all 1,200 employees at Snapper on all three shifts while wearing white aprons

| Go Big & Crazy with Pizza |

and tall chef's hats emblazoned with the red *SNAPPER*® logo. The local Pizza-Hut® manager in McDonough, Georgia, population 3,500 at the time, thought he had died and gone to heaven with over 400 super-extra-large pizzas delivered to Snapper that one day.   He was later promoted to Executive VP at Pizza-Hut headquarters based on that one order. Of course I'm kidding about his promotion, but can't you see and feel and even taste the fun in that kind of celebration?

Here are a few more fun tools and ideas: Try handing out $2.00 bills whenever you see someone doing a good job; get all senior managers to do the same. Serve lunch to everyone when a respected employee retires. Use tracking tools from chapter three to know you're actually doing recognition. Remember WGMGD: What Gets Measured Gets Done? Tracking really works. Get others to help in the fun stuff, especially if you're the moody type or an introvert – many of us CEOs and managers are both. Don't forget that the definition of having fun always includes making a profit. It's hard to celebrate one group's win, or hand out awards and bonuses, or have fun, if the overall company doesn't make a profit. Make profit a "condition precedent" to all celebrations.

4. Personal growth. More and more, opportunities for personal and professional growth play a key role in getting and keeping good people. One easy way to attend to people's personal growth is to give them some good business books and perhaps pen a personal note on the title page. Pick out the books you want them to read. Use the *Business Week*® business best-seller list as a source; it's on their web site at businessweek.com. Personally give the books to your employees. This sends a powerful message that you really care about them, both professionally and as people. Today, many of my very best performing clients have extensive training and/or learning programs. One has both performance objectives (POs) and learning objectives (LOs) for every employee. Take a look at the Executive Development Planner (EDP) in the Summary chapter for ideas on learning objectives for yourself and those around you. Another of my clients has repetitive and post-graduate refresher courses in every aspect of their operations. We now know that you can't train once and expect it to take. Training and learning are like communication; they must be repetitive and late-breaking/updating as our business world evolves.

5. **Challenge.** People need challenges. When people retire and have no challenges, they die. Literally. As a frequent speaker to the American Society of Pension Actuaries, my talks often include the statistic that 50 percent of men who retire at age 65 die within about

three years, for women longer. This is improving every year, but those are scary statistics. Why do so many die? It's almost certainly lack of challenge. As we grow older, we need to keep our brains agile and challenged, much as we do our bodies. My dad is my hero in this respect. At this writing he's 84 years young and still active as a stockbroker five days a week. He doesn't need to work, except to stay alive! It's all about challenge, isn't it? Satchel Paige, the great baseball player captured it most eloquently: "People don't quit playing because they get old, they get old because they quit playing."

The same is true in the workplace. When people have no challenges they die on the job, meaning slow down to a crawl.

| Challenge with BAG, QPM, QBR |

You've experienced the ones who retire without ever telling you; they do keep showing up, but they slow down, do less work, yet keep on collecting the same paycheck. The best way to keep a happy, highly motivated workforce is to create ongoing challenges for yourself and

CEO Tool
QPM

the people around you by jointly developing big audacious goals, doing quarterly priorities management, or quarterly business reviews. For those that really want to slow down some, you can accommodate them by converting them to part-time workers. Many people want to work, but only two or three days a week. Find ways to do just that with them.

| Harley Hot Button |

Remember the fun challenge arranged with Ken Clark in chapter one involving the Steinway piano? Find ways to apply this Harley Hot Button tool as a challenge to key players on your team.

6. Convenience. Make it convenient for people to work for you. Your people will celebrate privately if you create more personal time for them. You're probably saying, almost out loud, "Kraig, are you crazy? I need them to work *harder*, not *less*!" Yes, and most will work harder for you and have more personal time if you cut their

| Turn Commute into Productive Time |

commute time. Moreover, they'll cheer out loud if they know you not only did it but also are continuing to try to do it more. Try changing your hours to 7 a.m. to 4 p.m. or 6 a.m. to 3 p.m. and be willing to manage the exceptions for those that have to drop kids off and the like. Try instituting telecommuting. We as a nation have not delivered on that telecommuting promise (viz. *Wall Street Journal* article headlined "Telecommuters' Lament", October 31, 2000), and it's simply because we didn't even try to do it. Commit your company to averaging two days a week overall for telecommuting and you'll keep more, if not all, of your people. They'll applaud you for translating just a little of their traffic time into productive and/or personal time. Another tool is to give your managers an audio library to learn more about management or their hobbies as they commute. TEC (The Executive Committee) sometimes has a free tape with no strings attached at their www.TEConline.com website. TEC is an organization whose goal is to enhance the business and personal lives of CEOs and senior officers of companies all around the world.

Another longer-term approach is to hire people who live close to your place of business or consider moving your business to where it is more convenient for most of your great employees. Look for ways to make it easier for people to work for you. In an ongoing climate of low unemployment, people will leave companies over this issue alone.

7. Communication. We covered this topic extensively in chapter two, but here are a couple of tools that specifically help with communication and celebrating. When we consultants go into companies and ask your employees, "what don't you get enough of?" we only get two answers. Your people will say they don't get enough *communication* or enough *recognition*. Please grab some communication tools from chapter two and some recognition tools from this chapter for your people.

8. Security. People need to feel secure in their jobs: physically secure in their persons, intellectually secure with the application of their ideas, mentally secure in being open and honest, and spiritually secure in their personal beliefs. How are you providing for these needs in your company?

Some thought-starters in making people feel more secure:

- Recognition leads to feelings of job security; install recognition now.

- Consideration about parking lot safety and a company culture of trust both build physical security feelings; get a security audit.

- A culture of listening and not criticizing generates good emotions for employee openness; read a "listening" book.

- Practicing use of employee ideas with attribution whenever possible does wonders for intellectual safety.

- A well-centered business values statement that is lived each day helps with spiritual security; cite actual values-supporting anecdotes often.

Of course this attention to security shouldn't be confused with, or lead toward, complacency or lack of challenge. That's a very old definition of security. We're not talking about labor-leader Samuel Gompers' job security here. His labor union initiatives might have been appropriate in the 1920s and 30s but could stand a little 21st century update.

You might be asking at this point, how does security tie into celebration? Well, one plausible definition of celebration is

| Practice Happiness Frequently |

"happiness practiced as frequently as possible," and a sense of security in everything we do sure feels like happiness. Since security is at the bottom of behavioral scientist Maslow's needs hierarchy, people cannot rise to higher levels which include happiness and self-actualization until after security becomes a given. Another way of saying that is, people will perform at much higher levels once their basic needs are met, when basic needs stop being distractions. Here's a nifty example from my insurance company experience: we had a part-time assistant who would do things for employees like take their cars for smog inspections, pick up their laundry, and so on. This simply eliminated many of life's daily distractions and enabled employees to perform at higher levels.

Celebrating Milestones

Too many companies approach celebration as an all-or-nothing deal. They wait until they achieve the year-end numbers, the big audacious goal or some other overall goal that has a long timeframe before breaking out the balloons and banners. That's probably not how reward and recognition are best used. If we wait to reach the finish line before acknowledging and rewarding the efforts of our people, we lose a lot of them along the way. Think of running the *Iron Man Triathlon*. Certainly it's one of the ultimate physical challenges, but mostly it's a mental and even spiritual game. The successful finishers have prepared mentally, including rewarding themselves and re-assuring themselves as they progress through the 14-hours or so of swim, bike and run. Those focusing on the pain perish. Instead center on the celebration to come at the end. This creates a continuing aspiration to win. We envision ourselves crossing the finish line. It's this that keeps us going despite all odds.

It's important to celebrate the milestones on the road to success, yet people don't often do this for themselves in their jobs. This is the very definition of tracking we outlined in chapter three. It's our job as managers and leaders to cheerlead, thank, and praise for performance all along the way. Plus when the big goals are broken down into smaller pieces, they become a lot easier to achieve. So how do you do this "along the way" recognition and encouragement? You already have many tools for this from earlier chapters. Best among these are the CEO's monthly letter from chapter two, the monthly superstars letter from chapter three, the consummate communication tool of walking your four corners from chapter two, and even chapter three's trailing 12-months

> Celebrate
> As You Go

> W4C Tells
> Them You're
> Listening

charts and trailing 52-weeks charts posted publicly, or accompanied by a short note of encouragement from you.

A remarkable and impressive best-selling book by Gary Markle, *Catalytic Coaching: The End of the Performance Review,* reinforces the concept of recognition along the way. Gary shows us how to coach and bring along the performance of people without the hated and much-maligned annual review. His point is simply that celebrating or criticizing only at the end just doesn't work. It's along-the-way that matters the most. Thanks, Gary, for helping us highlight the powerful tool of repetitive communication and even more powerful tool of repetitive recognition.

Ban the Annual Review

Recognition Buck$

Recognition doesn't just come from the top down, although it's far more effective when it starts and is genuinely supported at the top. In the best performing companies, recognition is a way of life, going up, down, sideways and any other which-way it wants to go. One of the best tools for creating a culture of celebration is *recognition buck$.* These provide a fun way for employees at all levels of the organization to recognize and reward each other for outstanding performance on the job. Get all your employees together in a room, or football stadium if need be, and hand out recognition buck$ forms which you've custom-designed for your company. Ask them to do what best-selling author Ken Blanchard taught us over a decade ago, namely, "go out there and catch someone doing something right!" This turns every person in your company into a recognizer of good performance. You may need to fan the embers at first to encourage people to do this, but it will quickly become a wildfire of positive praise for performance.

Recognition Buck$

CEO Tool
Buck$

How about an example from GIR, the insurance underwriting firm, in which Margie Hicks as HR director brought this to me and asked if we could implement it? "You bet, fantastic!" was my immediate reply. Here's a form (Buck$ on the CD) that's very similar to the one we used at GIR. You can start using this in your company today to multiply your perform → praise → perform cycle.

Name of Your Company, Inc.
Recognition Buck$©

Customers & Profits

=

Recognition & Rewards

Issued To: _____

From: _____

Date: _____

For / Notes: _____

_____

_____

_____

_____

_____

_____

Use creativity to make it fun. For example, one company superimposes the CEO's face on a one-dollar bill while another encourages employees to actually draw a little face or scene in the center. Give employees a

Try Specific Recognition

designated amount of recognition buck forms and challenge them to catch people doing things right for a customer or another employee. That's a further adaptation of what Ken Blanchard taught us in his landmark book, *The One-Minute Manager*. Whenever employees give out recognition buck$, ask them to identify on the form who the buck is from, who is receiving it and why. Coach them to be specific on the why. "Frank went out of his way to serve the customer" is probably shy of the mark. "Frank spent hours helping Susan Rockrise from Esprit® solve a critical production problem" specifies the behavior that should be recognized. Recognition and reward leads to repeated instances of customer care.

Give the "recognizee" the original filled-in recognition buck and give a copy to HR, who then tracks the giving and receiving of all

| Add Fun To Recognition |

recognition bucks. Once a quarter, reward the employee who gives the most and maybe the one who receives the most. Make it a public recognition ceremony and make a big deal of it. Present the top recognizee each quarter with an all-expense-paid weekend with spouse to a special getaway, or maybe a gift certificate for $100 to Nordstrom®. Be sure to change this reward

| Keep Change a Constant! |

on a regular basis to keep it fresh and exciting so as not to set up feelings of entitlement. You can keep any tool we've talked about going a long time simply by changing it a bit as you go along, making it fresh and fun. In other words, *keep change a constant* in your company.

The Executive Committee takes a slightly different tack. They assign a value of one dollar to each TEC Buck. When employees earn enough TEC Bucks, they can redeem them for company merchandise such as jackets, shirts, travel bags and other items with the company logo. That way, everybody wins, not just the one or two employees who gave or got the most recognition buck$. It also automates the time and expense involved in tracking the distribution of recognition buck$. This tracking assures your recognition program is working. And it assures broadband employee recognition, resulting in repeated good performance.

Having mentioned TEC several times, perhaps the ultimate tool for presidents is membership. It's an international organization for CEOs, company presidents, and other senior management people, and is without question the first and foremost forum for CEO growth and development. Each month each local TEC group member sits around the table with 14 other local, non-competitor CEOs for a full day to wrestle with the major challenges and opportunities facing each of us in our businesses. If you've never experienced the power of

| TEC is the Ultimate Feedback Tool |

getting objective, unbiased feedback from a dozen or so of your peers whose only agenda is helping you run your company more effectively, you don't know what you're missing. As a continuing TEC member for over 15 years, please accept my assurance that this is the ultimate feedback tool for CEOs and senior managers. Those folks sitting around that table can see your management backswing and help you

CEO Tool
TEConline

improve it. If you own or run a business or report to someone who does, you owe it to yourself to look into TEC or a similar organization like YPO, Focus Point, and others.

Recognition Ads and Posters

Many larger companies can afford to place newspaper display advertisements that cite their employees with a headline celebrating a company-wide success. In reality, this kind of ad serves not just one, but four purposes: it's a recognition ad, an employment ad, an image building ad and a sales ad. Wow! It not only recognizes your employees publicly, it also sends a positive message to employee prospects, your customers, and your community at large. If you include employee pictures in the ad, the effect of the recognition is hyperbolic. The downside

| Broadcast Your Recognition |

is that although these kinds of ads certainly provide meaningful recognition, they can also cost a pretty penny and perhaps attract headhunters to your people. This shouldn't be a huge concern if you're celebrating the eight employee needs discussed earlier, since your employees won't want to leave.

Here's a better and more cost-effective recognition tool that eliminates the headhunter factor. Go to the computer store and buy some page-layout software for under $100 that will allow you to import your employee list. Then design and format your own full-page ad. Two examples come to mind, one from an Atlanta Business Chronicle ad by Saint Joseph's Hospital of Atlanta and another from an executive-friend at Team Industries, Inc. near Milwaukee. Both use the same technique of recognizing all employees by name in the advertisement or poster with the following headlines, respectively:

> **The Board of Directors Congratulates the Staff at Saint Joseph's Hospital of Atlanta.**

> **TEAM INDUSTRIES**
> **AND**
> **MILLER BREWING COMPANY**
> **PARTNERS IN EXCELLENCE**

Print your ad on an 8.5" x 11" page and take it to Kinko's; they'll blow it up to poster size for under five dollars each. Ask them to print 10 posters for you. Slip into your company after everyone has gone home. Make sure no night owls are burning the midnight oil, but if they are, recognize them. Put your posters up around the walls. Just watch the faces of your people as they come in the next morning. How about taking this same approach with posters in your offices, plant, and warehouse recognizing your customers by name, meaning the individual names of your customers' people with whom you work. After all, customers, suppliers, owners and community need recognition too.

Create Your Own Public Recognition

Don't ever be afraid to toot your own horn. There's nothing like a well-written press release to bring some well-deserved attention to your people for a recent big achievement. Like the personal recognition ads, press releases accomplish several goals. They raise awareness of the company in the public arena, they recognize important milestones or achievements, and they send positive images to customers and employees as well as potential customers and employees. Best of all, they don't cost anything other than a bit of staff member time to write.

When GAC printing crossed $100 million in annual sales, we celebrated many ways, including press releases and other ways of attracting attention. We put a colorful hot-air balloon on the roof of GAC proclaiming that we had crossed that noble $100 million number. We learned that our arch-competitors in other parts of the country heard about it and were more than a little dismayed by our success. As you might imagine, we shed crocodile tears.

> **Press Releases Get Recognition**

The Oregonian newspaper came over, took color photos, and ran the story as their lead business feature. Everyone in Oregon knew of GAC's success. And we got even more business because of this phenomenal publicity. Here are several helpful tools for writing your own press releases to get your company recognized publicly:

Use an appropriate format. Most editors are notoriously finicky when it comes to receiving unsolicited materials. If your press release doesn't fit the correct format, they'll reject it out of hand. Try mimicking the format of the example above.

Make sure it's newsworthy. The press release must focus on something big, such as hitting $100 million in annual sales, celebrating a 100th anniversary, launching a remarkable new product, landing a huge new brand-name client or doing something noteworthy in the community.

Make it short and sweet. Editors receive hundreds of press releases a week and don't have time to read long-winded tomes about how great your company is. For best results, limit your press release to one page, two at the absolute most – double-spaced.

Lastly, get your news release to someone you know at those publications, someone you really want to have cover the story, someone who can call you or your PR firm to build the story.

The following page provides an example of the press release we used to get the news out to everyone:

GAC

Graphic Arts Center

Corporate Offices
2000 N.W. Wilson Street
Portland, Oregon 97209
503 224 7777
503 222 0735: Fax

FOR IMMEDIATE RELEASE
February 6, 1989
Contacts: Kraig W. Kramers, President and CEO
J. D. Droge, Vice President – Sales Administration

PORTLAND PRINTER TOPS $100 MILLION SALES

PORTLAND, OREGON – Graphic Arts Center (GAC) of Portland announced today sales topping $100 million for its fiscal year ended January 27, 1989. What's unique about this is that Graphic Arts Center has become the largest commercial printer in the West, drawing clients to Portland from all across the nation to print their full-color corporate annual reports, upscale catalogs and colorful brochures of all types.

What has been the attraction? "A reputation for superb color printing plus attracting the most talented and customer-conscious employees in the country," says Kraig Kramers, GAC President and Chief Executive Officer.

How did this local Portland printer, doing just $11 million in sales ten years ago, become a $100 million company and gain the reputation of being one of only a handful of top quality, high volume commercial printers in the U.S.? "We've always focused on filling the customers' needs with the best quality color printing available," Kramers continued.

"We also strongly believe in a full-service philosophy, a total package from sparkling color printing to computerized addressing and mailing of our clients' catalogs and annual reports," said Kramers. That attention to detail carries into all phases of GAC's business. Over seventy annual reports were printed at GAC during the year – many for Fortune 500 companies from Atlanta to New York to Los Angeles to Portland. Thousands of different brochures are printed each year for other clients based all over America.

"We've become somewhat of an attraction, bringing new visitors to Portland every day," Kramers went on. "Our clients come to Graphic Arts Center to see their printing being done, and stay over to enjoy shopping, dining and recreating in the beauty of the Northwest." What's next for GAC? "We aim to continue our aggressive growth, providing the best in printing to local companies and other clients from all over the country. It's good for customers, employees, suppliers and it's good for Portland."

# # #

Personal Notes to Thank and to Recognize

Here's an expanded version of the personal notes tool presented in chapter two. As CEOs and managers, we have an obligation to write *thank-you notes* to our people. Why? Not just because Emily Post or Mr. Manners said we should, but rather because it's the right thing to do. We, and our organization, succeed through the efforts of those who work for and with us. It's simple common courtesy to thank the people who make us successful, even though the pace today often keeps us from even saying thank you when we should.

> Personal "Thank You" Notes

Doesn't it also make good business sense? You bet! In our highly competitive employment markets, it's hard to find and keep good people. Few things have greater impact on employee morale and engender more loyalty than a sincere personal thank-you note from the boss. Mailed to the employee's home, it's a grabber. Tom Peters, author and management guru, prefers to think of "thank you" as the two most powerful words in the English language. He's believable and he's right.

As CEOs, we should also write *recognition notes*, not only with enlightened self-interest in mind but because our people have earned that recognition. You can't carry it off if it doesn't come from the heart, so make sure it feels real. Dig down to that genuine gratitude that shows up at Thanksgiving or Christmas or whenever it is for you, and then work to turn it into an everyday experience.

> Personal "Recognition" Notes

Let's differentiate slightly between thank-you notes and recognition notes. The concept is thank for effort, recognize for results. There are many variations on the CEO's or manager's personal note, and writing them can be your own individual tool for repetitive recognition, that is, praising performance along the way. My favorite is a personal, hand-written note sent directly to the employee's home. If you skip management levels

> Thank for Effort...

> ...Praise for Performance

when doing this, always check with the employee's supervisors first as they may have some current issue to take into account. Even better, invite that supervisor to co-sign the personal note.

Until you experience it yourself, you can't imagine the impact these notes have. People hang on to them for life. Personal notes don't take much time, but they do take some discipline to do

| Mark Calendar To Do Recognition |

regularly. Find a time and a system that work for you and stick with it, so that after a while personal notes become automatic. Here's a simple tool for implementation: you can just mark your calendar a certain time on a day each month to do personal recognition and thank-you notes. It may sound a bit crass to schedule recognition, but it's hard to get in the habit any other way.

And try varying your format. One time, send a formal typed letter; the next time pen a brief, handwritten note card. It can be as simple as the following handwritten note: *"Dear Belinda, Great job! With best regards, Kraig."* Both you and Belinda will know what it's about. Here's a cardinal rule with personal notes: if you hand write the note, be sure to hand write the envelope too. Otherwise, it looks like someone else did it for you and that might come across as not genuine. If the employee doesn't feel like it came from you personally and totally, the personal note produces the opposite of the desired effect. So also always address the envelope personally. Above all, be genuine and generous with your personal notes.

Focus On Winners

As business people, we get the best results by using the proper leverage, meaning we focus our efforts on those areas within the

| Focus On Your Biggest $-Makers |

company that yield the biggest return on investment of our time, energy and attention. One of the key leverage points in any company is supporting winners and spending time with them. These are the people who produce the best results day after day, month after month, year after year.

You know who these folks are. They're the ones who are the top five in sales each year. They're the production managers whose lines have the lowest percentage of rework year after year. This winner might be the accounts receivable clerk who consistently has the lowest days sales outstanding. Or the new account rep that regularly brings in the most and highest-margin accounts. These are the people that, no matter what the job or the challenge, find a way to get it done. They find a way to win because that's what motivates them.

The #1 rule about recognizing winners is that you can't do too much of it. Try to make sure that your superstars know how much you appreciate their good work. Send meaningful messages to everyone else in the company by recognizing only great performers. For example, write individual, private letters to your winners on a regular basis, reminding them of how well they're doing and how much you appreciate their extra efforts and especially their repetitive results. At the same time, send a monthly letter to the entire sales force, focusing your recognition in the letter on those same top performers – meaning those who are beating their own prior performance consistently. Management should always pit people against their own prior performance, never against others' performances. An individual T12M chart is ideal for this. Don't ever mention the mediocre or bottom performers in your organization publicly. They know who they are and they know why they aren't in your letters, notes or public pronouncements. They'll figure it out and get themselves into your communiques by raising their performance. Else you'll be getting them gone, hopefully. While we're talking about salespeople, it applies equally well to any functional group or the entire company.

> **Send Meaningful Messages Indirectly!**

> **Pit People Against Prior Performance**

CEO Tool
T12M Chart

Finally, provide plenty of public praise and regular recognition through award ceremonies, newsletters, posters on the wall, Emails to the entire company, and words of praise as you walk your four corners. The greatest gift you can give your people is your time and attention. Help your employees become winners and stay winners by

> **Multiple Recognition Methods**

giving them more of your time and attention, but do it ratably, meaning a bit more for winners, a good amount for top performers and maybe a bit less for all others.

Spending most of your time with winners sure doesn't mean totally ignoring everyone else. The laggards and losers also deserve some of your attention, but only up to a point. Well-timed words of encouragement from you can sometimes help struggling managers or salespeople keep at it until they get over the hump. Send a short note saying, "you sure have had a tough go of it for the past month or two, but we have every confidence you'll attain your goals. Let us know how to help you get there." This will often provide enough incentive to see that person through to success.

In cases of chronic under-performance, however, a more strongly worded letter is in order. For example, "noticed you haven't made the winner's circle for four months in a row. If this doesn't improve within the next two months, we will have to part company." Give the person the letter, give them a day to think about it, and then set up a meeting to discuss it. Employees that respond with a genuinely positive attitude and willingness to succeed deserve your fullest support. But those exhibiting below average attitude should be exited immediately. Cut them a check and get them gone. Of course, make sure you have previously practiced progressive discipline and documented the lack of performance as counseled by your legal and HR experts.

> Get Bad Attitudes Gone!

When it comes to people in business, there are only two attributes that matter much – *performance* and *attitude*. You can teach almost any skill, but it's really hard to teach attitude. Recall that inimitable Winston Churchill quote, "I'm always willing to learn but not always willing to be taught." If a person wants to learn better attitude, then Dale Carnegie's or Norman Vincent Peale's great books and seminars work spectacularly – and perhaps even Tony Robbins up to a point. All offer proven motivational programs.

Winners have both good attitude and great performance. Commit to spending more of your time with winners and watch them get even better. We're always overly tempted to help the losers and laggards. But if you spend an hour a week with a $10-million a year salesperson versus the same time with a $1-million a year salesperson and increase both by 20 percent, which one yields the bigger return on your time investment? Yup, go with the winners every time.

Awards, Awards, Awards – You Can't Over-do Them!

Most companies give out annual awards like "top sales person of the year" or "circle of excellence" and the like. That's good, but why reward only the top one or two people in your company? Why not make as many people winners as often and as reasonable for your situation? At GAC printing, for example, we made a big deal of our highly sought-after Quarterly Sales Awards for any salesperson who hit their numbers for the quarter. We also celebrated Sales Region of the Quarter from GAC's seven regions. Each quarter we celebrated our success with the officers thanking and personally presenting some form of memento, like logo caps, specially minted logo silver dollars awarded when we hit the $100-million mark in annual sales, and logo jackets. You should have seen the seven officers guiding garment-district clothing racks like the workers in New York City, wheeling them throughout the 386,000 square feet of GAC on all three shifts, fitting logo jackets to every individual employee.

> Go Overboard
> With Awards

Sure this helps create the *Power of We* discussed in depth in the initial chapter, but it also creates the greatest of memories for you, the CEO or manager who doesn't get recognized very often. They say it's lonely at the top, but having spent some time on the other end, Kathy Mattea sure says it well when she sings *Lonely at the Bottom Too*. And most of us have been "stuck in the middle where the money gets tight," at some time in our lives as country/western singer JoDee Messina so aptly offers in her top hit tune *I'm Alright*. Here's where we managers get our recognition: it's those experiences and memories created along the way and the feelings you'll remember when you presented those awards and $ rewards to your people. If you're looking for recognition from bosses, better give them this book, since most managers who rise fast get their rewards from recognizing others. Another way of saying it: it's better to give than to receive.

Also please remember that our reality is not that of those

Plug Into Others' Realities

we're recognizing, in most cases. By plugging into their realities as described above, we can more appropriately recognize and celebrate in ways meaningful to them.

Each year our printing press operators and other manufacturing people at GAC got together and voted for the *Best Salesperson to Work With* award. Likewise the salespeople would vote for the *Best Press Operator to Work With* award. Can you imagine how coveted these annual awards were? They were presented by Sales to Manufacturing and by Manufacturing to Sales each year in front of hundreds of people. What a great way to break down those walls that build up in every organization between

Have Lots Of Awards

operations and marketing/sales. You might consider doing such awards quarterly, giving the awards different titles. Then make the annual version the biggest of all. A business associate in Atlanta is CEO of a franchising/operating company that runs about 1,000 fast food restaurants and has grown to more than $1 billion in sales by pursuing results through motivation. They recognize as many of their top performers as possible. Here's a sampling of their awards:

AWARDS LIST:		
Double Eagle Award	Best Crew	Service Awards
Award of Excellence	Manager of the Year	Top Ten Award
Biggest Dollar Volume	Go-Getter Award	Gold Cup
Biggest $ Improvement	Silver Cup	Bronze Cup
Biggest % Improvement	Top Region in Profit	Most Improved
Million $ Sales Award	Top Sales Region	Top Profit Region
President's Club	Circle of Excellence	Winners Circle

When it comes to awards, don't forget the along-the-way concept discussed earlier. Rewarding along the way pays off in even greater results in the end.

Obviously, many companies don't have the size and structure to give out this many awards. The point is to look for creative ways to recognize and reward your people both along-the-way and at the end of the year. Make big deals out of these opportunities. Have a nice awards banquet. Get people to dress up. Work hard to make it a special, fun occasion. How can I ever forget the skit and that gigantic six-foot poster the folks at GAC gave me at our $Q2 = \$2.00$ Christmas party in that first year? People treasure awards and will talk about the banquet and skits long afterwards. I know I do!

CELEBRATE SUCCESS
TO
REPEAT SUCCESS

Top 10 Tools To Be a *Better Recognizer*

1. Pat people on the back as they make headway on a job. Example, "It's great to see your progress on that project."

2. Talk positively about actual achievements of the company -- daily. Example: "Our productivity sure is picking up lately."

3. Listen to people's problems. Example: "Would you share that with me?"

4. Give encouragement and compliment people whenever possible. Example: "You should try your idea about …"

5. Find ways of being helpful to those around you. Example: "I saw this article that may tie into what you're working on."

6. Tell people you believe they can do it, that you have faith in them. Example: "Looks like you'll set a new sales record this year. Keep on keepin' on!"

7. Generate hope; there's always light at the end of the tunnel. Example: "This storm will pass; they all do. We'll be better for the struggle."

8. Find ways to give good news to those around you. Example: "Did you hear the news about our profit growth?"

9. Get people to feel better, no matter how the interaction started. Example: "What can we do to make this work out better for everyone involved?"

10. Thank them for their effort, praise them for performance. Example: "Thanks for the hard work. And congratulations on winning that bid!"

Top 10 *Recognition / Celebration* Tools

1. Personal notes home. Send individual *thank-you* and/or *recognition* notes to your people's homes to maximize the repetition of positive results.

2. Celebrate successes. Report against key goals and regularly celebrate the ones you achieve. Your people will respond with repeated superior performance.

3. Recognition buck$. To extend recognition, have employees recognize each other for positive actions. As Ken Blanchard said in *The One-Minute Manager*, go out and catch someone doing something right. When you do, give them a Recognition Buck.

4. "Harley" hot button. Your key players won't buy it for themselves. Match something they really want or need – but can't or won't acquire for themselves – to achievement of a key goal.

5. W4C - Walk your four corners. Recognize and celebrate daily successes just by walking around and talking with people. Get the company's officers to shake hands and congratulate everyone on all three shifts. Get the CEO to go out and say "thank you" to someone every day.

6. Awards, awards, awards! Have monthly, quarterly and annual awards. You can't over-do this unless you're the type that can't give awards. If so, get someone near you who can. Celebration is vital to an organization.

7. Recognizer's top ten tools. Take another look at the top ten tools for being a better recognizer. If there is one thing you take away from this chapter, it's go do your own version of employee recognition. Without question it's the biggest tool of all.

8. Two good celebration books. Read *1001 Ways to Reward Employees* and *1001 Ways to Energize Employees* by Bob Nelson.

9. Silver dollars. As noted sales expert Chuck Reaves says, "give 'em something hard and shiny!" People like hardware, so give them something that outlasts us mortals. Give them your version of silver dollars or a similar symbol.

10. YCDBSOYB. Regularly inject fun into your business to keep it fresh and interesting. YCDBSOYB? You can't do business sitting on your butt.

Summary – Get Started, One Tool at a Time

What's the best way to eat this elephant-sized tool kit? Certainly it's one bite at a time, one tool at a time. Here are some chewable chunks for making the process quicker, more palatable and more successful in your business or group.

> Implement
> One Bite
> At a Time

Start by selecting one or two, maybe three tools to use this month. Give yourself some time to practice and get comfortable with each tool and to see results. Involve your people with the implementation, wherever possible. Many tools can be delegated to others for implementation. An example is the Company Calendar (CoCal) from chapter six. Once two or three tools have become a regular part of your routine, crack open the book and choose a couple more. Repeat this process every month or so over the course of a year. Please be sure to calendar a date well in advance when you will implement the next tool or two. This will enable implementation in the face of day-to-day distractions. When you take a look back in six months or so, you'll be amazed at what you have accomplished and how your profits have grown.

Here's another approach: select a dozen tools up front, set up a calendar to implement a few tools each month and track yourself as you go along. Decide and mark the tools you want to implement, using a three-way selection criterion: the tools you will implement yourself mark M for Me, those you'll ask others to implement mark D for Delegate, and then spend time brainstorming with your management team those tools for Team (T) implementation. You'll see it's a bit like the industrial

> M = Me. I'll do.
> D = Delegate it.
> T = Team does it.

> Implement
> Via
> Division

225

revolution with division of labor to get the right people to implement the right tools. Try not to rush the process or get ahead of the schedule you've set for yourself, especially if the early returns aren't exactly as expected – either better or slower than anticipated.

Whatever approach you take to implement the tools, you'll find that – just like eating elephants – it's a lot easier to digest when you take it one tool at a time.

Why not get your management team to read this book for a thorough understanding of the tools before engaging them in the implementation? That way, it will be outside expertise bringing them the tools rather than you imposing the tools upon them. Often, this is a much better approach for most people – meaning, employees are much more accepting of us outside quote-unquote experts. There's no good reason why they're more accepting, since we consultants are no smarter than anyone else, in reality.

The tools most highly recommended for initial implementation are listed on the next several pages. These lists suggest tools that have proven immediately successful for most managers.

Please don't let me give you the wrong impression: there are over 100 powerful tools in this book and we've highlighted just a few of them here. The exactly right tool for you in your current situation, or to serve your current need, might not be one of these top 15 or 20 recommendations. So use the ensuing discussion and the checklists only as a guide. Why not go back to the specific chapter containing tools that match your current exact needs?

We've found the very best initial approach is to use tools that have worked again and again for CEOs and managers. Over the past ten years, these *CEO Tools* for exceptional managers have been presented to thousands of CEOs, executives, managers and MBA students in seminars and workshops. Recently, we took a poll that produced the overall top ten tools, ranked in priority order by about 10,000 senior executives:

Top Ten Most Effective CEO/Executive Tools

As picked by over 10,000 CEOs and managers of mid-sized companies

1. **Key customer-impacting jobs.** Find the key jobs affecting customers and put the right people in those jobs. Align their compensation, see to their recognition and really support them.

2. **What gets measured gets done.** WGMGD – three quick steps for profit growth now! Use W4C (walk your four corners) to communicate WGMGD.

3. **Big audacious goals.** Results happen by reaching higher, not just by setting logical goals.

4. **CEO's or manager's monthly letter.** Get your message to everyone, building trust, teamwork and results.

5. **One-page business plan with UBP.** Get your *unique business proposition* right, publish it in your one-page business plan and give it to all employees. Work to get their full understanding and focus their efforts on its achievement.

6. **12-month company calendar.** Show future events to *all* employees, creating coordinated teamwork. The results will astonish you!

7. **Trailing 12-month charts.** Track the sum of the 12 prior months, charted for three years by month. Chart sales, gross margin percent and the things that *cause sales to happen* (this early warning system allows you to take action long before an actual decline in sales).

8. **Regular recognition.** Praise people for performance on a regular, scheduled basis. It pays off 1000:1 over incentive compensation; you need both for best results. Use the W4C tool here as well to accomplish recognition.

9. **Quarterly priorities sharing.** This is the QPM (quarterly priorities manager system). Enables managers to share individual goals and help each other achieve them.

10. **One-to-one with direct reports.** Prescheduled, individual, short, uninterrupted weekly personal meetings will keep your team on top by building relationship and communication.

Fast-track Ways to Implement and Use Tools

You'll find some interesting, easily used aids to implement and apply the tools on the CD/Desktop Browser. Bring the browser up on your screen and click on "About the Book and Browser" and then on "Tour of Tools." Four different e-learning options are available: Streaming Media on the web (2-1/2 hour audio with PowerPoint®), Short Audio on the web (18 minutes), a PowerPoint version you can browse through at your own pace, and a Quick Reference Card in PowerPoint which you can print out in color or black-and-white.

Perhaps a few other suggestions on getting the tools to work in your organization will trigger your best approach. (1) Ask your board of directors or advisors to help, especially if they're involved in coaching roles with your managers. (2) Hire a consultant on a short-term basis to help with getting the tools installed. For example, many consultants can get the right key indicators installed quickly so you'll have the right trailing twelve months (T12M) charts. (3) Brainstorm with your team the *Tool of the Month* to implement. (4) Perhaps implement the company calendar (CoCal) first, showing right on the calendar which tools will be implemented and when over the coming 12 months. (5) Engage your Admin assistant in a planning session to select tools you will implement together over the next six months. (6) Get each of your senior managers to be champion of a different tool or two to expedite implementation of many tools at once. Pre-agree on dates the tools will be up-and-running as well as when they'll become finalized and ongoing in every respect.

Consider yet another proven approach: try the top-ten tool kit that's worked best for me in *every* situation. Once again, the tools are listed in priority order. These were implemented in my CEO role in eight businesses and again as consultant with hundreds of client companies. Here are the tools that would be tried immediately no matter what situation faced me in any industry and under any circumstances:

228

Kraig's Own Top 10 Tools for *Any* Business

1. **WGMGD.** Apply the principles of *What Gets Measured Gets Done*. Set an Overall Goal, then jointly set Big Audacious Goals. Work on communicating both while building trust, and finally track and feed back results. Stand back and watch your profits skyrocket.

2. **Serve your customers TOMA.** Top of Mind Awareness (TOMA) is a marketing technique, but use it to *serve* your customers and magic happens! Give your clients and customers free product and service and watch them buy *even more* from you.

3. **Key customer-impacting jobs.** Find the key jobs affecting customers and put the right people in those jobs. Align their compensation, see to their recognition and *really* support them.

4. **Trailing 12-month charts.** Track the sum of the 12 prior months, charted for three years by month. Chart sales, gross margin percent and the things that *cause sales to happen* (this early warning system allows you to take action long before an actual decline in sales).

5. **Set an electrifying strategy.** Use "What if?" and "Right Growth Rate" plus the price-volume-mix model to nail your strategy. You'll just know when it's right! Only then undertake changes in structure and process to effect growth. Get your people *excited* with the strategy!

6. **One-page business plan with UBP.** Get your unique business proposition right, publish it in your one-page business plan and give it to all employees. Then get their understanding and focus their efforts on its achievement.

7. **QPM.** The quarterly priorities manager (QPM) is your tool for self-accountability of your key people and direct reports. Help them align their five priorities with the company's goals and then actively support their efforts during the quarter to achieve them. You'll hit a home run!

8. **Walk your four corners (and listen).** Re-plug yourself into what's going on around you by walking your four corners. Spend 20 minutes each day walking and talking to your employees. Ask what they see that you don't, how to do things better, how to do better for the customer. They see stuff you don't! Try this "W4C" technique with customers and suppliers as well.

9. **Values, vision and passion.** Most executives have communicated their vision with passion. But most have not yet aligned the company's *business values* with their people. This is a must for ongoing, big-time success.

10. **Top five measures: daily + weekly + monthly.** Know the most meaningful measures in your business and track them religiously. Include monthly sales and profit re-forecasting plus daily cash report with weekly eight-week re-forecast. Change your Top 5 Measures periodically.

It was a great surprise to learn that only five tools made both of the lists just offered above. There are easily enough tools on the two lists to keep you busy for six months. So if nothing else in the book reaches out and grabs you, start with a few from one or both of these lists and take it from there.

Here's a pragmatic way to implement the tools: apply the five power-tools that appeared on both previous lists right away. Then try the other twelve tools one each month over the next twelve months. Use the delegation approach spelled out earlier and the enclosed CD/Desktop helper for a running jump in your situation. The following top five power-tools may be the very best way to start:

Top Five *First-Choice* Power Tools
As Practiced by Thousands of Managers

1. **Key customer-impacting jobs.** Find the key jobs affecting customers and put the right people in those jobs. Define "superb performance" for the customer. Give them tools, training, incentive compensation, and recognition. Genuinely support them!

2. **WGMGD.** Apply the principles of *What Gets Measured Gets Done*. Set an Overall Goal, then jointly set Big Audacious Goals. Work on communicating both while building trust, and finally track and feed back results. Stand back and watch your profits skyrocket!

3. **One-page business plan with UBP.** Get your *unique business proposition* right, publish it in your one-page business plan and give it to all employees. Then get their understanding and focus their efforts on its achievement.

4. **Trailing 12-month charts.** Track the sum of the 12 prior months, charted for three years by month. Chart sales, gross margin percent and the things that *cause sales to happen* (this early warning system allows you to take action long before an actual decline in sales).

5. **Quarterly priorities sharing.** This is the QPM (quarterly priorities manager system) using the format shown in chapter 3. Encourage managers to share their own individual goals and then help each other achieve them. Kick it forward each quarter.

For convenience, here's a combined list of power tools with recommendations for delegation and a key to which are CD-ready for your use over the next 12 months:

The Top Fifteen Power Tools
Quick Guide to Implementation

	Tool	Delegation	CD Tool
1.	Key Customer-Impacting Jobs = KCJ	Me and Team*	No
2.	What Gets Measured = WGMGD	Me and Team*	No
3.	1-Page Business Plan = 1-PgBP & UBP	Me and Team*	Yes
4.	Trailing 12-Mo Charts = T12M	Delegate*	Yes
5.	Quarterly Priorities Manager = QPM	Me and Team*	Yes
6.	Big Audacious Goals = BAG	Me and Team*	No
7.	Top of Mind Awareness = TOMA	Me or Delegate	No
8.	Regular Recognition = Buck$	Me and Delegate*	Yes
9.	CEO/Mgr Monthly Letter = CML	Me	Yes
10.	Walk Your Four Corners = W4C	Me and Delegate*	No
11.	One-to-One with Direct Reports	Me	No
12.	Electrifying Strategies = SWOT/PICKs	Me and Team*	No
13.	12-Mo Company Calendar = CoCal	Delegate	Yes
14.	Values + Vision + Passion	Me	No
15.	Top Five Measures = T5M	Me and Delegate	Yes

Key: M = Me, I'll do it!
　　　D = Delegate to one person (with full agreement) to get it done.*
　　　T = Team, meaning the team agrees to get it done together.*
　　　* = I will still take the leading oar to assure implementation.

Dedicate Yourself to Growth

Company growth is today accepted as the primary attribute of business success after the ever-present earnings per share. In fact, in many instances, we now see Wall Street downgrading stocks just because the company has slow growth even though its earnings are fine. Growth of an individual business need not be hampered by the industry in most cases, if the company has a good strategy. After all, when someone says, "our industry grows at eight percent per year," they really are saying that the industry's average growth is eight percent annually. That seldom keeps the industry leaders from growing at twice that rate and often three or more times the industry average.

Grow Your Business Faster

Many of my clients continue to grow way in excess of their industries today. And while at Snapper, Graphic Arts Center, Courtesy Coffee, National Airmotive Corp., Guarantee Insurance Resources, and Corporate Partners, we significantly outgrew our industries routinely. The chapters in this book reveal most of our growth secrets. The significance of double-digit growth rates, especially when they're 20 percent and higher, is twofold: first, we're creating wealth much faster than our industry, assuming we're not overly sacrificing current profitability just for volume. And secondly, rapid growth indicates the management group is growing, fast, else it's failing to stay abreast of the business pace and we'll see that pretty quickly. Think of it this way: if the business grows at 20 percent per year, it's doubling every four years, and we managers must grow at that rate just to keep up. How are you doubling your management and leadership capabilities every four years? How will you grow at a rate so as to stay ahead of competitive CEOs and managers who are growing themselves that fast? Many answers to these questions are in this book in the form of learning tools like T12M charts, Xyte.com's InSight, TEC, and the strategy and planning tools in chapter four.

Grow Yourself or Flatten Out

CEO Tool

Xyte

How about a tool to provide overall guidance for your personal executive growth? It's called the Executive Development

Planner (EDP). Here's a worksheet to personalize your executive growth:

EXECUTIVE DEVELOPMENT PLANNER

EDP WORKSHEET for _____
Scale: 1 - 10: (10 = Absolutely Perfect; 5 = Average for This Job; 1 = The Pits).

ATTRIBUTES & ACTIONS		DEVELOPMENT IDEAS ==> PLAN	PRIORITY
Track Record of Success	☐	_____	_____
Ties Ribbon = Completes Tasks	☐	_____	_____
Results Driven = Likes Tasks	☐	_____	_____
Good Communicator	☐	_____	_____
Hard Worker	☐	_____	_____
High Energy	☐	_____	_____
Forthrightness	☐	_____	_____
Is Forthcoming	☐	_____	_____
Positive Outlook & Demeanor	☐	_____	_____
Acceptance of Authority	☐	_____	_____
Good Listener; Open to Ideas	☐	_____	_____
Organizes Self & Others	☐	_____	_____
Acts the Leader	☐	_____	_____
Looks the Leader	☐	_____	_____
Entrepreneurial	☐	_____	_____
Works Well with Others	☐	_____	_____
Promotes Teamwork	☐	_____	_____
Is a Cheerleader	☐	_____	_____
Good Teacher	☐	_____	_____
Considerate of Others	☐	_____	_____
Is a Tracker; Accountable	☐	_____	_____
Good Planner	☐	_____	_____
I-Q (Intelligence)	☐	_____	_____
I-Can (Confidence)	☐	_____	_____
I-Will (Commitment)	☐	_____	_____
Consistency	☐	_____	_____

MANAGEMENT KNOWLEDGE & SKILLS

Communication Skills	☐	_____	_____
Industry Knowledge	☐	_____	_____
In-Job Management Knowledge	☐	_____	_____
Marketing Skills	☐	_____	_____
Finance Skills	☐	_____	_____
Tracking Skills	☐	_____	_____
Planning Skills	☐	_____	_____
People Skills	☐	_____	_____
Good Judgment	☐	_____	_____
Introspection	☐	_____	_____
Professional Growth	☐	_____	_____
Success Expectation	☐	_____	_____
Customer Orientation	☐	_____	_____
Big Picture & Vision	☐	_____	_____

233

The EDP allows you to self-assess which areas to grow yourself as manager and leader. This tool encourages the involvement of mentors or bosses and the use of individual personality assessments in order to focus initially on your highest and greatest managerial growth area. It's a tool that can be used for years of continuing, exhilarating individual improvement. And once again, this tool is included in the CD/Desktop tool kit.

CEO Tool
EDP

How does it work? There's a detailed approach at the end of this chapter including an example of a filled-in EDP worksheet with improvement action steps under the *development ideas* → *plans* column. But you can start by simply scoring yourself on a 1 – 10 scale on each of the executive attributes/actions and management knowledge/skills shown in the table above. To the right of each attribute/action item and knowledge/skill item, jot down a bullet about how you'll grow in that area. Ideally, get a mentor, spouse or trusted peer/superior to score you as well, since most of us can't see our own management backswings. Finalize your scores and select the ways you'll grow in each key area. Again, many suggestions and ideas on ways to grow are at chapter-end and on the CD. Prioritize which areas to work on first, using A, B or C and go to work on the A items right now. Some items might not even rate a C currently and get no priority. Mark your calendar now to re-address your EDP in six months. At that time, re-score the items on the EDP list, re-prioritize them, and work on your new A-list again. Keep this up for a year or so and see the progress. You'll be amazed.

Use EDP
To Grow
Yourself!

Working with Multiple Tools

Quite a few of the tools work very well together. They comprise what you might call tool systems. An obvious combination is the unique business proposition – those 13 words that describe what's special about your business – and the 1-page business plan. Others complement each other as well, like the big audacious goal supported by the CEO/manager monthly letter, other communication tools and most of the celebration tools. Perhaps you can envision putting four charts on a single page utilizing the T12M chart for sales, 12MMA chart for gross margin percent, T12M chart for net income, and OpExp% chart. This might be very revealing for your business!

See if your management team will implement tool systems to assure maximum success in your situation. Try to understand each tool not only in its own context but also in the bigger application. Your personal success and that of your company or group will soar as you become more skilled in utilizing these tool systems.

The Job of the CEO and How to Get There

The primary job of managers and CEOs alike is to lead the setting of direction for the business. Our second fundamental task involves aligning and supporting everyone around us in achieving that direction. Sounds easy, right? In order to succeed, we need to understand that this really is our role: to lead the goal setting together with our people and then provide the necessary support to everyone in getting us there. In reality, the same holds true for any manager at any level. After all, that's what management is all about – directing the skills, talents and abilities of others to achieve desired results.

If you're using this tool kit to become a CEO someday, please answer a critical question: *are you sure you want to get there?* Believe it or not, a lot of people don't. And you can tell by their behavior that they don't want to be top dog. Because along with the acclaim and the perks of the job comes a tremendous amount of responsibility to employees, the company, owners/shareholders, customers, suppliers, your community and now, our Government more-and-more.

Paraphrasing President Abraham Lincoln, you can please some of these audiences all the time, all some of the time, but not all very much the time. The burden of responsibility can take a terrific toll on families, friends and personal lives – physically, mentally, emotionally and even spiritually. It's no surprise, therefore, that many people choose not to go there. It's a long, hard road with surprises at many a turn.

Plus, not everyone buys into the CEO's particular form of success. One time as a hired gun CEO, someone falsified a search firm offer and sent it to my boss, even though I was definitely not in the market for a different job. Another time, a recently fired employee called in a fake bomb threat to disrupt operations. And at one company, my wife received an anonymous call from a woman who alluded to having an affair with me. It was a total fabrication, and fortunately my marriage was strong enough that my wife took it for what it was – a crank call from a disgruntled troublemaker.

The point is that life at the top isn't all peaches and cream. In my opinion, you can't beat the view and some of the perks that come along with it. But at the same time, we shouldn't go after it with our eyes closed tight. We have to accept that there will be some interesting and personally challenging bumps along the way.

Whether you're aimed at becoming CEO, division president, managing partner or whatever, the real question is: are you sure you want to get there? If so, these tools will work to make your company, division or group and you successful in that endeavor.

If your answer is that you want to be the best manager you can be and make more money, then the tools in this tool kit will get you there as well. You might be surprised to learn that my personal vision did not consciously contemplate becoming a CEO at first, but then all of a sudden, there it was, dangled right in front of me.

If you do want to get to the top, take a few chances. Go where it's uncomfortable, try things you've never tried before. Let the right people know you want to be CEO someday. Read and be ever-learning about CEOs and how they do it. Take the tough jobs that will lead to being CEO. Get an MBA, even if it's after-hours and really tough to do. Get a few good mentors to help you with advice as you face those challenges that you might otherwise decide not to undertake. And always stick to your principles and a well-founded set of business values, no matter what.

But most of all *have fun!* Remember the allusions we've made to eating elephants? One of my fondest memories is when Steinway-winning Ken Clark and his top-performing San Francisco sales team had won Region-of-the-Year at GAC printing. They all came up to receive the award together. Right after presenting it, Ken turned around and donned an elephant nose, which fit over his own nose and mouth; his nine San Francisco cohorts also suddenly were wearing elephant noses, and in unison they presented me with their surprise *Elephant Award.* What a scene: ten fully-grown adults wearing elephant noses and kidding around! Yes, they had an extra elephant nose for me to wear, which of course I did. The assembled sales and officer group went wild. I have never laughed so hard or had so much fun even to this day. That's what business success is about, isn't it? It's making money and having fun along the way.

The seven-step management process and tools learned along the way from others sure made it happen for me. It's been a fun ride so far with even more to come. My greatest wish is that by sharing these tools with you, your management ride will become more fun and more profitable for you and for your business.

IMPLEMENT THE TOOLS ONE BITE AT A TIME

Top 10 *CD* Tools for CEOs/Managers

CEO Tool
QPM

1. Quarterly priorities management (QPM). Set five quarterly goals or priorities tied into your vision; get your direct reports to do the same. Quarterly helps link the day-to-day to the longer-term, big picture. Review weekly and communicate these among yourselves to broaden teamwork and success toward your vision.

CEO Tool
T12M Chart

2. Trailing 12-month charts (T12M). Chart the sum of the prior 12 months, monthly, for three years. Use T12M to track key indicators, especially gross margin. You'll be amazed how you'll see your business differently.

CEO Tool
1-Pg BP

3. 1-page business plan with UBP. Create a one-page plan to plug all employees into a common direction. Let it shout out your unique business proposition (UBP), goals, purpose and strategy. Give it to everyone to reinforce the message.

CEO Tool
Buck$

4. Regular recognition form. Use this format for your regular recognition program. Just put your company name/logo on this form, give it to all employees, and coach them to recognize each other for performing. Feed the effort by talking it up with everyone around you for about six weeks. Keep encouraging them and your company will produce more profit through everyone's well-deserved recognition.

CEO Tool
Cash

5. Track cash daily & re-forecast cash weekly. Cash crunches sneak up on most of us because we're not watching. Track your cash, don't grow too fast and stay well capitalized.

CEO Tool
BestFin

6. Best Financials reporting format (BestFin). This reporting format will zoom you up to 30,000 feet to take a look at what your business is doing "Big Picture." You will start seeing things that lead to your vision for the company or group. You'll communicate better with everyone about what's needed to achieve overall goals of the organization. This truly is the best tool for tracking financial performance.

7. 12-month company calendar (CoCal). Show all key future events to all employees, creating coordinated teamwork. The results will surprise you! Each quarter, delete the prior quarter and append it for next year so it's perpetual!

CoCal

8. Executive development planner (EDP). Assess yourself and then grow yourself with this exceptional personal growth tool. When your company doubles in four years, you must double your management and leadership skills too.

EDP

9. Right growth rate. Use Profit Mentor or similar software to determine the best and fastest growth rate without running out of cash. Grow slower and you'll get steam-rolled by those around you.

Right

10. Re-forecast sales, profit & cash-flow monthly. Not knowing you're about to grow too fast or suffer an ongoing string of monthly losses are excuses your banker will never understand. Try the RefCast Tool on the CD.

ReFcst

Executive Development Planner (EDP) Tool

Executive Development Planner

edp.xls

Background, Instructions and Use

This Executive Development Planner is a quick and comprehensive way for managers in a business to evaluate how to improve their knowledge, business skills, and effectiveness. Both the developing executive and his/her mentor should complete the form in an open and learning-oriented frame of mind. This is not a "review" of the executive, nor is it meant to be critical. Instead, it's meant to form a solid basis for an ongoing learning experience. This process should be used by the executive with mentors or a trusted superior. The executive should fully "buy into" both the concept and the need for continuing education and must have the desire to want to improve.

Here's how to use the Executive Development Planner:

1 - Both executive and mentor should take time to review this 5-page document. Any items on the form that the executive is not comfortable with should be excluded and not scored.

2 - Both should agree to use either the +/-/= format or the 1-10 scale. Both should agree to write comments to the right of scores.

3 - Then, both executive and mentor should complete the form, taking several days to think about their own scorings and written comments in the "Development Ideas" space provided.

4 - Get back together and compare scores and comments. Agree on the need for development in certain areas. Don't try to design a "total, comprehensive plan" yet. Do try to agree on about ten "Development Ideas" for the Plan. Complete a formal, joint, final version of page EDP 2 or 3. Include specific seminars, books, actions, and attach copies of AMA seminar writeups or other pertinent information.

5 - The executive should take 2 - 3 weeks to plan selected dates and times over the next 18 months to attend seminars, read books, view or listen to tapes, and take agreed-to actions.

6 - A date should be jointly calendared 6-months out to meet and compare notes on progress and re-direct the course if necessary.

7 - Consider a completely new iteration of this process in about 12 - 18 months.

Note: For some people it is much more comfortable to use the +/-/= format than the 1 - 10 scale, since the latter seems to feel like a "rating" rather than a directional indication of where learning should be undertaken. Either format works fine, but it is more important for executive and mentor to agree as fully as possible on the relative need for growth in a given area than to agree on the actual scoring system or score chosen.

If the 1 - 10 scale is used, 1 is no knowledge at all, 10 is absolutely perfect with no room for improvement, and 5 is average for managers in the same job with similar size companies.

Executive Development Planner - Example

EXAMPLE of Executive Development Worksheet
Scale: (+ Above Average; = Average; - Needs Improvement)

CEO Tool

ATTRIBUTES & ACTIONS		DEVELOPMENT IDEAS ===> PLAN
Track Record of Success	+	*Work on a selective sense of urgency.*
Ties Ribbon = Completes Tasks	=	*Ask: Are there any loose ends? AMA Time Management course.*
Results Driven = Likes Tasks	+	
Good Communicator	=	*AMA Writing course; begin writing monthly progress reports.*
Hard Worker	-	*Be mindful of how leaving "on time" impacts others.*
High Energy	=	*Consider a regular exercise program.*
Forthrightness	+	
Is Forthcoming	=	*Try leaving daily voicemail updates with key people.*
Positive Outlook & Demeanor	-	*Read Dale Carnegie book.*
Acceptance of Authority	+	*Try to learn to roll with the punches more.*
Good Listener; Open to Ideas	=	*Leave to later date to take Emory's "Listener" course.*
Organizes Self & Others	=	*Implement "Priorities Management System" in your group.*
Acts the Leader	=	*Take "Developing Executive Leadership" course.*
Looks the Leader	+	
Entrepreneurial	=	*Improve planning/tracking to grow here.*
Works Well with Others	=	*Work on "right brain" knowledge & style; creativity course.*
Promotes Teamwork	+	*Build more relationships with other departments.*
Is a Cheerleader	=	*Attend "CEO Toolkit" sometime soon.*
Good Teacher	-	*Learn in order to teach; do payables for 3 weeks.*
Considerate of Others	+	
Is a Tracker; Accountable	-	*Build analytical tools; set up formal tracking system.*
Good Planner	-	*Write the narrative for '96 Budget.*
I-Q (Intelligence)	+	
I-Can (Confidence)	+	
I-Will (Commitment)	+	
Consistency	+	*Very consistent in all the above areas.*

MANAGEMENT KNOWLEDGE		
Communication Skills	=	*Toastmasters; make presentations at employee meetings.*
Industry Knowledge	+	
In-Job Management Knowledge	+	*Learn Lotus version 4.0 in Windows.*
Marketing Skills	=	*AMA marketing seminar.*
Finance Skills	=	*AMA financial analysis seminar.*
Tracking Skills	-	*Set up departmental tracking system; see "CEO Toolkit".*
Planning Skills	=	*Attend AMA planning seminar.*
People Skills	+	
Good Judgment	+	
Introspection	-	*Read Meninger and "Psychology Today".*
Professional Growth	=	*Consider joining TEC.*
Success Expectation	+	
Customer Orientation	+	*Visit a customer a month.*
Big Picture & Vision	=	*Take AMA business strategy seminar; Steiner book.*

Executive Development Planner - Worksheet

Executive Development Worksheet for _____

Scale: +, -, =.   (+ Well Above Average, - Well Below Average, = Average for This Job)

ATTRIBUTES & ACTIONS

Track Record of Success
Ties Ribbon = Completes Tasks
Results Driven = Likes Tasks
Good Communicator
Hard Worker
High Energy
Forthrightness
Is Forthcoming
Positive Outlook & Demeanor
Acceptance of Authority
Good Listener; Open to Ideas
Organizes Self & Others
Acts the Leader
Looks the Leader
Entrepreneurial
Works Well with Others
Promotes Teamwork
Is a Cheerleader
Good Teacher
Considerate of Others
Is a Tracker; Accountable
Good Planner
I-Q (Intelligence)
I-Can (Confidence)
I-Will (Commitment)
Consistency

MANAGEMENT KNOWLEDGE

Communication Skills
Industry Knowledge
In-Job Management Knowledge
Marketing Skills
Finance Skills
Tracking Skills
Planning Skills
People Skills
Good Judgment
Introspection
Professional Growth
Success Expectation
Customer Orientation
Big Picture & Vision

DEVELOPMENT IDEAS ===> PLAN

Executive Development Planner - Worksheet

Executive Development Worksheet for _____

CEO Tool

ATTRIBUTES & ACTIONS

DEVELOPMENT IDEAS ===> PLAN

Track Record of Success
Ties Ribbon = Completes Tasks
Results Driven = Likes Tasks
Good Communicator
Hard Worker
High Energy
Forthrightness
Is Forthcoming
Positive Outlook & Demeanor
Acceptance of Authority
Good Listener; Open to Ideas
Organizes Self & Others
Acts the Leader
Looks the Leader
Entrepreneurial
Works Well with Others
Promotes Teamwork
Is a Cheerleader
Good Teacher
Considerate of Others
Is a Tracker; Accountable
Good Planner
I-Q (Intelligence)
I-Can (Confidence)
I-Will (Commitment)
Consistency

MANAGEMENT KNOWLEDGE
Communication Skills
Industry Knowledge
In-Job Management Knowledge
Marketing Skills
Finance Skills
Tracking Skills
Planning Skills
People Skills
Good Judgment
Introspection
Professional Growth
Success Expectation
Customer Orientation
Big Picture & Vision

243

Executive Development Planner - Sources
Specific Sources for Executive Growth and Development

(CEO Tool)

| American Management Association | Numerous business seminars. | (800) 262-9699 |

Books
"The Little Engine That Could" by Watty Piper		I Can = Confidence
"The Go Getter" by Peter Kyne (out of print)		I Will = Commitment
"How to Win Friends and Influence People" by Dale Carnegie		Communicating / Confidence
"Listening" by Madelyn Barley-Allen		Listening / Communicating
"The Goal" by Eliyahu M. Goldratt & Jeff Cox		Results Orientation
"The Genius of Sitting Bull" by Emmett C. Murphy		Goals / Vision / People Skills
"The One Minute Manager" by Ken Blanchard		Planning
"Strategic Planning" by George Steiner		Planning
"Managing Through People" by Dale Carnegie		Organizing Others
"How To Get Control of Your Time & Your Life" by Allan Laiken		Organizing Others
"Jonathan Livingston Seagull" by Richard Bach		Leadership
"Man Against Himself" by Karl Meninger		Consistency / Introspection

| Corporate Partners Inc. | Management consultant to help you select the right training and growth steps for executives. | (770) 389-8511phone & fax email: kwker@mindspring.com www.ceotools.net |

| Institute for International Research | Industry-specific and function-specific seminars. | (212) 661-8740 (800) 345-8016 |

| Leadership Development Associates, Inc. | Extensive workshop seminars to develop leadership skills. | (201) 666-9494 |

| Movies | "Patton", "12 O'Clock High", "Hoosiers" | |

| Speaking & Verbal Communication | Toastmasters Rotary Ron Arden, Consultant | |

| Strategic Research Institute | Strategic-based seminars. | (800) 599-4950 |

| The Executive Committee (TEC) | Organization of Presidents and Key Executives that meets monthly in local groups to "mentor" each other. Monthly expert business speakers. | (800) 274-2367 |

| Xyte, Inc. | InSight Assessments   www.xyte.com | (608) 327-1000 |

244

Appendix for *CEO Tools*

Please utilize the unusual features that follow to facilitate your use of the CEO Tools. The ensuing sections will assist in locating tools, identifying sources, and getting more information on actual application of the tools in your business situation:

Also please try out the CD/Browser included on the inside back cover. It offers 24 easy-to-use tools in automated format for IBM-compatible personal computers. Moreover, the CD/Browser contains a number of *learning aides* and *e-tools* for more quickly applying the CEO Tools. Please click on "About the Book and Browser" and then on "Tours of Tools" for audio, streaming media, and other helpful hints for using the tools.

Tool Finder: to locate tool information quickly, please see page 257 in the Topical Index under *Tools* for page number location, and see the CD/Browser listing on page 249 for most of the abbreviations.

The 24 CD/Browser Tools

1.	**1-PgBP**	One-page Business Plan. Communicates your plan to all employees.
2.	**8-Score**	8-Score Tool. Score your company's ability to provide your people's eight work needs.
3.	**12MMA**	Twelve-month Moving Average. Key indicator for percentages and ratios.
4.	**Backlog**	Backlog Tool. Manage your future before it occurs!
5.	**BestFin**	Best Financial Statements. Look down at your business from 30,000 feet up for faster success.
6.	**Buck$**	Recognition Buck$. Recognition tool to get employees much more motivated.
7.	**Cash**	Daily Cash Report. Future cash management now.
8.	**CEO360**	CEO 360. Decide what's important in your business and improve it.
9.	**CEOMoLtr**	CEO/Manager Monthly Letter. Monthly letter to all employees communicates goals and how we're doing.
10.	**ceotools.com**	CEO Tools Website. Frequent updates and new tools.
11.	**CoCal**	Company Calendar. Helps people manage themselves.
12.	**EDP**	Executive Development Plan for each manager.
13.	**MST**	Managerial Success Traits. Scorecard for personal growth.
14.	**OpExp%**	Operating Expenses as % of Sales. Key indicator.
15.	**QPM**	Quarterly Priorities Manager. Manage major team initiatives quarter-to-quarter. Best management tool ever.
16.	**QRC 7-Steps**	Quick Reference Card. Seven-step management process.
17.	**QRC Top-10**	Quick Reference Card. Top ten tools pictorially.
18.	**ReFcast**	Reforecasting Tool. Reforecast every month to act sooner for results.
19.	**Right**	Right Growth Rate. How fast should you grow?
20.	**T12M**	Trailing 12-Month Charts. Exception report for all key indicators.
21.	**TEConline.com**	The Executive Committee website. Enhancing CEO's business and personal lives.
22.	**Time**	Time Audit. Benchmark and manage your time.
23.	**UBP**	Unique Business Proposition. Thirteen words to communicate your vision and lead your people.
24.	**xyte.com**	Xyte, Inc. website to profile self and others for better communication and teamwork.

CEO Tools Topical Index

Topical Index (continued)

Topical Index (continued)

Topical Index (continued)

Topical Index (continued)

Topical Index (continued)

CEO Tools Bibliography

Ash, Mary Kay. *Mary Kay You Can Have It All: Lifetime Wisdom from America's Foremost Woman Entrepreneur.* Prima Publishing, 1996.

Basch, Michael. *CustomerCulture: How FedEx and Other Great Companies Put the Customer First Every Day.* Financial Times Prentice Hall, 2002.

Berra, Yogi. *The Yogi Book: 'I Really Didn't Say Everything I Said'* Workman Publishing Company, 1998.

Blanchard, Ken and Johnson, S. *The One Minute Manager.* William Morrow and Company, Inc., 1982.

Bleech, J. *Let's Get Results, Not Excuses! A No-Nonsense Approach to Increasing Productivity, Performance and Profit.* Lifetime Books, 1995.

Carnegie, Dale. *How to Win Friends and Influence People.* Pocket Books, 1994.

Churchill, Winston. Book by James C. Humes, Richard M. Nixon (foreward). *The Wit and Wisdom of Winston Churchill: A Treasury of More Than 1,000 Quotations and Anecdotes.* Harper Perennial, 1995.

Einstein, Albert. *Ideas and Opinions.* Bonanza Books, 1988.

Einstein, Kurt. Harvey Mackay's website at www.mackay.com, 2002.

Emerson, Ralph Waldo, et al. *The Essential Writings of Ralph Waldo Emerson (Modern Library Paperback Classics).* Princeton Review, 2000.

Faust, G., Phillips, W., Lyles, R. *Responsible Managers Get Results: How the Best Find Solutions – Not Excuses.* American Management Association, 1998.

Gillespie, Jack, et al. *Harnessing Desktop Publishing: How to Let the New Technology Help You Do Your Job Better.* Scott Tilden, 1987.

Gitomer, Jeffrey. *The Sales Bible.* William Morrow and Company, Inc., 1994.

Groen, David and Jay. *Huey.* Ballantine Books, 1984.

Harvey, E. *180 Ways to Walk the Recognition Talk.* The Walk the Talk Company, 2000.

Hemingway, Ernest, et al. *The Complete Short Stories of Ernest Hemingway: The Finca Vigia Edition.* Scribner, 1998.

Horan, Jim. *The One Page Business Plan.* The One Page Business Plan™ Company, 1998.

Kelly, Walt, et al. *Pogo, Volume 10.* Fantagraphics Books, 1999.

Lakein, A. *Give Me A Moment and I'll Change Your Life: Tools for Moment Management.* Andrews McMeel Publishing, 1997.

Lakein, A. *How To Get Control of Your Time and Your Life.* New American Library, division of Penguin Putnam Inc., 1973.

LeBoeuf, M. *Working Smart : How to Accomplish More in Half the Time.* New York, NY: Warner Books, Inc., 1979.

Lindberg, Charles. Book by Barry Denenberg. *An American Hero: The True Story of Charles A. Lindberg.* Scholastic Trade, 1998.

Maguire, Francis X. *You're the Greatest! How Validated Employees Can Impact Your Bottom Line.* Saltillo Press, 2001.

Markle, Gary. *Catalytic Coaching : The End of the Performance Review.* Wesport, CT: Quorum Books, 2000.

Marshall, Susan, et al. *How to Grow a Backbone: 10 Strategies for Gaining Power and Influence at Work.* Contemporary Books, 2000.

Maslow, Abraham Harold. *Motivation and Personality.* Addison-Wesley Publishing Company, 1987.

McDermott, Brian. *Managing the Training Function - Book One: Trends, Politics and Political Issues.* Lakewoods Publications, 1990.

Nelson, Bob. *1001 Ways to Reward Employees.* Workman Publishing Company, Inc., 1994. Also *1001 Ways to Energize Employees.*

Oncken, Jr., W. *Managing Time Management.* Prentice Hall, Inc., 1984.

Peale, Norman Vincent. *The Power of Positive Thinking.* Ballantine Books, 1996.

Peters, Thomas J. *The Pursuit of Wow!* Vintage Books, 1994.

Piper, Watty. *The Little Engine That Could.* Grosset & Dunlap, 1978.

Post, Emily. *Emily Post's Etiquette (16th Edition).* HarperCollins, 1997.

Reaves, Chuck. *Theory of Twenty One: Finding the Power to Succeed.* M Evans & Co., 1983.

Rifkin, G. and Matthews, D. *The CEO Chronicles.* Lanham, MD: Knowledge Exchange, 1999.

Rogers, Will. Book edited by Bryan Sterling. *The Best of Will Rogers.* M Evans & Co., 1992.

Shechtman, M. *Working Without a Net.* Prentice Hall, Inc., 1994.

Steiner, George A. *Strategic Planning: What Every Manager Must Know.* Free Press, 1997.

Sutton, Walt. *Leap of Strength : A Personal Tour Through the Months Before and Years After You Start Your Own Business.* Silver Lake Publishing, 2000.

Vermeil, Dick, et al. *Burnout: Keeping the Fire.* Learn, 1996.

Welch, Jack. *Jack: Straight from the Gut.* Warner Books, 2001.

Wilde, O. Book by Richard Ellman. *Oscar Wilde.* Vintage Books, 1988.

Williams, M., et al. *Only the Best On Customer Service.* Alan Press, 1996.

Illustrations at Beginning of Chapters

Major Illustrations within Chapters

Illustrations at End of Chapters

Acknowledgments – The people behind the scenes of *CEO Tools*

There are so many people who made this book happen. Thanks to every one of you, even if you're not mentioned by name here. You know who you are because you touched my life at just the right time with the learning each of us needs so much. To name those who must come up first:

> Ted and June Kramers – my parents who loved me and scrimped for me to get degrees from both MIT and Stanford, and who taught me to be stubborn, dedicated, focused and to work very hard.

> Janet Ivarie – my wife and life-partner, who loved me so amazingly through the toughest times that led to this book, and who taught me patience, persistence and a modicum of self-control.

> Charles "Red" Scott – my boss of a dozen years and my mentor, who taught me so incredibly much, including many of the tools in this book. Red fired me once, and thank goodness for that – it was a quantum-leap learning experience that took over a decade for me to appreciate fully.

> TEC 180 and TEC 151 – Two groups of CEOs who gave me the guidance and encouragement to be successful and to write this book. The chairs of those two groups must be included: John Amond and Bud Carter, who deserve much of the "blame" here, too, for holding me accountable to myself.

Some well-known people who contributed in big ways include: former CEO Clark Johnson of Pier One Imports, president and CEO of The Executive Committee (TEC Worldwide) Richard Carr, CEO Glenn Hemmerle (formerly CEO of Crown Books, Athlete's Foot, Pearle Vision, and Miracle-Ear), senior business writer Susan Harte of the Atlanta Journal-Constitution newspaper, and author/speakers Ken Blanchard and Spencer Johnson, Alan Lakein, Gerry Faust, Walt Sutton, Larry King, Jim Cecil, Pat Murray, Jerry Goldress, Steven Covey, Michael Basch, Michael LeBoeuf, William Oncken, Jr., Jim Horan, and professional football coach Dick Vermeil.

Many thanks to a few others who contributed their company's practices to the work: Carl Herndon and Marty Robinson of W.H. Bass, Gerry Hull of Automated Logic Corporation, and both David and Jay Groen of Groen Brothers Aviation. Two very special people got me started on CEO Tools in the first place: Judy Starkey of Chamberlin Edmonds & Associates and her TEC Chair at the time, Rick Houcek. Thank you both!

The hugely important *support and help* people include: software genius Dinny McIsaac and CEO/supporter Linda McIsaac and her wonderful assistant Kelly Reigel, CEO and IT expert Andy Vabulas (I.B.I.S., Inc.) and two of his key people, Ken Grabowski and Steven Wilkes, writer/author Doug Matthews, art manager Larry Goldstein, CEO and marketing expert Doug Pickert and his incredibly helpful creative director Jim Loser of GBA/SourceLink, my attorney and good friend Rick Andre, CEO Russ Umphenour, my good friend and fellow CEO/speaker Ron Fleisher, author/speaker Gary Markle, my friend Belinda Bertholf, and all the literary agents and publishers who encouraged me to go forward.

Thanks a million to every one of you!

CEO Tools

About the Author of *CEO Tools*

Kraig Kramers has been CEO of eight businesses in widely diverse industries. He's an experienced executive who has had spectacular successes and a few phenomenal failures. He's captured the lessons learned and the tools for business success in this, his first book, *CEO Tools: The Nuts-n-Bolts of Business for Every Manager's Success.*

Kraig is a nationally acclaimed speaker and was recently selected *Speaker of the Year* out of nearly 2,000 business speakers by TEC Worldwide. Kraig offers audiences unique tools that make companies, managers and leaders successful. His topics include ways to accelerate profitable growth, tools for acquisitions that work, and how to strategically position companies for success. Kraig speaks to industry groups, managers, CEOs and universities 100+ times each year.

During his career Kraig has been manager and CEO, negotiated over 70 acquisitions, been on three-dozen boards of directors or advisors, and consulted with thousands of companies. Clearly, he addresses topics in *CEO Tools* that he has personally experienced. Kraig shepherded an amazing turnaround at Snapper (lawnmowers) from a $54 million loss in one year to a profit of over $13 million the next – and this was during the 1992 recession in an industry in long-term decline.

Other companies Kraig has run include Guarantee Insurance, Metro-One Telecommunications, Courtesy Coffee, and Munson Sporting Goods. At Graphic Arts Center printing, he guided this company's growth from $60 million sales to $120 million in four years while the industry grew slowly.

Today, Kraig is CEO of Corporate Partners Inc., the pre-eminent business-acceleration consulting firm. He coaches CEOs and managers throughout North America and is a frequently published business writer. He's an acknowledged authority on creating and improving boards, now serving on ten. He is an active member of TEC (The Executive Committee) and affiliated with the Association for Corporate Growth.

Kraig has a BS in physics from MIT and an MBA in marketing and finance from Stanford University.

CEO Tools – How to Install and Use the CD/Browser

CD/Desktop Browser with 24 Automated CEO Tools
from the book
CEO Tools: The Nuts-n-Bolts of Business
for Every Manager's Success

General: The enclosed CD contains a selection of automated tools from the book, *CEO Tools: The Nuts-n-Bolts of Business for Every Manager's Success.* The tools are described in the book, ready for your use in Excel®, Word®, PowerPoint®, and on the Internet.

System Requirements: IBM-compatible PC, Windows™ 95/98/NT/2000/XP, 16mb RAM, about 32mb Available Disk Space, and a CD/ROM Drive.

No Technical Support: This CD is provided without technical or software support. Please see the browser for legal policy.

To Install the CD/Desktop Browser: Insert the CD into your CD/ROM drive. The program should open automatically and ask to allow installation with the following message: "InstallShield Self-Extracting EXE. This will install *CEO Tools*. Do you wish to continue?" Click YES. It will save under the *CEO Tools* filename if you just click *Next* in the installer. Specify another location if you choose. If the Browser does not automatically load, click *Start*, then *Run*, and *Open* to load it. This is probably M:\setupex.exe on your PC.

To Use the CD/Desktop Browser & Tools: The installer will put the *CEO Tools* icon on your PC desktop. Double-click on it to access the browser and tools. Click on any icon at the bottom of the screen to see a list of automated tools in that toolbox (book chapter). Then click on the tool to use it. See the book for tool use information and see the browser for technical information.

Copyright © 2001-2002 Corporate Partners Inc. All Rights Reserved.
Please see Browser for Legal Policy.   *CD Instructions*

CEO Tools – How to Install and Use the CD/Browser

CD/Desktop Browser with 24 Automated CEO Tools
from the book
CEO Tools: The Nuts-n-Bolts of Business for Every Manager's Success

General: The enclosed CD contains a selection of automated tools from the book, *CEO Tools: The Nuts-n-Bolts of Business for Every Manager's Success.* The tools are described in the book, ready for your use in Excel®, Word®, PowerPoint®, and on the Internet.

System Requirements: IBM-compatible PC, Windows™ 95/98/NT/2000/XP, 16mb RAM, about 32mb Available Disk Space, and a CD/ROM Drive.

No Technical Support: This CD is provided without technical or software support. Please see the browser for legal policy.

To Install the CD/Desktop Browser: Insert the CD into your CD/ROM drive. The program should open automatically and ask to allow installation with the following message: "InstallShield Self-Extracting EXE. This will install *CEO Tools*. Do you wish to continue?" Click YES. It will save under the *CEO Tools* filename if you just click *Next* in the installer. Specify another location if you choose. If the Browser does not automatically load, click *Start*, then *Run*, and *Open* to load it. This is probably M:\setupex.exe on your PC.

To Use the CD/Desktop Browser & Tools: The installer will put the *CEO Tools* icon on your PC desktop. Double-click on it to access the browser and tools. Click on any icon at the bottom of the screen to see a list of automated tools in that toolbox (book chapter). Then click on the tool to use it. See the book for tool use information and see the browser for technical information.